D1475333

Drama and power in a hunting society

The Selk'nam of Tierra del Fuego

Frontispiece. Lola Kiepja in 1966, the year of her death.

Drama and power in a hunting society

The Selk'nam of Tierra del Fuego

ANNE CHAPMAN
Centre National de la
Recherche Scientifique, France

CAMBRIDGE UNIVERSITY PRESS

Cambridge
London   New York   New Rochelle
Melbourne   Sydney

Published by the Press Syndicate of the University of Cambridge
The Pitt Building, Trumpington Street, Cambridge CB2 1RP
32 East 57th Street, New York, NY 10022, USA
296 Beaconsfield Parade, Middle Park, Melbourne 3206, Australia

© Cambridge University Press 1982

First published 1982

Printed in Great Britain at the University Press, Cambridge

Library of Congress catalogue card number: 82-4286

British Library cataloguing in publication data

Chapman, Anne
Drama and power in a hunting society.
1. Ona Indians
I. Title
305.8'98   F2823.05

ISBN 0 521 23884 6

Contents

Contents

Contents

Figures

Figures

Acknowledgements

This book would not exist without the friendship and collaboration of the last few descendants of the Selk'nam with whom I was privileged to work, namely Lola Kiepja, Angela Loij, Federico Echeuline, Luis Garibaldi Honte, Esteban Ichton, Francisco Minkiol, Leticia Ferrando and Segundo Arteaga. I hope to return to the island to see those who are still living and other friends, and to continue my study.

It is thanks to the late Annette Laming-Emperaire that I first went to Tierra del Fuego in 1964. Dr Laming-Emperaire was an archaeologist who had worked extensively in Tierra del Fuego as well as in Brazil and her native France. She died tragically in Brazil in 1977. It was she who told me about Lola Kiepja, the only Selk'nam then still living who had been born before the colonization of her land, which began about 1880. Toward the end of 1964 I went to Tierra del Fuego as a member of Dr Laming-Emperaire's archaeological team (of the Mission Archéologique Française au Chili Austral) in order to meet Lola Kiepja, which I did in the Christmas vacation of that year. I returned to see her once the archaeological work was completed, at the end of January 1965, when I decided I would do my utmost to study with her.

Dr Laming-Emperaire's range of interests did not exclude the living descendants of the people whose past she so ardently researched. Her enthusiasm, dedication and generosity were an inspiration to all of us who worked with her and were her friends.

The Centre National de la Recherche Scientifique (Paris) made it possible for me to carry out the field work and the research for this book. I have been a member of the C.N.R.S. since 1961, and through the years this institution has funded my work. I wish to express my appreciation to the C.N.R.S. for this unusual opportunity to do basic research on subjects of my choice.

The Consejo Nacional de Investigaciones Científicas y Técnicas (Buenos Aires) also supported my field work during the 1972–4 period. I am especially grateful to this institution and to the many friends in Buenos Aires and in Tierra del Fuego who aided and encouraged me in my endeavour.

I also wish to acknowledge the Laboratoire d'Ethnologie and the library of the Musée de l'Homme (Paris) for many research facilities, and to thank my French colleagues who were very helpful in the realization of this book.

In memory of Lola Kiepja and Angela Loij,
the last Selk'nam women.

Introduction

The Selk'nam (Ona) people, inhabitants of the largest island of Tierra del Fuego in the extreme south of South America, were still living in accordance with their ancient traditions when, in 1880, the White man suddenly began to colonize their land.[1] During the final decades of the nineteenth century an unknown number of Selk'nam were massacred by the newcomers. Then and later, countless others died of imported diseases, against which they had no natural immunity. Paradoxically, internecine feuds became more violent during this final period of hardship and suffering and many Selk'nam were killed by their own people. In 1980, one hundred years after the beginning of colonization, only one or two direct descendants of these people remain.

The Selk'nam were hunters, their main prey being the guanaco, an American camel of the llama genus. They also hunted foxes, rodents and birds, and gathered shellfish and edible plants. They fished in the rivers, in the lakes and along the coasts of their island. The island which they inhabited, now called the Great Island (see figures 4 and 5), was divided into a large number of territories, called *haruwens*, 'earths', in each of which dwelt certain kin groups. Every person was known by the 'earth' in which he or she lived and the 'sky', called *shó'on*, with which he or she was associated. The sky concept was the organizing principle of the cosmology and had great social and ceremonial significance.

The main focus of this study is one ceremony, which the Selk'nam called the Hain (pronounced 'highn'), but which is more familiarly known in the anthropological literature as the *kloketen* initiation rite.[2] This ceremony, which served to initiate young men, the *kloketens*, into adulthood and train them in the ways of adult society, had numerous facets, a great wealth of meanings, and several vital objectives. These included the 'teaching' of the women, over whom the men expressed their superiority during the ceremony;[3] the bringing together of people who rarely met in ordinary life, thus mitigating inter-group conflicts — men who were enemies would nevertheless participate in the same Hain;[4] and the ritual expression of the continuity of society.

This ceremony will be discussed in detail in chapters 3 to 9. First, however, it is necessary to situate the ceremony in context, and chapters 1 and 2

WD

will be devoted to an account of the history and economy of Selk'nam society and its socio-economic structure.

The cultures of the Selk'nam and their neighbours, the Haush, are known to us primarily through the work of the Austrian ethnologist, Father Martin Gusinde,[5] who visited these people a number of times between 1919 and 1922 and who spent almost four months among them in 1923, during which time he documented a Hain ceremony. He estimated that the total population of both peoples in 1923 was 279 individuals, the great majority of whom were Selk'nam; some were Mestizos Selk'nam–Haush and very few were Haush. He calculated that the pre-White population (prior to about 1880) of the two groups was between 3,500 and 4,000. The first of his three large volumes on the Indians of Tierra del Fuego, entitled *Die Feuerland-Indianer. Die Selk'nam*, will undoubtedly remain the classical work on these people as well as one of the outstanding contributions to knowledge of hunting and gathering cultures the world over. He also wrote numerous articles in scientific journals on the Selk'nam and on the other Indian groups of Tierra del Fuego.

Another primary source is Lucas Bridges' *Uttermost Part of the Earth.* Bridges was a son of the first White settler in Tierra del Fuego, the Anglican missionary Thomas Bridges. His book is a fascinating history of his family and includes important data on the Selk'nam he knew. Although it was published in 1948, its most significant accounts of the Indians date from before the First World War. Carlos Gallardo, an Argentine who visited the Great Island about 1905, also wrote an important book, *Los Onas.* The Salesian missionaries of the order of Don Bosco, who established two missions in Tierra del Fuego in the late nineteenth century, made some very relevant contributions, outstanding among whom were Fathers José Beauvoir, Alberto Agostini, Maggiorino Borgatello, Antonio Coiazzi and Antonio Tonelli. Colonel Charles W. Furlong made an expedition to the Great Island in 1907–8 and subsequently published several interesting articles on the Selk'nam and Haush. Although the anthropologist John Cooper was never in Tierra del Fuego he should be mentioned as the author of an extremely well documented annotated bibliography of all the Indian groups of Tierra del Fuego. A North American archaeologist, Samuel K. Lothrop, excavated on the Great Island in 1924–5. His book, *The Indians of Tierra del Fuego*, contains cultural data on the Selk'nam and the neighbouring Yámana as well as reports of his excavations.

If very little ethnography was carried out among the Selk'nam after Samuel Lothrop's field work, this may in part be attributed to the reluctance of ethnographers to attempt the study of a people 'reduced almost to extinction' as Lothrop states on the first page of his book. Many ethnographers may not have been aware of the possibilities of studying with very few informants the survivors of a nearly dead culture. I was not, until I met Lola Kiepja.

The present study draws on all of these sources and will argue that, according to my informants and my analyses, a number of previous statements concerning the Selk'nam society have been inaccurate. My study of the Selk'nam culture began in early 1965 when I first met Lola Kiepja (frontispiece and figure 1) at her home on the reservation near Lake Fagnano, on the Great Island of Tierra del Fuego, Argentina. She was the last Selk'nam who had lived as an Indian and the only remaining shaman. She was also a person of extraordinary sensibility and intelligence. I returned the following year and spent three months with her. She especially enjoyed singing ancient chants for me to record, and to hear her voice played back on the recorder.[6] She also seemed pleased to have someone with whom she could share her memories of all that had disappeared. Lola and I became close friends and when I left in June 1966 I promised to return to see her the following year. Sadly, she died four months later, on 9 October 1966 at the approximate age

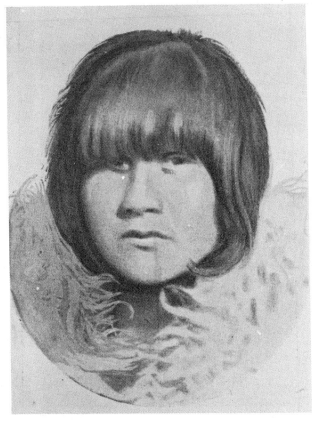

1. Lola Kiepja, Selk'nam, about 1900.

of ninety.[7] I did return in 1967, again for three months, when I worked mainly with Angela Loij (figure 2) whom I had met the previous year as a friend of Lola's. She helped me to translate the words of the chants I had recorded with Lola. This proved to be difficult because of the esoteric language the shamans employed while chanting. As Angela tried to explain the meaning of the phrases to me in detail I discovered that she also knew a great deal about the Selk'nam culture, even though she was born at the turn of the century at the height of the turmoil caused by the White occupation of the island. However, both her parents were Indian and she had lived her early years in the midst of her people. Later in life, she spent some ten years in the Salesian mission on the Great Island, living in daily contact with the old Selk'nam women who constantly evoked the past. Angela's first husband was Indian. Though she spoke Spanish as well as Selk'nam and was a

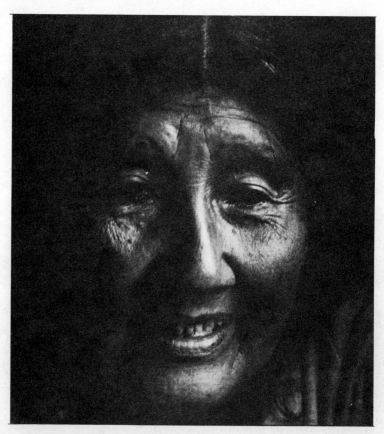

2. Angela Loij, Selk'nam, 1966.

Christian, she was profoundly involved in her ancestral culture. Like Lola, she had retained extraordinarily clear memories of the people she had known and of impressions and conversations from many years before. Again like Lola, Angela took pleasure in talking to me and acting as my teacher.

On my third visit, from September 1968 to April 1970, I spent the great majority of time in Tierra del Fuego working intensely with Angela. I also interviewed other descendants of the Selk'nam. Federico Echeuline, whose mother was Selk'nam and father Norwegian, told me a great deal about the Hain ceremony. He died in December 1980 at the age of seventy-five. Luis Garibaldi Honte (figure 3), of Haush descent, talked to me principally about his boyhood and the Hain. I also met Esteban Ichton, both of whose parents

3. Luis Garibaldi Honte, of Haush descent, 1968.

were Selk'nam, but I had been working with him for only a short while when he died in November 1968. Another friend was Francisco Minkiol, also of Selk'nam parentage, whom I often visited with Angela in Río Grande where he was confined to his home, being paralysed in both legs as a result of a horse-training accident. He died at the age of fifty in December 1970. He was not very familiar with the Indian life but he spoke Selk'nam quite well.

During these years (1968–70) I took part in the making of a documentary film about the last Selk'nam and the tragic end of this people.[8] I made two expeditions to the southeastern region of the island on horseback and on foot, and travelled in other parts of the island seeking to become familiar with the more remote areas in order to gain a better understanding of how the Indians had lived in their own time, as well as looking for archaeological sites. I made several surface collections of stone and bone tools, and excavated a few burials.[9] In Punta Arenas, Chile, I consulted historical documents at the Instituto de la Patagonia and interviewed two elderly Scotsmen who had worked on the sheep farms on the island at the beginning of the century when there were still quite a few Selk'nam alive.

I returned to Argentina a fourth time in June 1972 and remained there until September 1974, during which time I worked in the libraries in Buenos Aires and made three trips to Tierra del Fuego, continuing my study with Angela and the others. When I departed from Río Grande in April 1974 I expected to see Angela in Buenos Aires a few months later when she was to come on a second visit. I was very grieved to hear that she died suddenly the following month.[10]

I returned for the last time to Tierra del Fuego in 1976 for two months when I worked mainly with Federico Echeuline and with Segundo Arteaga, whose mother was Selk'nam and father Chilean. I also completed my survey on horseback of the entire Atlantic coast from Cape Espíritu Santo to Cape San Diego. That year I also interviewed Leticia Ferrando, whose mother was Alakaluf. She was born on Dawson Island and as a girl had lived in the Salesian mission near Río Grande. The original material on the Selk'nam and Haush which I have gathered is thanks to all these people, whom I will refer to by their first names throughout the text, except for Luis Garibaldi Honte who among friends was known as Garibaldi.[11]

1 History and environment

The prehistory of the Selk'nam

Fifty thousand years ago or earlier people of Asia passed into America over what eventually became the Bering Strait. At certain periods during the final glacial epoch there was an isthmus 1,000 or more kilometres wide connecting Siberia and Alaska. Man and prehistoric animals, such as the mammoth, traversed the vast land mass, although for thousands of years at a time this passage to the New World was blocked by immense glaciers. Dr Annette Laming-Emperaire, an archaeologist, wrote in one of her last articles:

> It is admitted today that the most ancient and most numerous ancestors of the American Indians penetrated [into the New World] through the region of Bering. And through this same region during the Tertiary and Quaternary, Asia and America exchanged their fauna. The principal entrance into America was Alaska and the passage of penetration was the Mackenzie Valley.[1]

People probably came in small groups searching for better hunting grounds or following their game. Some 40,000 years later, about 10,000 years ago, hunters were living at the southern extreme of this immense continent, on the shore of the Magellan Strait.[2] Across this strait lies the Great Island of Tierra del Fuego, the 'Land of Fire', where the Selk'nam lived until recent times.

Dr Laming-Emperaire discovered a site on the Great Island which produced evidence that it was inhabited by humans some 9,500 years ago. These people may have arrived there on foot, over a land-bridge, a terminal moraine, at the point which became the Second Narrows of the Magellan Strait. By then the glaciers which had covered southern Patagonia and Tierra del Fuego had retreated, and as the climate grew warmer forest, shrubs and grass developed. The largest known quadrupeds of the first prehistoric period in southern Patagonia are the ground sloth, a native horse and the guanaco. The sloth and horse became extinct soon afterwards and may never have reached the Great Island. But the guanaco (*Lama huanacos*) and other animals did penetrate the Great Island at an early date, perhaps as soon as conditions were appropriate. The hunters followed their game here as they had probably done at the other extreme of the continent so many thousands of years before. Geologists date the retreat of the last glaciers to 10,000 years ago. This coincides very closely with the date which archaeologists give for the arrival of the first humans on the southern fringe of Patagonia and on the Great Island.[3]

In recent times the Great Island was inhabited by two groups of hunters, the Selk'nam and the Haush.[4] It is not known when they arrived on the island and how many other groups, which have since become extinct, may have preceded them. There is no doubt, however, that the Haush arrived on the island before the Selk'nam,[5] although at least by the nineteenth century the Haush had been confined to the southeastern part of the island by their more aggressive neighbours. Both these cultures were part of the ancient hunting tradition which extended over an immense area of more than two million square kilometres from Uruguay and southern Paraguay in the north, through most of Argentina to the southeastern tip of Tierra del Fuego.[6]

Agriculture was never practised either in Patagonia or in Tierra del Fuego. Even today it only takes place on a small scale, mainly because of the short growing season, the climate and the nature of the soils. All the Indian cultures of Tierra del Fuego are authentic manifestations of an unbroken tradition of hunting, gathering and fishing. It is one of the few areas of the world in which the indigenous cultures have remained intact into modern times. This is of great importance for our understanding of all types of such cultures. These pristine cultures should not be confused with those groups, with the same type of subsistence economy, which in recent centuries have been forced out of their original habitat into much poorer areas, either by more aggressive neighbours or as a result of European world expansion. Furthermore, in the past few centuries many horticulturists, in the tropical forest of South America for example, were compelled to abandon cultivation when for similar reasons they were forced to take refuge in areas in which their traditional form of living was not possible and where they had to rely heavily on hunting, gathering and fishing. Thus many of these groups were unable to maintain their original cultures in their entirety and lost much of their heritage. These cultures should not be considered typical of the hunting and gathering traditions whose history is rooted in the most remote epochs of human existence. Examples of the latter are the Selk'nam and Haush and the Australian cultures.[7]

Unfortunately there has been little archaeological research in the Selk'nam—Haush region of the Great Island. The most significant work has been that of the late Annette Laming-Emperaire and her associates at a site on the shore of Useless Bay, in the northwestern section of the island. At this site, named Marazzi, located at the base of a huge boulder, a carbon-14 date of 9,590 ± 210 years was obtained for the earliest period of human occupation. This is the earliest date reported for the area south of the Magellan

Strait. The site was a temporary shelter of land-animal hunters, though bone of marine mammals and remains of shellfish were also found.[8] Dr Laming-Emperaire also discovered the only other stratified site thus far reported for the Selk'nam area, which she named the 'Last Ona Camp'. Located inland near the entrance to the Magellan Strait, it comprised two levels which were not dated but which contained a great number of stone implements, including crude choppers, and an abundance of guanaco bones.[9]

In the 1920s an Argentine archaeologist, Milcíades Vignati, excavated four shell mounds containing stone tools on the Atlantic coast between River Chico and Cape Viamonte. Among the material he found is a piece that resembles a 'fish tail' projectile point which, according to Junius Bird, is the oldest datable artifact in South America.[10] In the summer of 1924—5 Samuel K. Lothrop collected lithic material from three localities, also on the Atlantic coast, in the vicinity of River Fuego.[11] Neither Vignati's nor Lothrop's material was dated. From 1969 to 1976 I made a number of surface collections from sites all along the Atlantic coast from the vicinity of Cape Espíritu Santo, near the eastern entrance to the Magellan Strait, to Cape San Diego at the entrance to the Strait of Le Maire.[12]

The recorded history of the Selk'nam

On 21 October 1520, during the voyage which the historian Morison considered the most remarkable of recorded history, a fleet of four ships veered west into a channel and discovered a waterway connecting the two great oceans.[13] The channel was subsequently named the Strait of Magellan, after the fleet's illustrious captain general. Magellan and his crew encountered no humans during the five weeks they navigated the strait from the Atlantic to the Pacific, a total of 334 nautical miles. But they did see man-made fires on the island, which became known as the Great Island, to the south of the entrance to the strait. The Selk'nam who first sighted the astonishing craft moving silently along the shore of their island probably built bonfires to signal to their neighbours further along the coast and inland that something alarming was occurring. Angela told me that her people traditionally signalled from group to group in this manner. Because of the fires seen by Magellan and his crew, the Great Island and all the islands south of the strait were later named 'Land of the Fire' (Tierra del Fuego).

The Selk'nam first encountered Europeans in 1579 in the person of the Spaniard Pedro Sarmiento de Gamboa and some of his men. The meeting occurred on the west coast of the island at a place which Sarmiento named Bahía de Gente Grande (Bay of the Tall People) in honour of the Selk'nam. Despite the peaceful reception they were accorded, the Spaniards proceeded to kidnap one of the Selk'nam. The volley of arrows which ensued wounded a Spaniard but the Selk'nam was still abducted.[14]

Olivier van Noort, commander of the second Dutch expedition to the Magellan Strait, landed in 1598 on 'Penguin Islands' (now Martha and Magdalena Islands) near the Bay of the Tall People. Here they encountered about forty tall people who, this time, attacked first, wounding three or four of van Noort's crew. In reprisal, van Noort killed all the men and took four boys and two girls as captives. Sometime later, one of the boys learned Dutch and spoke of his country and his people's enemies. From his account, it seems very likely that his people were Tehuelche Indians from the mainland in Patagonia and his enemies were the Selk'nam.[15]

The first Europeans to meet the Haush Indians who lived in the far tip of the Great Island were the Nodal brothers, whose vessel anchored in Good Success Bay on the Strait of Le Maire in 1619. The contact was friendly, even though the Spaniards attempted to capture some of the Indians. Apparently the Haush did not bear a grudge as they helped their would-be captors fetch drinking water and collect fire-wood. They learned to recite a Sunday prayer to the pleasure of the Christians and accepted their gifts of trinkets.[16] A Dutch ship put in at nearby Valentine Bay in 1624 and received skins of 'sea dogs' from the Indians in exchange probably for goods such as pieces of red cloth.[17]

In 1711 another expedition remained for five days in the Bay of Good Success, but the navigators did not see the Indians until the eve of their departure. Among the crew was a Jesuit, Father Labbe, who wrote, 'Those people seemed quite docile and I think it would not be difficult to instruct them.'[18] In December of 1769 the Haush once again played host to Europeans in the same bay, this time to Captain Cook and his crew of scientists and sailors. But the Captain's legacy concerning his polite hosts was harsh. 'In a word', he wrote, 'they are perhaps as miserable a set of people as are this day upon earth.'[19] The most renowned scientist of all to have visited the bay arrived in 1832 in the person of Charles Darwin, sailing on the *Beagle* under the command of Captain Fitz-Roy. Again the newcomers were welcomed. But Darwin was hardly more flattering than his predecessor, though he seems to have favoured the Haush over 'the stunted, miserable wretches further westward',[20] meaning the Yámana Indians.

Sometime during the latter part of the eighteenth century, Yankee sealers began exploiting the fabulous rookeries on the islands and along the coasts of southern South America. According to the Chilean historian Mateo Martinič, by 1890 the fur seal had been virtually annihilated and the decimated herds had taken refuge in the most inaccessible parts of the islands along the south Pacific littoral.[21] The contacts between sealers and Indians were often brutal. Fitz-Roy, writing of the period between 1827 and 1836, notes that the sealers frequently robbed the Channel Indians of the seal and otter skins.[22] My informants knew of Haush who had died from eating seals or beached whales which had been deliberately poisoned by the sealers in the nineteenth century. But the Selk'nam had little, if any, contact with sealers, since there were no large rookeries in their part of the island.

From the early seventeenth century many ships were wrecked along the rocky coasts of the Great Island, particularly near Cape San Diego at the Atlantic entrance to the Strait of Le Maire. The survivors, if there were any, would attempt to gain the northern part of the island in the hope of hailing a ship passing through the Strait of Magellan. These men, who were truly 'miserable', were often aided by the Indians.[23] It was good news for the Indians when the hull of a ship was thrown up on the shore. Those nearby would pick through the wreckage and salvage anything that might be of use to them, such as pieces of iron from which they fashioned cutting instruments, or glass for arrow heads. Bottles and barrels with iron hoops quite often drifted on to the coasts from passing ships or from those which had sunk in off-shore waters. The Indians sighted and hailed the ships which through the centuries passed along the shores of their island. Though the Selk'nam had far less contact with the Whites than the other groups of Tierra del Fuego, they were probably aware of their presence in the zone since Magellan's voyage. And there were undoubtedly more encounters between Indians and Whites than were reported.

The Selk'nam, however, were not prepared for the death blow they were to receive when, in about 1880, the Whites began seriously to occupy their land, lured there by the discovery of alluvial gold and of rich grassland suitable for sheep raising. Throughout the two final decades of the nineteenth century the Indians, men, women and children, were attacked by professional killers in the employ of sheep-farm owners, by farm administrators and by gold seekers. In the beginning of this period they were also shot by the military. The farm owners justified the genocide they were perpetrating by stating that they were safe-guarding their property – the sheep. The Indians did 'steal' some sheep because they were hungry or for vengeance. They sometimes counter-attacked too and killed a few White men but, armed only with bows and arrows, they were doomed to lose against an enemy with fire-arms, horses, and dogs trained to attack.[24] A number of Selk'nam were also shipped out of the region, to Patagonia and even to Buenos Aires, and were mostly never heard of again.

Internecine strife among the Indians themselves was aggravated by the usurpation of their territory by the Whites.[25] The Salesian order of Don Bosco established two missions in the area; the first in 1889 on Dawson Island in Chile in Alakaluf territory, and the second in 1896 on the east coast of the Great Island near the town of Río Grande in Argentina, on land belonging to the Selk'nam. Many of the adults suffered great hardship because of the radical change from their former free life to confinement in the missions. Entire families were captured and taken by force to the missions, especially to the one on Dawson Island. Some escaped from the

11

latter with the help of the Alakaluf who rowed them back to the shores of their island. Others were eventually allowed to leave. But at times the Indians went voluntarily to the missions to avoid being killed by other Whites, or because they were starving, or because they wanted to be with relatives who were in one of the missions. The children adapted more easily to mission life than the adults and were quick to learn from the schooling they received there. But if they remained very long in the missions the great majority of children and adults alike succumbed to the new diseases brought by the Whites, against which they had no immunity. These diseases, such as tuberculosis, influenza, pneumonia, measles, scarlatina and venereal infections, also caused considerable mortality in the countryside.

At different times the Indians also took refuge in the sheep farms owned by the sons of the protestant missionary, Thomas Bridges. In the farm called Harberton, on Beagle Channel, on the land of the Yámana Indians, many worked as farm-hands and shepherds. In 1903 another farm, Viamonte, was established on the east coast by the missionary's son, Lucas Bridges, with the help of the Selk'nam. The Indians who lived in that area urged him to settle there so that they might have a safe place to live, where they would not be endangered by attacks of the White killers. But these farms too became centres of contagion. So for the vast majority, despite efforts made to save them by the Bridges family, the Salesian missionaries, and a few other Whites, such as government officials and private persons in Chile and Argentina, there was no escape. During this final period (from 1880 to approximately 1905) the population of the Selk'nam and the neighbouring Haush dropped from 3,500 or 4,000 to about 500.[26] By 1905 the genocide had subsided, though sooner or later most of those remaining died of the new diseases. In 1980 there are about five Mestizos on the Great Island and one person both of whose parents may have been Indian. There are a number of people having one Indian grandparent (usually grandmother) but they are completely assimilated to modern life. These are all that remain.

Geography of the Indian territories[27]

The Great Island is roughly the shape of a triangle. The base, which faces south and west towards the Pacific, runs along the shores of the Beagle Channel and a great mountainous peninsula to a point called Brecknock. From here a line can be traced across Dawson Island to the apex of the triangle at the northeastern section of the island, bordering the Atlantic entrance to the Magellan Strait. The northeastern coast of the island, facing the Atlantic, represents the third side of the triangle. With the exception of one large bay (San Sebastian) it descends in a regular line terminating at the entrance to the Strait of Le Maire. Conflicting currents from the two great oceans make this strait and the Drake Passage beyond to Cape Horn one of

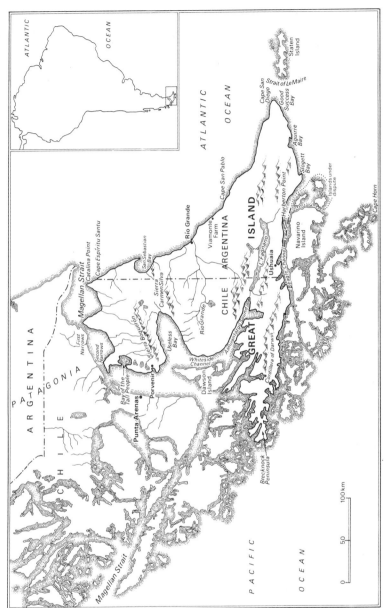

4. The Great Island, Tierra del Fuego (Argentina and Chile).

13

the most turbulent waterways in the world. The opposite side of the Strait of
Le Maire is formed by the massive rock mountain range of Staten Island
which is often shrouded in fog.

The Great Island lies between 52° 27' and 55° 59' South latitude. Its total
area is approximately 48,000 square kilometres of which, assuming about
10,000 square kilometres for the uninhabited areas of the cordilleras in the
southern section, roughly 38,000 square kilometres were inhabited by the
Indians.[28] In the town of Ushuaia on the Beagle Channel, the winter temperatures range from 10 °F to 80 °F with a mean of 34.7 °F, and the summer
mean is 50.2 °F. In the northern steppe zone, the annual temperature may
range from −4 °F in the winter to above 80 °F in the summer.[29] However, on
the northern and eastern coasts (the coast bordering the Magellan Strait and
the Atlantic coast of the Great Island respectively), the winter temperature
tends to be about five degrees warmer than that of the south coast (along the
Beagle Channel and further south).[30] The summer months (December to
March) are notable for their long days, with a maximum of daylight lasting
from about 4 a.m. to after midnight, and for their harsh winds sweeping up
from the antarctic. In the shortest days of the winter (which lasts from June
to September) the sun rises at about 10 a.m. and sets at about 4 p.m. During
this season the winds are calmer. Sunny though windy days are frequent in
the summer, and during the winter there are also days of pristine clarity.

The Great Island is now divided politically between Argentina and Chile at
the meridian of Cape Espíritu Santo (68° 36' W.). The eastern half (21,339
square kilometres) is part of Argentina and its provincial capital is Ushuaia,
located on the shores of Beagle Channel. In 1975 the population of Ushuaia
was 5,677. The largest town on the island, Río Grande, is situated on the
Atlantic coast, and is also Argentinian. In 1975 it had a population of 7,754.
The Chilean side of the island (27,000 square kilometres) includes the peninsula with the great Cordillera of Darwin, which extends along the southern
coast. Porvenir, a small town on the shore of Magellan Strait, is the Chilean
capital of Tierra del Fuego. Across the strait from Porvenir, on the continental coast of Chile, lies the urban centre of Patagonia, Punta Arenas.

During the last Indian period, a group called the Yámana or Yahganes, a
'canoe people', inhabited most of the south littoral of the Great Island,
especially along the Beagle Channel. Another canoe-faring people, the
Alakaluf or Halakwulup, also occupied the Great Island; part of the shore of
Useless Bay and the coast of Almirantazgo Sound. 'Foot people' (the hunters)
lived in the remainder of the island: the Selk'nam, who occupied most of the
island, and the Haush in the southeastern tip (see figures 4 and 5).

Yámana territory

The cordillera which is the terminal part of the Andean chain
stretches along much of the south coast of the island. Brecknock Peninsula,

at the western extreme of the island, extends almost to the Pacific ocean, but otherwise the entire southwestern coast is fronted by numerous islands including Cape Horn at land's end. The Yámana inhabited most of the area from Whale Boat Sound, near Brecknock Peninsula, in the vicinity of Alakaluf territory,[31] to Slogget Bay where they were neighbours of the Haush.[32]

In the Cordillera of Darwin, which extends over the long peninsula of the island, is found the highest mountain in Tierra del Fuego, Mount Saramiento (some 2,400 metres). High altitude lakes and lagoons are interspersed by glaciers, some of which reach down to the peninsula's shoreline. The latter, with its deep fjords, is carpeted with a dense forest of evergreen beech (*Nothofagus betuloides*). The cordillera diminishes in altitude along the Beagle Channel. In Indian times, as today, one of the best areas for human occupation in the south Pacific was the shore of the Beagle Channel, especially the Bay of Ushuaia. Recent constructions in the town of Ushuaia and the building of an air base nearby have destroyed much of the extremely rich remains of Yámana settlements in this bay. Fortunately, however, some

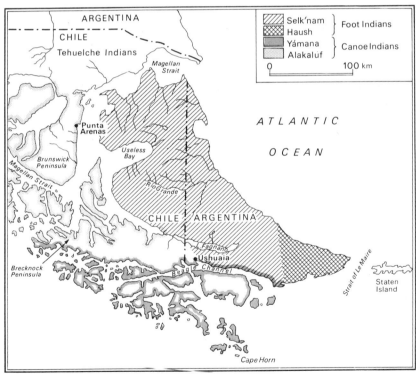

5. Tierra del Fuego, indicating the location of the four Indian groups.

Argentine archaeologists have been excavating in the last few years in coastal sites on Beagle Channel and on the Atlantic coast.[33]

Alakaluf (Halakwulup) territory

The Halakwulup Indians, better known as Alakaluf, inhabited an immense area of the archipelago, which is now part of Chile, from about 54° 30' S. latitude near Brecknock Peninsula to 47° S. latitude in the vicinity of the Gulf of Penas, where they were the neighbours of another fishing people known as the Chonos, who apparently became extinct about the end of the eighteenth century. The Alakaluf also occupied the entire south-western coast of the continent (Chile) where they were neighbours of the Tehuelche, a hunting people of Patagonia (Argentina). On the Great Island the Alakaluf had settled on the south shore of Useless Bay, where they were surrounded by the Selk'nam (see figure 5).[34] This zone, including the coasts of Almirantazgo Sound, is forested and while the interior south of Useless Bay is mountainous, there are no glaciers here.

Selk'nam territory

The Selk'nam described the land in which they lived as *párik*, the steppe region north of River Hurr (Río Grande), and *hérsk*, the forest area to the south. The Río Grande, which is the longest river on the island, originates in the mountainous forested area south of Useless Bay, and traverses the island almost horizontally, emptying into the Atlantic at the centre of the coastline where the town of Río Grande is now located. The northern steppe region is quite well watered by rivers and streams and has many salt and fresh water lagoons. Along the coasts of *párik*, that is the shores of the Magellan Strait and the Atlantic, there are a number of ancient moraines which form high cliffs. But in many parts the coastline is flat and covered with smoothly worn stones or extensive sandy beaches. In this northern *párik* zone there are two ranges of hills formed by morainic plateaux. One, called Carmen Silva, stretches across the central part of the island above the Río Grande. The other, Sierra Boquerón, attains its highest elevation on the northern shore of Useless Bay and terminates on the Atlantic coast as a vast shrub-covered plateau comprising the huge cliffs which line the shore from Cape Espíritu Santo to San Sebastian Bay. *Párik* is far more exposed to the violent western winds than is *hérsk*, the central zone to the south of the Río Grande, where the cordillera forms a bulwark against the winds and where the forests provide shelter.

Hérsk is characterized by its forests, the most common trees being two summer-green species of beech (*Nothofagus pumilio* and *N. antarctica*). There are also wide expanses of hard grass and bush lands, as well as vast peat bogs. Many of the bogs have dried up in modern times owing mainly to the extensive grazing of sheep and the construction of roads. Cords (*cordones* in

Spanish) of elongated rounded hills, formed by ancient moraines, cut across the island and terminate as bluffs on the Atlantic coast. Numerous streams and rivers, whose sources are in the cordillera, flow through this part of the island and empty in the Atlantic. All of the island's lakes are located in *hérsk*; the largest, now named Fagnano (K'ámi in Selk'nam), is over 100 kilometres long. The densest forest, which lies in the lake area, stretches over cordillera to the south and reaches out to the Atlantic coast in certain sections. The cordillera formed a natural boundary between the Selk'nam and the Yámana territories.

Haush territory

Haush is apparently a Selk'nam term; according to Gusinde the authentic name is Manekenkn. The territory of this group bordered on that of the Selk'nam in the vicinity of Cape San Pablo on the Atlantic coast and inland from there. The Haush inhabited the entire southeastern zone from Cape San Pablo to Slogget Bay on the opposite side of the island, where they were neighbours of the Yámana (see figure 5). While the Haush area in the centre of the island is similar to that of the Selk'nam, in the southeastern tip of the island hail, rain and snow storms are more frequent than in the central area; the forests are also more difficult to penetrate, and the peat bogs more extensive. In addition, tangled bushes about a metre high carpet some of the valley floors and make walking over them tedious, although there are many tracts of open moorland in this zone. Much of the coast around the tip of the island is rocky and lined with great cliff walls, although again there are a number of wide sandy bays which are ideal for camping. On a clear day this area is extraordinarily beautiful with the sea a deep blue, although the stark mountain ridges of Staten Island across the Strait of Le Maire at the tip of the island are seldom visible but are usually shrouded in fog.

For the period shortly before 1880, when the colonization of the Great Island began, the estimated population of the 'foot people' (Selk'nam and Haush) was between 3,500 and 4,000 individuals, while the 'canoe people' (Yámana and Alakaluf) may have numbered 7,500. If so, a total of 11,000 to 11,500 people inhabited Tierra del Fuego, the adjacent archipelagos along the Pacific coast and the southwestern extreme of the mainland. All the Indians of 'greater Tierra del Fuego' have now ceased to exist, with the exception of a few families (of Mestizos) and lone individuals scattered over southern Argentina and Chile.[35]

The resources of Tierra del Fuego

The terrain on the Atlantic side of Tierra del Fuego (the northern portion of the Great Island) is an extension of the steppe region of Patagonia. In contrast to this relatively flat area, the southern section of the Great Island is mountainous. The terminal Andes extend down into much of this area while many of the southern islands are formed by peaks of the cordillera. There are deep fjords along the coastline in this part of Tierra del Fuego while the forests are typically so dense as to be virtually inpenetrable, and they often border the shoreline. The habitable parts of this area are therefore reduced to stretches of rocky or sandy beaches. However, the difficulties of the terrain and also the climate of the Pacific area in general are compensated for by an extraordinarily rich aquatic fauna, particularly sea mammals and shellfish. In the Atlantic area the rigorous climate was compensated for by an abundance of game, especially the guanaco, different species of rodents and a great variety of birds. This area was ideal hunting ground while the Pacific area attracted sea-faring peoples. These ways of life, from the sea and off the land, represent the two traditions of non-agricultural economies.

It is important to note, however, that all these economies were multi-faceted. This is one of the main reasons why these people were able to exploit their environment efficiently. The canoe people, for example, hunted if they sighted a guanaco, just as the landsmen fished and collected shellfish, especially during the winter when guanacos were thin. They occasionally feasted on beached whales and the canoe people even killed whales off-shore. Certain sections of the coast also abounded in different species of seals before the advent of the Whites. A variety of edible plants and a great diversity of birds were available throughout Tierra del Fuego. These were consumed along with the staple seafood and game, or when the latter were scarce or lacking. It is now too late for quantitative research on the exploi-tation of their environment, but it does seem clear that sea and land peoples alike took advantage of much, if not all, of that which nature offered.

Tierra del Fuego has often been termed a marginal zone, and its societies 'simple'.[36] It has the aura of a no man's land where nobody would go if he could avoid doing so; a survival land of the last resort, fit only for the most primitive. The Indians of Tierra del Fuego were, supposedly, a brand of marginal primitives whose ancestors had somehow been forced to evacuate the better lands to the north under the pressure of energetic and enterprising cultivators. Once their ancestors had reached land's end, since they could go no further they were said to have languished there, generation upon gener-ation in splendid isolation, somehow surviving but more out of habit than a creative will to live. Early explorers and nineteenth-century scientists alike were appalled at the nakedness of the 'native' and shuddered to imagine the hardships which such a violent environment imposed upon these reputedly pitiful creatures. The Indians also gained notoriety as thieves. These early reports read as if it were the Indians' Christian duty to receive the White man's embrace of death with a courteous smile.

The inability of the explorers and nineteenth-century scientists to under-stand the life of these people is not surprising, but it is surprising that in the twentieth century, when knowledge of their cultures increased decisively, misconceptions about them still persisted.[37] Like other peoples the world over whose heritage had profound roots in the past, the Fuegian cultures were complex and rich.

The Europeans, for the most part, did not comprehend the nature of the hardships which were the lot of the Indians, such as, for example, the occasional severe winters. They were appalled because they compared the environment they found there with their own. Most of them ignored the fact that as one travels further south from Patagonia to Tierra del Fuego, the land does not become increasingly difficult for human existence; the southern archipelagos along the Pacific are much more habitable than those further north,[38] and on the Atlantic coast of the Great Island the rainfall is greater, the pastures are greener and the guanaco larger and fatter than in the southern Patagonian mainland. Again, the winters are normally less severe and the terrain is more varied on the Great Island than on the continent, north of Magellan Strait.[39] The extraordinary number and variety of birds which migrate in the spring to the Great Island, including humming birds, parakeets and geese, testify to the diversity of ecospheres to be found there.[40] The Great Island of Tierra del Fuego is marginal only in terms of its locality, at the end of the world. For hunters it was a good land. For sheep farm owners today, it is likewise.

Living as a hunter[41]

Normally, Selk'nam families migrated within their own territories (called *haruwen*) in search of food. According to Gallardo, they rarely remained more than a week in one camp site.[42] During the winter the family and a few additional relatives moved as a unit from site to site, but from late spring through into autumn, when game and other foods were more abundant, several families usually camped together or in close proximity. The families, except the wives, were members of the same patrilineal lineage.

If people from one territory entered a neighbouring territory it was understood that permission should be obtained from the occupants. However, trespassing (*haruwen airen*) did occur, especially when hunters were pursuing game and the owners of the territory were not nearby. Nevertheless this was done with extreme caution because it could motivate an armed attack, an act of individual aggression or group combat, particularly if tension already existed between the neighbouring lineages. As Lothrop stated, 'Each group had definitely located hunting rights, and to trespass on another's territory was a cause for war.'[43] Apparently, however, permission was often sought to hunt in another territory. A messenger (*oshen*), usually a boy, was sent to the camp where the owners were living. If permission was granted, some of the local men accompanied their guests on the hunt. The hosts offered hospitality to their guests in the form of sustenance for the duration of their visit. They expected recompense for the hunting rights and the hospitality, and were given bows, arrows, capes, sea lion skins and the like. The guests might also make arrow heads for their hosts during the visit. Gusinde commented that the rights of possession of the land were maintained in this way.[44]

I was able to obtain information concerning some 3,386 individuals, including the Whites who married or lived with Indian women and the Mestizo descendants, of whom a certain number are alive today. These individuals are contained in seventy-nine genealogies which my informants helped me to draw up over the years. Each genealogy corresponds to a lineage which inhabited one of the eighty-two territories into which the Great Island was divided. Sixty-nine of these *haruwens* were Selk'nam, eleven were Haush and two were Alakaluf (see figure 5). Correspondingly, there are sixty-nine Selk'nam genealogies, eight Haush genealogies (I have no genealogies for three Haush territories) and two Alakaluf genealogies. The number of generations covered in the genealogies varies from eight to only two in one genealogy. The oldest individuals of the first generation were probably born at the end of the eighteenth century and died about 1850.

The data testify to a certain fractioning of the lineages and an instability in the number and the boundaries of the *haruwens*.[45] For instance, two Selk'nam *haruwen* groups had conquered neighbouring Selk'nam *haruwens*, probably sometime before 1850. Some of the former inhabitants of the conquered *haruwens* had been killed while others, undoubtedly the women and children, had been adopted by the victors, or the women (with their children) had returned to their own *haruwen* group (see chapter 2). Two other Selk'nam *haruwen* groups had occupied neighbouring territories some time before 1880, thus increasing their land. These *haruwens* had not been conquered, but the former inhabitants had died, probably from starvation. Unfortunately, my informants could not identify any of the former inhabitants of these four extinct *haruwens*. On the other hand, the genealogies do reveal that shortly before the conquest of the island by the Whites six Selk'nam lineages (the *haruwen* groups) had broken into smaller fractions: five had divided into two groups and one into three.

Of the eighty-two *haruwens* which are documented, forty-four had coastal lands (including the two Alakaluf territories) while thirty-eight were exclusively inland. During the coldest months, from May to November, the hunters preferred the shoreline as the climate was milder and there was less snow than inland near the cordillera. The guanaco migrated out of the cordillera and the adjacent forests into the open lands and near the coasts for the same reasons. Those people who lived near the cordillera and had no coastline in their *haruwen* occupied the open valley and steppe or prairie land during the winter. In the warmer season, from December to April, the piedmont and forests were sought because the guanaco tended to gather there, and because the forests offered edible resources and provided more protection against the strong summer winds than the treeless coastal areas and inland prairies.

Even though the coast was apparently preferred for winter living, not all the groups had this choice. Nearly half of the *haruwens* known for the late Indian period had no coastal terrain. Moreover, many of the *haruwens* were quite small, so that the variations in seasonal temperatures would hardly have affected migratory patterns. Even the four largest *haruwens* did not have sufficiently extensive tracts of shoreline to offer adequate food resources for all of their members to remain on the coast during the entire winter season.

Although people typically moved within their own *haruwen*, there were numerous occasions which brought together groups from different *haruwens*. For example, whenever a whale was stranded or had died on a beach, people came from distant territories to feast upon it. Other such events were communal bird hunts, Hain celebrations, gatherings called *kuash-ketin*, competitions of different kinds, peace treaties, mourning rites of famous persons, and so forth. On these occasions people camped in the same vicinity for at least a few days and often, as in the case of a whale feast or a Hain, for many months.

Concerning the migration of people from camp site to camp site, Gallardo remarked: 'the fact of having killed three guanacos was sufficient motivation for the transfer of their dwelling to the locality where the guanacos had fallen, as this was easier than carrying the meat to the camp'.[46] Normally they changed camp during the day, although they sometimes travelled on moonlit nights. They were familiar with the smallest significant geographical detail of their *haruwen*[47] and with the advantages and the limitations of the habitable sites. Once a decision was made as to where they would go, they calculated the time necessary to reach their destination according to such factors as conditions of the weather, the physical state of the members of the group, the weight of the loads the women carried, the nature of the terrain over which they would travel. The women with their heavy burdens (often as much as 100 kilos),[48] the children and the elderly normally took the easiest route. The men went by a longer route if they had reason to believe they might find game by doing so. Lothrop wrote: 'In moving camp the women and children followed the valley floors while the men kept on higher land on either side. Feeding guanaco startled by the former fled to the heights where the hunters were waiting for them.'[49] Alternatively, the hunters led the group, Indian file, some distance ahead of the others, carrying only their bows and quivers full of arrows ready to pursue guanaco if they were sighted. The men aided the women with their burdens over difficult terrain – uphill, or across a swamp, a peat bog, a stream or river – and especially helped pregnant women.[50] If no game had been killed on the way and little food had been brought along, the men set out to hunt upon arrival at the site, while the women built the shelter, fetched water, gathered fire-wood and lit the home fire. The men might also help in these tasks.

Hunting provided the principal sources of food, clothing and dwelling. Its economic importance far outweighed that of gathering and fishing. Gallardo, writing at the beginning of this century, described the men's passion for hunting in the following terms: 'The hunt occupies most of their time and they give themselves to it with body and soul, with an unextinguishable ardour, and with real and very intense passion, as it is the greatest pleasure of their existence.'[51] The guanaco provides an excellent resource for human subsistence. Its lean meat, marrow and blood are nourishing food. Its hide, with or without the fur, its sinews and nerves provide materials for clothing, dwellings and utensils. Its shin bone makes an ideal flaking tool because of its length and hardness. A large guanaco gives over 100 kilos of meat and bone.[52] As it is a swift runner, the guanaco is difficult to kill with a bow and arrow. It has, however, a natural curiosity which may make it pause when it sights an object moving on the horizon and even slowly approach a would-be killer. The guanaco was hunted all year round, but the best seasons were the spring for the young guanacos and the summer and autumn when the herds were well fed. In the winter they could be tracked in the snow, as their relative weakness slowed them down. I was told that when they became stuck in the snow drifts the dogs could kill them by biting their heads.

The men often hunted singly, although a group of three to eight men might cooperate for such work.[53] Hunting on the northern steppe of the island was more tedious than in the forest area to the south, because the guanaco could easily sight a hunter and would often gallop away before it could be killed, despite its curiosity. Under these conditions the hunter approached the animal stealthily, slowly dragging himself along the ground and pausing for long periods. The hunter attempted to kill or mortally wound his game with the first shot, even if this meant passing long hours in silent pursuit or running down a bleeding animal after striking it.

The only domesticated animal was the dog, of which there were several breeds.[54] Dogs were highly valued and carefully trained to track and to keep silent until the game was cornered. Though proper names were given to them, they were usually not treated as pets. Women sometimes hunted young guanacos with their aid, using a large stick to kill the animal. Lola told me how sorry she felt to kill baby guanacos in this fashion.

Dogs were also used for fox hunting. The fox (*Canis seu cerdocyon*) was sought above all for its fur, which because of the warmth it provided was preferred as clothing to guanaco fur. Fox meat was also eaten, though apparently with little enthusiasm. Foxes, like the guanacos, inhabited the entire island except for the rocky heights of the cordillera. This species is now extinct and a smaller imported fox now plagues the sheep on the Great Island.

Two species of rodents, the tucotuco (*Ctenomys feuguinus*) and the cururo (*C. magellanicus*), were very much sought after, particularly in the northern zone where they were abundant. It was easy to kill many at a time,[55] and their meat was deemed tasty. The fur of both species is very soft, although numerous pelts and a great deal of sewing were required to make them into a garment. These rodents were hunted by the entire family or by the women and children alone. The only weapon needed was a pointed stick with a leather covering on the blunt end to protect the hands while dealing blows at the burrows. The rodents were roasted in a hearth on hot ashes. The meat was preserved for some time, smoked or dried in the wind, and was an item of barter.[56] Gusinde remarked that the people of the south (of *hérsk*) spoke with amused contempt of the northerners (of *párik*) as 'cururo eaters'.[57] Lola, a southerner, used exactly the same expression, deriding the cururo hunters.

Before the whaling and sealing businesses began on a large scale in the eighteenth century, Tierra del Fuego was one of the earth's paradises for whales and seals. Vast numbers of these creatures swam through the Magellan Strait, along the Atlantic coast of the Great Island, back and forth through the Le Maire Strait, around, and in and out of the Pacific archipelagos. The bodies of dying or dead whales were occasionally thrown by high tides on the shores of the islands. When this happened, the Selk'nam or Haush in the vicinity built bonfires to signal to all who could see them, and a great feast ensued. According to Gallardo, such a feast might last many months or even a year.[58] The Hain ceremony was sometimes celebrated when a whale was beached. Under any circumstances, it was a happy event, for it permitted the gathering of large numbers of people from different *haruwens* for an extended period of time, during which concern about the acquisition of food was relaxed.

Certain species of seals lived almost all year round in the caves and on the rocky and sandy beaches along the coast of the island. From November to January the fur seal arrived there to breed[59] and others migrated from the Antarctic to Tierra del Fuego at almost any time of year.[60] Seals were abundant in the Haush area where some herds still come to breed today. Lola, Angela and Federico told me of other rookeries in the Selk'nam area along the east coast, along the shores of Magellan Strait and in Useless Bay, all of which have long since ceased to exist. Seals are not difficult to kill. They were often simply clubbed to death, shot with an arrow at close range or harpooned. They were also sometimes caught in specially made nets. If the seals were swimming near the shore, a decoy pup might be made of seal hide stuffed with grass. The decoy was moved on the shore by a cord held at the other end by a hidden hunter who imitated the cries of the pup, thus attracting the adults to shore where they could be easily killed. Seal meat was not a favourite with those unaccustomed to it from childhood, although its oil and fat were universally appreciated. Those who did consume it preferred the pups to the adults. Lola wrinkled her nose when I asked her if she liked seal meat. However, her first husband, who was part Haush, was fond of it. The Haush relied more on this game for meat and hides than did the Selk'nam because it was more abundant than the guanaco in their area, although the guanaco was generally preferred by both groups. Seals were especially esteemed for their hides which were used in the fabrication of quivers. If necessity demanded, the hides were also made into clothing. Certain bones were employed for harpoon heads, particularly by the Haush; these very harpoons were then used to kill other seals.

Bird hunting was an important activity.[61] Sometimes hundreds of birds were killed during a hunt in which as many as twenty-five to thirty men and women cooperated. Gallardo wrote an excellent description of one of the simpler methods of communal hunting of lagoon birds:

> On the north side of the large island there exist innumerable lagoons which always provide abundant game and where the Indian from this region goes in search of birds which he takes in a rather curious fashion. He chooses one of the best lagoons, where there is an abundance of ducks, geese, swans and flamingos, and for two or three months he abstains from hunting here, though he visits every now and then to accustom the birds to seeing people. After this lapse of time, on a dark and rainy night, twenty-five to thirty Indians make their way to the lagoon, taking along torches made of dry bark rolled around a filling of dry leaves, secured by guanaco nerves. The torches are lit but only smouldering. Once the hunters have surrounded the lagoon they raise a great hubbub to frighten the birds into taking flight. At this moment the torches are waved so that they flare up brightly. The panic-stricken birds fly into the lagoon waters and the Indians wade in holding a torch in the left hand and a stick in the right with which they kill the dazzled birds and throw them to the shore of the lagoon. In this manner they make extraordinary killings.[62]

Cormorants, which nested in holes in the cliffs along the sea, were killed at night by specialized hunters whose honorific title was *horn*. The hunter was secured around the waist by a strong hide thong, the other end of which was held tightly by his assistants. He was lowered down the precipice to where the birds were sleeping. Seizing them one at a time with both hands, he killed them by biting their heads or necks before they had time to cry out. One author, Bridges, commented that this 'was dangerous work, for the rain and droppings from the sea-birds make the ledges terribly slippery'.[63] Angela told me of a cousin of the *horn* hunter known to Bridges. He was also a *horn*, and was killed performing this work. After his death he was spoken of as Tarsitin, 'he whom the cliffs ate'.

For hunting land-birds, various types of traps and snares were used. They were made of cords of guanaco nerves or whale whiskers and some measured forty-five to fifty metres long.[64] Birds were also killed singly with a loop of cord tied to the end of a long pole, with slings or with bows and small arrows.

For the Great Island alone 168 species of birds are documented, including 515 subspecies and varieties in all.[65] Many are ocean birds, while others are continental migratory birds. Besides the ducks, geese, swans, flamingos and cormorants mentioned above, the Indians ate parakeets, penguins, ibis, wood-peckers, owls, gulls, and terns; almost any bird except scavengers and a few others. Egg-gathering was an important activity of the women and children during the spring.

Shellfish, especially mussels, limpets, conches, razor clams and ordinary clams, were common in certain localities along the coasts where the Selk'nam and Haush dwelt, although they were not nearly as abundant as they were further south in Yámana territory. In recent times the giant crab (*centolla* in Spanish), so common in the latter region, was found in at least one locality along the Atlantic coast of the Great Island. Shellfish were available all year round. The women, aided by the children, gathered them at low tide and carried them to camp in loosely woven baskets which allowed the water to drain out.

Fishing was done along the coasts as well as in the rivers and lakes. For coastal fishing the women would simply wait until the tide had receded and then hand-catch the fish which had been stranded in pools formed among the rocks. Spears and nets were also used. Weirs were made for river and lagoon fishing. Robalo, trout, eels, rock fish, blenny, smelt, sprat and other small fish are most frequently mentioned in the literature. Robalo was especially valued and was preserved by being dried in the sun or smoked over the fire. Dried robalos were strung on guanaco nerves and hung up in the dwellings.[66]

A recent ethno-botanical study by Raul Martínez-Crovetto describes 179 plants named by the Selk'nam, but only thirty-five or so were actually used as food. Although plant foods were not normally quantitatively important, they were sought as a complement to meat or fish, and even as the main meal to quiet hunger if the staples were not available. In times of famine, when no game or land plants could be found, algae were eaten.[67] Women did the systematic gathering of plants and everyone picked berries and mushrooms. Different varieties of fungi, including mushrooms, were popular. The latter were stored dried in leather bags. There are no hallucinatory mushrooms in the entire region. Sap was obtained by scraping the bark of the dwarf beech tree (*Nothofagus pumilio*), and various kinds of roots and tubers were roasted and consumed. The entire plant of the wild celery (*Apium australe*) was eaten. Because of its high vitamin C content, this plant was sought as a remedy for scurvy by the crews of ships when they moored along the coast, especially in Good Success Bay.

In *párik* there is a plant called *taiius* (*Descurainia antarctica*) whose seeds, according to Lola, when prepared as a paste, gave a chocolate flavour. Gusinde remarked that the children were particularly fond of it.[68] The seeds were first rubbed between the palms of the hands to remove the husks, and then roasted on a large flat stone especially selected for the purpose. The stone was placed on hot ashes at the edge of the fire and while the seeds were roasting the women ground them with a cylindrical shaped stone. The roasted seeds were sometimes stored away for later use. To make the paste, water and seal fat or oil were added; it was consumed immediately or reheated later and eaten. Gallardo called it 'bread' and observed:

> In order to eat this bread certain rules must be observed, among which the most important is that small pieces should be thrown into the mouth and these should not be chewed but rather dissolved with saliva in order to be swallowed. If this bread is chewed the results would be rather annoying because the upper teeth would become stuck to the lower teeth, paralysing the jaw.[69]

Except for periods of hunger, or famine, caused by exceptionally cold or prolonged winters, it seems that the Selk'nam and Haush had a varied and abundant diet. Perhaps they tended to consume an excessive amount of protein in the form of guanaco meat. According to Gallardo, a stout or fat woman was prided by her husband as a sign that he was a proficient hunter.[70] The big eater was, however, derided by the term *chiteré*, glutton. Bridges remarked: 'The Ona [Selk'nam] were not greedy people. They had healthy appetites, as is natural in those who go long periods without food, but they never overfed themselves for the sheer love of eating. In all my years with them, I met but one who could have been called a glutton.'[71]

Dwellings[72]

The Selk'nam had two basic types of dwellings or *kauwi*: the rarer solid conical hut and the much more common tent or windbreak. The former was only used in the forest regions of the island, where suitable wood was available. The wall consisted of thin trunks and long branches which were driven into the ground and braced against one another at the apex, forming a circle. Lumps of grass, moss and mud were packed around the base of the wall to a height of about thirty centimetres to make the wooden frame firm and afford added shelter. Scraped guanaco hides were either secured to the wall with leather strips or thongs which ran through holes in the hides and were tied around the trunks, or simply inserted under the trunks and branches at intervals. They were placed around the part of the hut where the wind hit the most strongly. The entrance faced the opposite direction, usually the east. Gusinde described this type of dwelling as being from three to four and a half metres in diameter, the size varying with the number of people destined to occupy it, which may have been from one to three families.[73] With only stone axes to hew the wood and only human power to transport it to the site, a hut took much longer to construct than the tent type of dwelling, and it was probably repaired and reoccupied when its inhabitants returned to the locality. Such dwellings were also constructed for the families during a Hain ceremony when people remained on one site for extended periods of time. The ceremonial hut itself was in fact a variant of this type of dwelling (see chapter 4).

There was also a more or less conical construction which was built in a much simpler fashion using specially made poles, branches and usually a guanaco or seal hide covering. This was a more temporary shelter than the log hut and may be termed a windbreak or tent. It was a far more usual type of dwelling than the hut, mainly because it was transportable, quickly set up and, apparently, afforded an adequate shelter. It was well suited to semi-nomadic life. Most of the necessary materials for its construction were transported by the women from one camp site to another, and the women also built the tent. The poles (*léul* or *léwush*) were pointed at one end and forked at the other and were about one and a half metres long. Anywhere from six to twelve of these poles were driven into the ground, approximately equidistant from each other and inclined toward the centre, thus forming a half or three-quarters circle. During adverse weather, the circle was almost completely closed leaving only a small opening for an entrance. The tent covering (*ta'ix*) consisted of from six to as many as sixteen carefully sewn together guanaco hides or pieces of hide, although seal skins were sometimes used as a substitute. Guanaco nerves served as thread. The hides were scraped and painted or rubbed down on either side with a mixture of red ochre and fat (*ákel*). The covering is usually described as being several metres long and about half as wide, although there is one report of it being four metres long and two and a half metres wide.[74] Along its top edge the covering had holes at more or less equal intervals, through which the forked ends of the poles were inserted to secure and tighten the covering around the frame. If it were set up in a wooded area, the covering might be tied by thongs to nearby branches. The lower edge of the covering was extended a short distance on the ground. Rocks, stone and mud were placed on this flat in order to secure it firmly and to afford added protection against the wind, rain and snow. Branches were often propped up against the wall in order to give it greater solidity. The tent or windbreak was sometimes built in a depression or a hole in the ground.[75] Four reports from the early expeditions of the last century (1874 and 1883) state that the ground where the dwellings stood had been scooped out to a depth of between twenty-five and forty centimetres, with a diameter of one and a half to three metres.[76] As with the huts, the entrance usually faced the east because the prevailing winds rarely came from this direction. The fire was built in or near the centre of the dwelling, the rest of

27

the floor being covered with grass and twigs, when available, to keep the guanaco furs used as bedding from the ground. The utensils, tools and weapons were hung from the poles or set up against the inner wall.[77]

The tent or windbreak was obviously designed to adapt to varying circumstances in terms of the social arrangement, the landscape and the climate. It could be used either as a single or a multi-family dwelling. As its essential materials were transportable, it could be set up anywhere and the topography and the vegetation of the locality where it was constructed could be taken advantage of. During the summer or fair weather it was built simply as a semicircular windbreak, while in the winter it was more securely made and completely closed as a tent. When several families were camping together and each had its own materials, the dwellings would be located about twenty-five to forty metres apart, if the site selected afforded sufficient open space and if there was no threat of being attacked by an enemy.[78]

Lola, as other Selk'nam, clung to the ancient form of dwelling to the very last.[79] A few years before she died in 1966, when she was living on the reservation, the employees of a nearby saw mill had built a one-room house for her, where she slept and cooked. But at the back of the house she had a conical log hut where she passed many hours of the day alone sitting by the fire, weaving a basket, mending her clothes or knitting woollen socks.[80]

Clothing and ornaments[81]

The clothing of all the Indians of Tierra del Fuego was made exclusively from animal fur and skin. The hide of the guanaco was ideal for this purpose, as Lothrop observed: 'The skin of the guanaco, however, from which most of their clothing was made, is very suitable for garments, as the thin parchment-like hide soon becomes softened by use without tanning, and the shaggy wool of the adult animal is nearly water-proof and extraordinarily warm.'[82] However, for the larger capes worn by both the Selk'nam and the Haush, the warmer fox fur was preferred to guanaco fur. As an alternative to these skins, those of seals and rodents were used. The manufacture of clothing was women's work. The skins were stretched, staked on the ground or suspended on a tree or bush, and treated in the same way as tent coverings: the flesh side was scraped with a hafted stone tool and rubbed down with a mixture of red ochre and animal fat (*ákel*). The garments became soft with wear. The skins were sewn together with guanaco nerves or sinews, using a bone awl to make holes.

The principal garment, the fur cape, was worn by everyone. In contrast to the Tehuelche of Patagonia, who used their capes with the fur turned inside, the hunters of Tierra del Fuego wore theirs like a fur coat.[83] The comparatively heavier rainfall in Tierra del Fuego probably induced the Indians to wear the fur outside because wet fur dries much faster than a soaked hide.

The cape was sometimes decorated on the fur side with red stripes of *ákel* paint,[84] but the complicated geometrical designs of the Tehuelche robes were absent in Tierra del Fuego, perhaps because the fur was worn outside. Two large guanaco skins were required to make an adult-sized cape. The woman's cape was knee length, while the man's reached almost to the feet, but both were worn simply in the manner of a wrap-around. However, the woman's cape had straps sewn on its upper edges and could be tied across the chest, thus freeing the hands. The men sometimes wrapped the cape tightly around the body securing it under the right armpit, thus leaving the right shoulder and arm exposed while the left hand clutched the cape. Gallardo wrote that the man's cape 'covers the body to the feet and is held on simply by the arms, without any fastenings what so ever: thus when the Indian does not pay attention and lifts his arms, the robe falls off him and he is left completely naked, revealing his splendid physique.'[85] The cape served as a sleeping cover, and was also used as a shield. When attacking an enemy, two men held up a cape while a third warrior between them dodged out from behind it and shot arrows at the adversary.[86] The men were almost naked while fighting or hunting.

When there was snow on the ground the Selk'nam and Haush wore moccasins; those of the adults were made with the fur turned outside and the children's with the fur inside. When it was very cold they were lined with dried grass to afford greater warmth. Bridges, who often camped with the Selk'nam, was impressed with these shoes:

> In his *jamni* [moccasins] an Ona might walk for hours through icy water, often above the knees. When he camped for the night, he would wring the water out of his *jamni* and replace them on his feet, to which they would cling so closely that soon the feet would become very warm, though the fur outside might be frozen stiff. With his *jamni* on his feet and his robe swathed tightly around his body, he would pass a comfortable night, despite the fact that the temperature might be many degrees below freezing point, with his bare legs exposed from ankle to knee to the stars.[87]

The men also used leggings, laced up in front, made of fur-free guanaco hides, for protection against snow and thorny bushes.

The head band (*kóchil* or *goöchilh*) worn by the men consisted of a triangular piece of guanaco fur about eighteen centimetres at the apex, secured around the head by a string of plaited sinew tied at the back. It served more for camouflage during the hunt or in combat than for warmth. Also a symbol of manhood, it was ritually tied on the novice's head during the Hain ceremony. Both men and women sometimes wore a fillet made of woven guanaco nerves which, like the head band, was bound around the head and knotted at the back.

The men carried a bag, called *hasi*, made of fox skin with the fur turned out, in which they put small items such as pyrites, down for tinder, balls of *ákel*, stone tools, and feathers for arrows. Lothrop wrote that the *hasi* served as a pubic covering when the robe was discarded.[88]

The women had two garments exclusive to their sex: a wrap-around skirt

6. Two young Selk'nam men, probably in 1896 at the Salesian mission near Río Grande.

and a pubic covering. The former, called *kohi-aten*, 'hip tie', was worn usually like the cape with the fur outside. It encircled the body about one and a half times, reaching from the armpits to the knees, and was secured over the breasts by a thong. The pubic covering was a small triangular piece of furless guanaco skin.

The children were dressed in long capes, tied under the chin by a strap. However, around camp the children often ran naked even during the winter. According to Bridges the little girls were never seen without their pubic covering, though while playing it often slipped far out of place.[89]

Infants were swaddled in specially softened fox skins and lashed with strips of hide onto a cradle which was like a small ladder. The feet of the cradle were pointed so that by thrusting them into the ground, the baby could be placed upright while its mother was busy at work. In order to protect the infant's eyes from the glare of the sun or snow, a flap of softened guanaco hide was tied around its head, like a visor. The mother transported her infant in the cradle on her back, and in cold weather secured it inside her cape to give the baby added warmth. It was held in place by a net made of guanaco nerves or sinews, tied around the outside of the cape and the mother's body.

The women adorned themselves with necklaces, wristlets and anklets worn singly or in pairs; these were made of braided guanaco nerves or sinews, or plaited grass. The more elaborate necklaces and bracelets consisted of small lagoon shells or incised bird bones strung on nerves or sinews. A strip of guanaco skin was worn as an anklet. Occasionally, the men tied around their upper arm a band made from a nerve string, to which feathers of a swallow were attached. Bridges stated that this armlet was worn during foot races, to increase the swiftness and resistance of the runner.[90]

There were a number of different styles of feather head-dresses, most of which were worn by the men. One type consisted of a crown of feathers, called *ohn* or *oon*. It would be particularly admired if it were made of the blue head feathers of the cormorant; these were very difficult to obtain as blue feathers rarely grow on these birds.[91] Both male and female shamans donned special head gear when they were in a trance attempting to cure sick people or participating in a ritual. The feathers of the shaman's crowns had mystical significance (see chapter 3).

The Indians wore their hair long, except for fringes which were carefully trimmed. The hair was tonsured as a symbol of grief during the mourning rite. A mussel shell tweezer was used to extract all the body hair, except the eyelashes. Lola considered body hair repulsive and scowled with disgust when I mentioned the heavy eyebrows of one of the other Selk'nam. Both she and Angela had their eyebrows extracted when they were young. Tattooing was commonly practised and considered beautifying. Small incisions were burnt into the forearm and charcoal was rubbed into the wounds, thus producing a pattern of dark blue dots.

Body paint was important, if not essential, for everyday living, special designs being employed for the hunt, sporting competitions, combats and peace meetings. It played a highly significant role in the Hain ceremony, in the shamanistic performances and in the rites held upon occasions of female puberty, marriage, death, and the eclipse of the moon.

In normal times, when no special event was taking place, body paint had a practical as well as an aesthetic and a symbolic function. Ochre mixed with fat was used frequently to protect the skin and cutis against the wind and cold. The Selk'nam took dry baths by rubbing down the body, and rubbing yesterday's paint and grease off, with a lichen (*Usnea campestris* or *U. magellanica*, called 'the beards of the trees' in Spanish) or another plant (*Cladonia laevigata*).[92] Before setting out to hunt guanaco the men painted their bodies, their bows and their quivers with dark red, yellow or white paint, depending on the season, to blend in with the landscape.

Red was considered the most beautiful colour. The red paint called *ákel* was made from heated or burnt ochre mixed with animal fat, and was patted into balls. Everyone had his or her own supply of these balls which were kept in a small bag made of skin or from the bladder of a seal or a guanaco. *Akel* was an important trade item. Other colours, tones from yellow to tan and shades of grey, were obtained from different clays. Charcoal from the fire place, termed *háuk sa'a* (fire excrement), was employed to make black paint. White paint was made of natural chalk or limestone or guanaco bones, which were burnt and ground.

The body, sometimes omitting the face, was rubbed down with *ákel* and patterns were painted over this base using different colours, while the face was painted white all over or simply with designs of dots and lines using red and white colours. The designs were composed of round forms, ranging from dots to rather large circles, and lines of different width and length. At least six patterns, each distinguished by a name, were used on the face.[93] Gusinde describes the practice thus:

> Women who want to appear most beautiful powder themselves with red powder as they choose – on the chest and arms and even on the head-hair; the men however on their entire body. For a joyful event a mixture of fat and *ákel* is smeared evenly on the face. On a happy occasion, weather permitting [dry weather], all the members of the camp paint themselves in the same way early in the morning, with red on the entire body. Over this they paint two parallel white finger-wide lines around the upper arms near the elbows and on the upper thigh a little above the knee; moreover three lines from one shoulder to the other over the collar bone and from the breast bone down to the navel. Then the men don their capes as loosely as possible [around their body] so that the colour does not rub off.

The women sometimes only paint their upper body as they never leave the hut without a skirt.[94]

Raw materials and products[95]

Most of the domestic ware and 'hardware' was manufactured from more than one raw material, although a given substance (a type of stone or rock, a species of fauna or flora) was usually deemed superior for a particular purpose. The availability of the materials and the factor of preferences are also relevant for the study of the utilization of the natural resources. For example, according to my informants, arrow heads and spear heads could be made of at least seven different types of rock which in the Selk'nam language were named *héur* (also the term for arrow head), *haii, halp, mistr, pal, yar* and *seul*. As far as I can establish, these names refer respectively to flint, quartz or quartzite, silt stone, obsidian, slate or shale, rhyolite and possibly chert. Basalt was employed, and it is possible that diorite was also used.[96] Bone was apparently also used occasionally to make arrow heads.[97] Through the centuries since the era of Magellan, bottles floated ashore from passing or sunken ships, and very small arrow heads made of glass, suitable for killing birds, have been found in the archaeological sites in the Selk'nam area. Large ones are reported by three authors.[98] However, glass never replaced stone as the major raw material for the manufacture of projectile points or even the smaller arrow heads.

Stones and rocks also afforded material for a great variety of knives, blades and scrapers. Other common tools of the same material were hammers, choppers, axes, chisels, chipping tools, arrow shaft straighteners, stone sharpeners, rubbing stones and fist wedges. Stone bolas (the size of a tennis ball or larger) are found in the archaeological sites on the island or even on the surface of the ground, but according to all reports they were not employed by the Selk'nam during their final period.[99] Pyrites, used with flint to make fire, were only found in certain sections of the island. Mortars and pestles used to grind the 'chocolate' seeds described previously were only used in the northern zone where the plant which produces this seed grows. The mortar was simply a large slab of natural hard stone, and likewise for the pestle an appropriate natural form of stone was sought, although sometimes it was slightly reworked. The mortar and pestle were left near the camp site and reused when the owners returned. Bands of steel or iron which, like the glass mentioned above, were found on the beach offered good substitutes for cutting instruments and chisels which were traditionally made of stone.

Ochre was a vital item and, as stated above, it was mixed with animal fat to produce *ákel*. It was used almost daily to decorate the body and to protect the skin against inclement weather as well as to adorn the bags and capes and to preserve and soften the hides of which they were made. Great quantities of *ákel* were consumed during the Hain ceremony. Different tones of clay and limestone were also used to make paint.

Wood was a very important resource. The three species of beech on the island were used to make the bow, although the one most generally cited is the *Nothofagus antarctica*.[100] Bridges mentioned the *N. pumilio*[101] and Gusinde the *N. betuloides*[102] as having been employed for this purpose. Pickwood (*Maytenus magellanica*) was also used for bows.[103]

In the manufacture of arrow shafts the branches of almost all the small trees and bushes were employed. However, some had qualities only suitable for certain types of arrow shafts and others were considered superior for other reasons. Heath (*Pernettya mucronata*) was described by some authors as being the best for shafts.[104] It produces a relatively heavy wood suitable for arrows destined to kill guanacos, foxes and seals. But pickwood was considered by one author and several of my informants as the best for hunting this larger game.[105] The currant bush (*Ribes magellanica*) was sought for arrow shafts used to hunt aquatic birds[106] because it is lightweight, and shafts made of it would therefore float. Barberry (*Berberis ilicifolia*) is also lightweight, but employed for more general kinds of hunting than the currant bush.[107] *B. buxifolia* tends to have many knots on its branches, but even so it was frequently used for shafts.[108] A pampa bush called *mata negra* in Spanish (*Chiliotrichium diffusum*) is lightweight and another pampa bush termed *mata verde* (*C. amelloideum*) were both less suitable for shafts than the other woods.[109]

Other objects made of wood included spear and harpoon shafts, tool handles, fire tongs, and cradles. Any large heavy piece of wood might be used as a club. The poles employed as the frame for the dwellings, the digging sticks, and the canes the women used to steady themselves while carrying heavy loads were all made from specially selected woods. Torches were fashioned from strips of bark. Sewn bark cups are also reported,[110] although they were far more common among the neighbouring Yámana. Fire-wood was, of course, a primary necessity and was available in most parts of the island, although it may have been scarce in sections of the northern steppe lands. In addition products were made from other species of flora. Reeds of the *Marsippospermum grandiflorum* were employed for weaving the half-hitch coiled baskets, and loosely woven baskets were made from the stems of the *Agropyron patagonicum*. The powder of certain dry fungi was used as tinder. A tree parasite, called *barba* (beard) in Spanish, served as we saw earlier to rub down and clean the body. Black paint was made from charcoal mixed with fat and the white paint from ashes. The masks of the Hain ceremony were made of bark, although guanaco hide was also used for the purpose.

The island's fauna was of course essential for the manufacture of many products. Animal skins and fur were not only used to make clothing, tent or hut coverings, a variety of ropes and straps including the pack harness and different types of bags, but also for arrow shaft polishers, slings and quivers. Dolls made of sticks were also dressed in guanaco furs. The pelt of the hair seal, *Otaria byronia*, was preferred for quivers, but if not available guanaco skin served as a substitute. The nerves and sinews of this animal were made into thread and string for sewing clothing, dwelling coverings and bags, for tying the arrow heads and feathers onto the shafts, for making the cord of the bow, bird snares and fish nets, and for different types of body ornaments. Whale whiskers also supplied material for bird snares. Seal and guanaco bladders were used as containers to preserve objects from the humidity, and the fat of these animals was used to produce paint.

Certain tools were made from bone; for example, the tibia of the guanaco or the fox was used for retouching and sharpening arrow heads. Bones of certain birds were used as awls for sewing. Incised bird bones were fashioned into necklaces. The Haush and perhaps also the Selk'nam made harpoon heads out of seal bones, although guanaco and whale bones were also used for this purpose. Whale bones were employed to make wedges. The shoulder blades of guanacos and seals, because of their form, made handy shovels, plates for serving fatty meat, pallets on which to mix the paints and receptacles for gathering sap. The jaws of dolphins and porpoises were sought as combs.

Feathers of certain birds were highly esteemed for their symbolic significance or beauty and employed in the manufacture of head-dresses and forearm bracelets, and were an indispensable part of the arrows. Down was used in the disguise of the 'spirits' of the Hain ceremony and it was used as kindling, as was dry fungi.

Small lagoon shells were gathered for making necklaces and bracelets, and mussel shells for tweezers, knives and scrapers. The conch, a large spiral shell, was highly prized as a drinking cup.

Exchange of goods[111]

According to Gusinde, the Selk'nam never spoke of gift exchange and lacked a developed sense of gift-giving. He observed that:

> This was restricted to an uncle gratifying his nephew with a bow and an aunt or a neighbour making a doll for a girl. That which a male kin takes along when he visits a female relative, he does not deliver himself but rather his wife, mother, aunt or sister-in-law passes it on. 'So is the custom.' No one considers the gift a recommendation nor an obligation and no dispute would arise from this. Never would it come to the mind of a man to make a present to a woman who was not his kin. If a youth wanted to give a small ornament to a girl of his preference, he had to find a secret way of doing it.[112]

However, Lola and Angela told me that the Selk'nam did exchange gifts, in quite a formal manner, and this was confirmed subsequently by Federico, although gift exchange undoubtedly ceased to be practised when the Whites began to colonize the island.

Families from all parts of the island met from time to time to exchange objects and to engage in shamanistic and sporting competitions. These reunions were called *kuash-ketin* which Federico translated as signifying 'the encounter or meeting of many people'. Those who wished to organize a *kuash-ketin* sent a messenger (an *oshen*) to invite the inhabitants of certain *haruwens* to the reunion and to stipulate its place and the approximate day it would take place. At least in the latter pre-contact period, the Haush were sometimes invited to these reunions.

Shamanistic competitions, which were part of the *kuash-ketins*, were termed *kas-wáiuwen-jir*, translated as 'the profound speaking of the power of the shaman'. It involved a sort of competition between two shamans who had agreed to vie with one another to demonstrate what their respective 'powers' (*wáiuwins*) could accomplish. During the seance, the shamans normally attained a state of trance by chanting for long hours and thereby became imbued with what may be termed the energy force of their *wáiuwins*. The intensity of the trances, their duration, the symbolic richness and relevance of the words recited were all compared and it was decided which of the two per-formances was superior. On such occasions the shamans also made exhibitions of the force of their *wáiuwins*, which my informants referred to as *pruebas* in Spanish, 'proofs' of supernatural powers by means of certain demonstrations and ordeals.[113] The sporting competitions consisted of wrestling matches, foot races, arrow-shooting and ball games (see chapter 2).

During the *kuash-ketins* goods or gifts were exchanged among kin and friends from different *haruwens*. Each family or family group resident in the territory where the gathering was held traditionally received the same family from another territory. These arrangements had existed 'since the times of the grandfathers', in the words of Angela. The relationship was reciprocal, for the guests would later invite their hosts to their *haruwen* during a *kuash-ketin* organized by them and other members of their patrilineal group. The guests were offered a meal, called *hamis*, which was prepared by the male host rather than his wife. Large quantities of meat, fish and whatever else was available would be served. The meat was served on a plate consisting of the shoulder blade of a guanaco or seal. Angela commented, 'They wouldn't eat everything because there would be too much.' During or after the feast, gifts were exchanged. According to Federico the expression *wiik haijen*, meaning 'to make a present to one another', referred to this sort of exchange. But not only gifts were exchanged; if the guest desired some special object he or she would ask the host or hostess for it. Here the term *wiwewan*, meaning 'to ask for something without giving anything in return', was used. However, the following year or whenever another *kuash-ketin* took place, the person who had received an object in this fashion would normally offer something equivalent in value to his host of the previous reunion. Moreover, on these occasions anyone could barter for goods they needed or desired.

Lola told me about a *kuash-ketin* in which her maternal grandfather had participated. Federico heard of another which had taken place in *párik*, on the shore of San Sebastian Bay, where a whale had just been beached. It was organized by the patrilineal group from that part of the bay with the assurance that there would be an abundance of food for many families. Two famous champion wrestlers (*sórrens*) were to fight. One, whose name was Kuakas, lived in a nearby *haruwen* while the other, Alhila, was a Haush from a *haruwen* on the southeastern coast, a distance of some four days' walk. The latter won the contest. During this *kuash-ketin* people from Federico's mother's territory (at Cape Penas, south of the Río Grande) had brought along bows and quivers to barter or exchange as presents. People from the K'ámi (Lake Fagnano) *haruwen* brought arrow heads. Those of the Useless Bay area offered branches of a barberry bush from which arrow shafts were made. Arrow straighteners were presented by the inhabitants of an inland northern *haruwen*, famous for the stone from which these tools were made. Others, from *hérsk* (south of the Río Grande), came with fox fur capes. Those nearby, around the Bay of San Sebastian, provided roasted rodent in abundance for everyone. 'Each brought whatever he had', Federico finally commented.

Barter was a feature of the *kuash-ketin* but was not limited just to these occasions; it occurred at almost any time or place. As kin were not obliged to exchange gifts they could freely barter among themselves and with non-kin. Other writers have noted this. Gusinde states:

> Barter was a real necessity. The north group lacked the Nothofagus wood which was used for bows and the Berberis for arrows. The people of the south did not barter natural wood because the difficult job of making the object would remain, but rather they took along ready made bows or arrow shafts. For these they asked sea lion skins, mostly made into quivers. Thus sea lion skin, which was almost exclusively used for quivers, moved from the coast to the hinterland; in the same direction went resin and barrel loops. The north [misprint for south] lacked the Chiliotrichum little bush whose branches were good for making arrow shafts. The best little stones for arrow heads were found in the vicinity of Cape San Pablo, from where they found their way over the Great Island.[114]

A Salesian missionary, Coiazzi, observed:

> Among the Indians from diverse regions were exchanged barberry wood used for arrow shafts, clay for painting themselves, reeds for

baskets, the cyttaria mushroom for eating and skins with which they covered themselves. They undertook journeys for two or three days in order to acquire these raw materials.[115]

And Gallardo wrote:

> Such is the fame of the wood of the south that the Indians of the north offered *tucotucos* (a rodent), dried in the smoke and wind, for partially finished arrow shafts, an exchange which the Indians of the south undertook with pleasure.
>
> The same Indians of the interior traded their arrows with the tribes of the north, for fox skins, cururos (another rodent) dried in the fire, and stones for producing sparks.[116]

Finally I quote Angela:

> Around Kasims, near Ushuaia, and also Axtepec, near the lake [Lake Fagnano] there was *haiiko* (pickwood) used to make arrows. It also grew in Amshen, on the Chilean part of the island. Only in these three places. The women from these *haruwens* carried it, already scraped down, *charen*. They traded these sticks for *hamker* (arrow straighteners), for feathers, *chaitr*, for the arrows, for stone to make fire and for other things depending on the place [where they went]. In the *haruwen* of Ilk, on the coast of San Sebastian Bay, there was *aur* (conch shells) used as cups to drink water. They too were exchanged for pickwood. There was the transparent stone from which arrow heads were made: this was traded too.

The Selk'nam as a 'simple' society

To define the technology of the Selk'nam as 'simple', as many authors do when characterizing such hunting—gathering societies, is a misrepresentation. In itself, the technology was neither simple nor complex; it was adequate for the realization of the tasks for which it was destined. A more 'complex' technology is inconceivable in this context. I do not intend to imply that the technology of hunters and gatherers was as greatly developed as it might have been. But since no technology realizes its absolute potential, this is a false problem.

The classification of hunting—gathering technology as simple and industrial technology as complex elicits comparison on other cultural levels of these types of societies. How, for example, can the spiritual, mythological, symbolic and ceremonial aspects of Selk'nam culture be classified in terms of these facets of modern society? It could be argued that these religious domains of culture were relatively more complex among the Selk'nam than they are in any given contemporary industrial society.

The technology of certain hunter—gatherers may perhaps be considered simple in comparison with the superstructure of the same culture. For instance, Gusinde, in his principal work on the Selk'nam, dedicated only 113 pages to their habitat, clothing, ornaments, tools, weapons, subsistence and camp movements, while 760 pages concern their social organization and religion (600 pages on the latter). And if even more can be said about Selk'nam technology than Gusinde wrote, the same is true of the Selk'nam social organization and religion, as my informants proved some fifty years later. The Selk'nam 'tool kit', with the exception of the bow and arrow, does indeed appear rudimentary to modern eyes. In itself it gives little indication of the knowledge and training involved in the food quest, and even less of the elaborate social and religious life of the tool-users. Were the Selk'nam known only through archaeology, their culture would certainly be classified as a simple hunting tradition.

In many ways, the Selk'nam can be compared with Australian aboriginal societies. The latter have been viewed in the anthropological literature as having exceptionally complex social organizations, coupled with typically primitive technologies. Because of its complexity, in the past many anthropologists regarded the Australian society as an aberrant case of the evolution of human society from the simplicity of hunting—gathering ways of life to the complexity of contemporary modes of living. Yet Selk'nam society may be ranged in the same category as the Australians, with allowances being made for the great difference in the population of the two groups, the variety of the social institutions in Australia and the vast extent of the Australian continent as compared to the small island inhabited by the Selk'nam. Both societies may be viewed as having a technology which is simple relative to their own social organization and religious traditions.

This raises the question of whether any society can be classified as simple. Is the technology a sufficient or adequate criterion upon which to found such a sweeping hypothesis? If two of the better-documented pristine hunting—gathering societies cast doubt on the hypothesis of the evolution of society from simple to complex, does this not challenge the validity of the hypothesis itself?

2 The socio-economic structure

One of the main aspects of the Hain ceremony, the central subject of this book, was that it dramatized and symbolized the relationships between the sexes in ways which were vitally meaningful both to the men — who directed the ceremony and participated in it — and to the women — who were its audience and its inspiration. This account of the socio-economic structure of the Selk'nam will thus focus on the relationships between men and women, with special reference to the latter. These themes will be discussed again in the last chapter.

Selk'nam society had no chiefs, no council of elders and no law-enforcing agencies of any kind.[1] Within the male sphere, adults had authority over the young, especially over the initiates during the Hain ceremony, but otherwise the exercise of power was largely situational. The counsellors of the Hain had a certain authority during the ceremony; an expert hunter could organize a hunting expedition; a reputed warrior could lead a combat; but their authority was only operative for the particular context and was not coercive. A man took part in a Hain ceremony, a hunt or a combat if motivated by personal or group interests. There were no means of obliging him to do so, although a request to participate might carry more weight if made by a notorious shaman. The individual adult male assumed responsibility for making his own decisions, though he might consult with kin, friends and allies. In this sense, the society was egalitarian and individualistic. But it was also egalitarian in certain areas of the economic structure. No one but children, the old and the infirm was exempt from subsistence labour. Men of the greatest prestige, such as shamans, sages and prophets, were hunters like all other men, and female shamans fulfilled their economic role in an analogous fashion. There was no tribute system of any kind, no form of non-reciprocal gift-giving, no accumulation of wealth except the preservation of small quantities of food for use in the future. But there were variations in the extent and resources of the territories (haruwens), and there was a fundamental disparity in the sexual division of labour. Social distinctions also existed; some occupations had high status and those who fulfilled them formed what may be termed an elite. Moreover the social organization was strongly patriarchal.

Economic distinctions and the division of labour

Certain individuals were recognized as being exceptionally efficient or gifted in one or more of the economic activities in which everyone participated. In production activities, this category of persons was termed *haalchin*, which may be translated as 'expert artisan' (*chin* signifies 'hands') and could include both sexes. A woman who was especially adept at making clothing was distinguished by the term *haalchin ulion* (*ulion* meaning 'cape' or 'clothing'). An expert basket maker, who would invariably be a woman, was honoured by being called *haalchin tai-u*. Though most of the men could make bows, some were more talented than others and were probably designated *haalchin haa*. Similarly, almost all men made arrow heads but those who excelled at it were called *haalchin héur*. Bridges commented on this work:

> The Ona bows and arrows were beautiful pieces of workmanship . . . When fashioned by a good bow-maker (the experts were called *k'haälchin*), the wood was not smoothly rounded, but had some twenty-five flat faces, each of which diminished in width as the bow grew thinner from its centre to its end. In making the bow, the bending of it edgeways was a most difficult task. The finished article was most ingenious, combining strength with lightness . . . In Paraguay and Brazil, the natives have far better and more springy wood than that from the dwarf beech of Tierra del Fuego, yet I have never seen — either in those places or anywhere else — an aboriginal weapon to compare in workmanship with the Ona bow and arrow.[2]

The products of the expert bow maker were sought after and might be exchanged for other goods if he chose to barter.[3] But constructing bows was not a full time specialization and the bow maker was also a hunter.

The proficient hunter was called *hoipin* or *paautin*. The renowned archer, who shot with extraordinary precision in the hunt and in combat, was referred to as *kian-seren*. This term and *paautin* may be considered honorary titles. *Hoipin* simply means 'hunter', but when it was applied consistently to someone, this indicated that he was exceptionally successful as such. The fruits of the hunt were shared more or less equally among those who took part in the hunt as well as among the people in the camp. Women, particularly wives of the hunters, had the task of distributing the meat and the man who had made the kill usually received the brisket. Guanaco meat and fur capes were sometimes exchanged or bartered. Meat was shared generously with visitors but it was considered to be the property of the hunter rather than his wife.[4] A hunter of renown usually had more than one wife and even lesser hunters might also be polygamous. A classic case is that of Kausel, a famous hunter who had four wives.[5]

The cormorant hunter, the *horn*, was referred to in chapter 1. Because of the difficulty and danger involved in such hunting, the title was considered to be an honour. Certain shamans were also famous for hunting specific game with which they had mystical associations; they employed their shamanistic power to attract the game. Outstanding in this category was the *ochen-maten*, who 'killed' beached whales (*ochen*) with what might be termed 'magical arrows'. The guanaco-shaman (*johwn-xo'on*) was said to dominate the guanaco by his power. By chanting he rendered the guanaco so tame that the animal approached him and was easily slaughtered. According to my informants there were at least six other specialists of different game. All of these designations may be considered honorary titles because they connoted prestige.

As mentioned in chapter 1, during the final period of Selk'nam and Haush cultures (before 1880) the Great Island was divided into at least eighty territories, each of which was occupied by and considered to be the property of a lineage.[6] There was no unclaimed land on the island. Four of these territories were considerably larger than the others, but although this disparity existed, it could not become the basis of a consolidated hierarchy. Property claims over basic resources (game) could not be made because the animals were not domesticated. Moreover there was no institutionalized means by which one territory might expand at the expense of another and create a landless or dependent sector of the population.[7]

Hunting with bows and arrows was an exclusively male enterprise. Fishing and hunting with simpler weapons were performed by both sexes. Gathering was principally women's work. Dexterity with the bow and arrow required a long training which began when the boy was old enough to hold a small version of the weapon. The hunter had to have a great capacity to resist hunger, fatigue and cold. He had to be a swift runner and to be knowledgeable about the habits and characteristics of the game. A woman was never taught to use the bow and arrow, nor was she exposed to the physical and intellectual demands of a large-game hunt. She could kill rodents by stamping on their nests or striking them with a pointed stick and smashing their heads with a rock; she might also kill baby guanacos if she had well-trained dogs.[8] Lola, in her later years, hunted guanacos with a rifle. In contrast to hunting, gathering was relatively easy, though it may have been tedious. All the equipment needed was a basket or leather bag and sometimes a pointed stick, and although a detailed knowledge of the flora was required, the flora on the island was not exceptionally varied.[9] Moreover, everyone ate 'off the bush'.

The manufacture of stone, bone and wood tools was also confined to the males. This work called for considerable practice and know-how, and had to be taught, while women's productive work, like the manufacture of baskets, the preparation and sewing of hides, and cooking (roasting) could be learned by attentive observation. The women also took care of the children, transported the domestic equipment on their backs during the trips from one

7. The cordillera of Tierra del Fuego, near Ushuaia.

camp site to another, gathered fire-wood, fetched water and constructed dwellings.

Although men sometimes aided women in their tasks, a fundamental aspect of the Selk'nam sexual division of labour was that while men could perform most of the women's work the converse was not true. Moreover, men controlled the 'means of production' (tools) and provided the main sources of food, clothing and dwellings. While the men were dependent on the women for the perpetuation of the group and hence the society, the women were economically subject to the men even though the products of their labours and services were indispensable, and despite the fact that they worked as much (and perhaps more) than the men. The division of labour is a cultural invention, not a biological imperative:[10] the inability of the women to carry out the work of the men was mainly a result of socialization and teaching.

The sexual division of labour was patterned differently among the neighbouring 'nomads of the sea', the Yámana and Alakaluf. Here the women handled the canoe, only they could swim, and only they had the ability to remain under water long enough to gather certain aquatic foods.[11] These activities were indispensable for economic survival, but the Yámana and Alakaluf men were unable to engage in them because they lacked the requisite early training. On the other hand, they were responsible for hunting large game (seals, sometimes guanacos and even whales) for which the Yámana and Alakaluf women lacked training. Thus the economic relationships between the sexes among the 'land nomads' and the 'sea nomads' in Tierra del Fuego exhibits a distinct contrast. Among the former, the women were economically subordinate to the men, while among the latter the relationship was far more egalitarian.

Status occupations

The status positions which constituted what may be called a religious elite were the shaman (*xo'on*), the sages (*lailuka-ain* and *lailuka-am*, the father (*ain*) and mother (*am*) of *lailuka*, the oral tradition), and the prophets (*chan-ain* and *chan-am*, the father and mother of *chan*, the word). The persons of status who are represented in table 1 belong to the first four generations of the genealogies I collected (see chapter 1). These generations number approximately 2,850 individuals: 2,500 Selk'nam, 180 Haush, 70 Mestizos and 100 Whites who lived with Indian women, only some of whom had offspring.

Among the Haush there is a disproportionately large number of shamans, sages and prophets who were remembered by my informants. This also applies to the Selk'nam genealogies, though these are more representative than those of the Haush, because they are more complete. The number of women sages among the Haush is notable. I am not as yet able to offer a coherent or plausible hypothesis for this high ratio. It may in some way

Table 1. *Numbers of shamans, sages and prophets for four generations of Selk'nam and Haush Indians*

				Selk'nam		Haush	
Status	Total	Men	Women	Men	Women	Men	Women
Shaman only	186	151	35	144	33	7	2
Shaman–sage	18	16	2	12	2	4	–
Sage only	51	27	24	14	5	13	19
Sage–prophet	9	7	2	4	1	3	1
Prophet only	–	–	–	–	–	–	–
Shaman–prophet	3	3	–	2	–	1	–
Shaman–prophet–sage	6	6	–	5	–	1	–
Total	273	210	63	181	41	29	22

illustrate the difference between the Haush and Selk'nam cultures, but unfortunately the source material on the Haush is relatively meagre and difficult to analyse.

Bearing these qualifications in mind, we can assume that among the Selk'nam these elite status holders formed about 7% of the population as a whole during the final Indian period; that the proportion was higher among the Haush; that among the Selk'nam the ratio of male to female status holders was about four to one; and that among the Haush women held a greater percentage of these statuses than among the Selk'nam.

Shamans[12]

The shamans, called *xo'on*, had great prestige in Selk'nam society. They exercised their power, their *wáiuwin*, in activities where the element of chance intervened, such as in the wars and in the hunt, and they 'controlled' the weather. They participated in all the rituals and ceremonies and they held special seances during the *kuash-ketin*, referred to in chapter 1. The shamans gained access to the outer world while in a state of trance, which was induced without any external stimuli. Hallucinatory plant derivatives and tobacco did not exist in Tierra del Fuego. Trance was brought on by self-hypnosis induced by profound concentration while chanting for hours at a time. All shamans were able to cure (*soipin*) by drawing the sickness out of the body of the patient, but not all could 'kill' or inflict illness. Naturally the 'killing' shamans were feared. Many though not all male shamans were of this category, while very few female shamans had such power. Angela had heard of only two among approximately seventy female shamans (Selk'nam as well as Haush) whom she knew about. There were two sorts of such shamanistic power. One was termed *xo'on uhan té*. *Han* signifies 'killing by shamanistic power'; *té* has several meanings, the most common being 'obscurity'. Shamans having this power could 'kill' anyone and do so from a distance, without seeing their victims. The other was called simply *xo'on uhan* and shamans having this degree of power could only 'kill' other shamans. The two women shamans whom Angela told me about were of this type. Shamans who could only cure had a power called *xo'on unitern* and Lola, like the vast majority of shamans of her sex, was of this category. She treated Garibaldi often and treated me in the last year of her life.

The shamans might receive recompense for curing and I have specific reports of a guanaco cape, a basket of berries and an arrow straightener being given in return for such services, but no shaman could demand payment.[13]

In order to become a shaman one had to spend years as a novice under the guidance of one or more older shamans. Eventually the novice would have a dream during which he or she would receive the *wáiuwin* from a recently deceased shaman, with whom there would almost invariably have been a kinship tie.

Sages

The *lailuka* 'mothers' (*am*) and 'fathers' (*ain*) were the depositories of the mythological tradition and were the scholars of the society. Their erudition and their role differed from that of the shamans. They did not have supernatural power, they were not knowledgeable about the shamanistic lore and they did not chant. The word *lailuka* has a more general meaning than *hoowin*. The latter refers specifically to the mythical ancestors: their histories, adventures and ultimate transformation into natural phenomena. *Lailuka* includes the *hoowin* tradition as well as other myths, such as those concerning the origin of human life. The great number of Haush *lailuka* sages (see table 1) confirms the statements made by Angela and Garibaldi, that the Selk'nam had learned a great part of their oral tradition from the Haush, as was the case with important aspects of the Hain ceremony.

One of the functions of the sages and the prophets was name-giving. There were two distinct types of names among both the Selk'nam and the Haush: the common names, and prestigious names which were drawn from the *lailuka*. The former originated in a physical characteristic or flaw of the individual, a personality trait or the souvenir of an event which had occurred when the person was a baby or young child. These names were given by the family. Everyone had such a name but if a young child showed signs of special intelligence, or perhaps for other reasons, the parents would seek out a sage or prophet to give the child a *lailuka* name.[14]

The sages also played an important role in enhancing the prestige of their respective *haruwens* through interpretations of the *hoowin* tradition, as they were more knowledgeable concerning it than anyone else.

Prophets

The 'fathers' and 'mothers' of *chan* (the word) had the faculty to predict or foresee the future attributed to them. They had what Angela called 'visions of the future'. The most renowned 'father of the word' of the last half of the nineteenth century was Lola's maternal grandfather, Alakin, who was killed by the Whites about 1886 when he was very old. All the Selk'nam I knew spoke of him with admiration and veneration.

The status of prophets was apparently superior to that of sages and shamans. It is undoubtedly significant that as table 1 shows there were relatively few male prophets (eighteen in all) and only two female prophets in late Indian times, and that these were also shamans and/or sages. The prophets had detailed knowledge of the lore concerning the skies, which was the organizing principle of the symbolism of the Hain ceremony. This may explain why a prophet was usually, and in former times perhaps always, chosen to be a counsellor of the Hain and why woman prophets were so rare.

Other statuses of prestige

Prestige of a different nature was given to a person deemed to be unusually beautiful. A man or youth who was considered to be exceptionally well proportioned and handsome was called *hauwitpin.* According to my informants the Selk'nam were far more likely to acknowledge beauty in males than in females.

Warriors who excelled in battle, champion wrestlers and runners were all honoured by special titles.

Warriors[15]

The generic term for warrior was *pawin*; those who achieved great fame were called *kemal*, while an experienced warrior was called 'father of war', *aien-ain*. Gusinde considered the *kemal* to be the person who most resembled a chief. He stated that there was a *kemal* in each extended family group. This person was the respected elder, the counsellor whose word was backed by experience, sound judgement and familiarity with the tradition. Gusinde stated that the *kemal* had great moral prestige, that he mediated between contending groups and that his advice was often followed when war threatened. On the other hand, Angela, Federico and Garibaldi insisted that while the *kemal* was a great, honoured, or feared warrior, he was neither a respected elder nor a moral leader. In late Indian times there were very few *kemals* and only three are designated in all the genealogies I collected.

Women were usually excluded from the front line of combat. They could not handle the main weapon, the bow and arrow. Angela told me that women did fight with spears in the northern part of the island by coming to the rescue if their husbands or some close kin were being defeated. But women did not normally form part of an attacking party nor could they achieve recognition as warriors.

Women and children were rarely killed in the skirmishes,[16] but women were captured by the victors and abducted to become wives of the men who had slaughtered their husbands, fathers or brothers. I was told many stories by Angela and Lola of the suffering of women who had been wrenched from their families during combat. The captive was forced to live with a man whom she resented because he had killed her husband or kin and disrupted her life. Quite frequently a captured woman succeeded in escaping and returned to her husband's *haruwen* or to her own; sometimes, however, she was overtaken by her new master, brought back to his territory and punished. Gallardo remarked: 'When the captive woman tries to escape, she is punished in a barbarous fashion, even wounded with arrows, principally in the thigh, because of the lesser possibility of killing her by shooting her there.'[17]

Wrestlers[18]

Wrestling matches were a pastime and a sport but they could also be serious affairs. All the males, including the boys, wrestled for fun, to match their strength and abilities, and for practice. Serious wrestling was motivated either by private interests or by communal concerns. If a man had a grievance against another of a different *haruwen*, he could seek him out and challenge him to a bout. The challenger was usually accompanied by his male kin or friends who would witness the fight, but a larger audience might gather, including women and children from several *haruwens*. Gusinde described the enthusiasm generated upon such an occasion:

> People in the camp spoke for a long time about that match. They discussed each round separately as well as the positions, the grips and the movements of the fighters. Even at times they explicitly requested a prompt continuation of the match. Such an event concerned the entire sib and the distant neighbours, for every Selk'nam enjoyed a fight.[19]

A group of people of one or several allied *haruwens* could challenge another group to a wrestling contest. This was often done to avoid a combat, when, for example, the degree of hostility between the groups did not warrant the risks of outright warfare. An old woman, preferably kin to both parties, normally acted as the go-between and arranged for the time and place of the contest. On a selected day, the men, women and children from one group formed a semi-circle around the space designated as the ring, facing their rivals who did likewise. Nearly all the able-bodied men of the contending parties participated in the match. The contest was opened by an old man of the challenging party who harangued and insulted the opponents, relating the wrongs and treachery his people had suffered from them. Someone from the accused group responded, returning the insults. Despite the incriminations, the matches were fought with great decorum. The audience ensured that the rules were respected; these included not smiting the ears, eyes or sexual organs, not pulling the hair, nor scratching, biting or choking the opponent. The onlookers would be just as likely to protest if one of their wrestlers disobeyed the rules as they would if an adversary did. They also cheered and exclaimed over a good performance, *merrém*, 'well done', or to the contrary shouted *merr-són*, 'badly done'.

Usually the challengers opened the match. One of their best wrestlers appeared at the edge of the ring and dropped his cape to the ground revealing his body, painted red with white vertical stripes. He then stepped forward into the ring, his left arm stretched out horizontally in the direction of his opponent who advanced in a similar fashion. In the centre of the ring they grasped each other, either by crossed forearms or by laying both arms on the other's hips and clasping their hands behind each other's lower back. Then the fight was on, sometimes with several bouts proceeding simultaneously. One fighter replaced another until the last member of one team had dropped out from exhaustion, or until one team had shown greater capacity than the other by forcing their opponents to the ground. The victors and their supporters shouted cheerfully but the losers had the possibility of challenging the victors to a further contest later on, and there might be several such contests before the final outcome was determined.

Wrestling was also a sport. During the *kuash-ketin* reunions one champion wrestler, or *sórren*, could challenge another *sórren*, even though he had never met him. During such bouts reputations were at stake and the outcomes of the fights might be the subject of comment for decades. Champion wrestlers, the *sórrens*, were men of great renown and since the title was a relatively rare achievement, they were famous throughout the island.

Racers[20]

According to my genealogies, there were considerably more champion runners, called *sóijens*, than there were *sórrens*. Racing was also a competitive sport, but it was not a means of resolving conflicts. Anyone who had the disposition to do so participated in the races, though apparently they were never 'mixed'. Informal racing occurred when one group visited another and the men and boys or women and girls decided to race up a hill, around a lagoon or along a beach. There were also a number of racing tracks, open flat spaces some 500 metres long, and their locations were recalled by Angela and Federico. Apparently only the men competed in the more formal races for which they painted their bodies and wore the bracelet of feathers described in chapter 1. People from two or more *haruwens* gathered for such spectacles, which usually took place on one of the tracks. The arbitrators, two old men from each side, indicated a line halfway down the track by setting objects on the ground at each end. The two competitors placed themselves at the opposite ends of the track, equidistant from the centre line. The arbitrators stood beside the centre line and simultaneously signalled for the race to start by throwing a leather ball on the ground. Upon setting out the racers let their capes drop and began at a trot, slowly gaining speed. The first to reach the centre line would be acclaimed the winner.

The Selk'nam men were great racers and some were known to run down a galloping guanaco. In this context Julio Popper, the chief of the military expedition to the Great Island in 1883, observed:

> The Ona Indians are extremely agile. Obliged to hunt guanaco on foot they have acquired the ability of running with extreme velocity. Out of curiosity I measured the foot prints in the mud left by an Indian who had fled upon seeing us. The distance which separated one foot from the other was one metre and ninety centimetres.[21]

All the status titles mentioned here, with the exception of *hauwitpin* (perfectly formed) and sage, were employed as suffixes to the name of the honoured person's *haruwen*. These composite titles were not however exclusive to one individual if there was more than one having the same title in the same *haruwen*. Tenenésk, one of Gusinde's principal informants, was known as Kalu-xo'on, a shaman of the territory or *haruwen* named Kal. A woman shaman from a *haruwen* on the edge of Lake Fagnano was called K'amiu-xo'on; K'ámi was the Selk'nam name for this lake. Lola's grandfather, Alakin, had the title Naken-Chan-ain, 'father of the word from Naken'. Further examples abound. The titles of women were partly composed of the name of their own *haruwen*, even though they might never have lived there after their marriage.

Social organization[22]

The social organization of the Selk'nam and Haush in their final period consisted of four units or categories of relationships: divisions, kindreds, localized lineages and families.

Divisions

The largest exogamic unit was called *shó'on*, 'sky'. In anthropological terms it may be considered as analogous to the 'sections' of Australian society. There were three skies among the Selk'nam and three among the Haush, each representing one of the four cardinal points. The Selk'nam skies were the north, the south, and the west, while those of the Haush were the north, the south, and the east. Each territory (*haruwen*) was associated with a sky in a way which loosely corresponded to the spatial location of the *haruwen* on the island. This explains why the east was lacking among the

Table 2. *Status positions possible for men and women*

Status	Men	Women
Shaman: *xo'on*	√	√
Top rank shaman: *xo'on uhan té*	√	very few
Sage: *lailuka-ain* and *lailuka-am*	√	√
Prophet: *chan-ain* and *chan-am*	√	very few
Warrior: *kemal*	√	x
Hunter: *paautin*	√	x
Archer: *kian-seren*	√	x
Runner: *sóijen*	√	x
Wrestler: *sórren*	√	x
Artisan: *haalchin*	√	√
Cormorant hunter: *horn*	√	x
Beautiful: *hauwitpin*	√	few

Selk'nam and the west among the Haush. In chapter 1 it was shown that the Haush had been obliged by the Selk'nam to retreat or confine themselves to the southeastern zone, where they lived on the eve of White colonization. Before the arrival of the Selk'nam, the Haush had occupied the entire island, and so the division system as it existed in the last period was a kind of patched-up version of the original system. The Selk'nam probably took it over from the Haush and adapted it to the new reality. The Haush, instead of having the four traditional sections, were then reduced to three because they no longer inhabited the western part of the island, just as the Selk'nam could only make use of three sections because they did not have any *haruwens* in the east.

The fundamental organizing principle which the Selk'nam and the Haush employed to elaborate their cosmology was a circle divided into four quadrants. The circle symbolized totality. In the outer world it represented the universe. Within each division, each sky, resided the sources of all power (or energy), the greatest being that of the east. The souls or spirits (*kaspi*) of human beings returned, upon death, each to his or her own sky. The circle was reflected or manifested on the earth (the island) by the associations of the 'earths' (*haruwens*) into which the island was divided with the four skies (*shó'ons*). This concurrence, the harmony of the universe, of the skies and the earths, was symbolized in the ceremonial Hain hut, which was circular. In the hut, the centre of the universe was expressed by a fire, which rose from the entrails of the earth. Each sky, with the possible exception of that of the east, was conceived as having both a 'centre' (*oishka*) and a 'periphery' (*shixka*) around the circumference of the circle. In the Hain hut the skies were symbolized by posts, the four 'central' ones having greater prestige than the three

51

'peripheral' ones (see figure 12 and chapter 4). Each of the eighty Selk'nam and Haush *haruwens* was assigned to either the centre or the periphery of a sky. But this principle did not affect the rules of exogamy which depended only upon the sky to which the *haruwen* was assigned, the position within the sky being irrelevant.

A person was normally born in his or her father's *haruwen* or earth, and following the patrilineal rule of inheritance, this was considered to be that person's *haruwen*. Each individual was thereby associated with the sky assigned to his or her own earth. Two people who were *sos-shó'on* ('one-sky'), who belonged to the same sky, should not marry even if they were not kin. This exogamy rule may not have been always respected, but it was very clearly stated by my informants.

After the arrival of the Whites and the drastic population drop and disintegration of the social structure which soon followed, this rule was seldom, if ever, observed, which probably explains why Gusinde was not informed about it. He describes how the men in the ceremonial hut were associated with the cardinal point of their 'homeland territory', but he was unaware of the great importance of this concept.[23]

There is no evidence that the skies or divisions were kinship units as they were in Australia. When, for example, some members of a lineage settled in a *haruwen* which was associated with a sky different from that of their original territory, they adopted the new sky and their children, when adults, would be advised to marry accordingly.

Kindreds or kin-range

One of the prevailing categories of kinship among the Selk'nam was the 'kindred'.[24] By definition it is ego-centred and therefore its members vary with every 'ego', with every individual, except full siblings. People having the same mother and father shared the same range of kin. Selk'nam kindred was bilateral and included all of the individual's consanguineous kin up to the third or fourth ascending generations, that is to the great-great or great grandparents (uncles and aunts as well), and down to the cousins three or four times removed. The kindreds traced webs of kinship among the entire population, over the whole island. Among the Selk'nam one of the main functions of the kindred was to eliminate, and at the same time specify, possible marriage partners. All cognates, anyone consanguineously related to an individual as far removed as the third or fourth degree of cousinhood, were proscribed as spouses, with the exception of one category. Among these distant cousins one category was in fact preferred as a marriage partner above all possible candidates. It was advisable and even laudable for a man to wed his mother's brother's daughter three or four times removed, a daughter of one of his *ch'é*. *Ch'é* is a generation term for mother's brother, which means that it applies to all the matrilateral 'uncles', the fathers of the first, second, third

52

and perhaps even fourth cousins. To state the relationship differently, a man should ideally marry a girl whose kinship links are traced through his maternal grandmother's line up two or three generations and down to a *ch'é*'s ('mother's brother's') daughter (figure 8).

I am not sure how this relationship was traced up, say four generations to the great-great grandmothers on the maternal line, across to their brothers and down to the fourth removed *ch'é*'s daughter. A man, could, of course, have quite a number of *ch'é* uncles at this degree and quite a number of marriageable cousins. With reference to these marriages, Federico commented, 'People from all over the island would marry as everyone had distant kin in far parts of the island.'

The same applied for a woman. She could have quite a choice of husbands among the sons of a 'father's sister' (*po'ot*) three or four times removed. This is simply stating the same relationship from the point of view of a female 'ego'. But due to the male bias of Selk'nam society the relationship was always described in terms of a man and his *ch'é*'s daughters.[25]

The kindred not only served to institutionalize marriage rules. Selk'nam society accentuated individualism, despite the need for communal living patterns. Not only were people keenly competitive on almost all levels of society but also each 'ego' had his or her own set of kin which was shared only by full siblings. It was important for the individual to establish his relationship with others outside his lineages (his father's lineage above all, but also outside his mother's lineage), to know whom beyond his near kin he could ask for a favour, who would give him hospitality on a journey and even whom he might be obliged to aid. For instance, when a Selk'nam arrived at a *haruwen* whose lineage included a member of his kindred, he would first

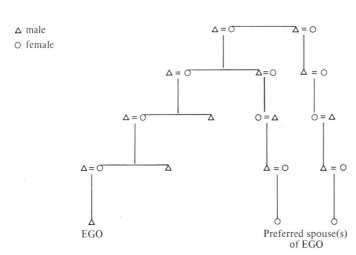

Δ male
O female

EGO

Preferred spouse(s)
of EGO

8. Simplified diagram of the mother's brother (*ch'é*) preferred spouse.

identify himself and then inquire if that person were present. If the answer were in the affirmative, he could expect to be especially well received. At all gatherings people commented upon and sought out members of their kindred. In combat a man would usually attempt to save the life of a fellow kinsman, if he recognized one among the enemy about to be killed.[26]

Lineages[27]

The third exogamic unit comprises the group of kin which normally occupied a given territory, a *haruwen*. Among the authors who had direct contact with the Selk'nam and described this category of kin, Gusinde rather confusedly called it a sib, an extended family (*Grossfamilie*), a kin group (*Verwandtschaftsgruppe*) and a tie of blood community (*Band des Blutsgemeinschaft*), while Furlong stated that it was a clan and Lothrop that it was a band.[28] Baer and Schmitz interpreted Gusinde's data as indicating that the *haruwen* group was a patrisib, that is a patrilineal clan, Lowie that it was a borderline case of the same while Steward and Service considered it to be a patrilineal band.[29] From my own data and an analysis of the literature, of which Gusinde's is by far the best documented, I have concluded that it was a localized patrilineal and patrilocal lineage.

A clan (or sib) is a unilineal descent group which traces its kin relations back to a real or fictitious ancestor.[30] It is a discrete group and relatively stable through time. In the case of the Selk'nam, Gusinde maintained that each *haruwen* (or district) group was founded by a mythological ancestor. He stated that the mythical Owl, K'aux, divided the island strictly into thirty-nine *haruwens* each with a mythical founder, that the limits of these *haruwens* or territories had remained unchanged and that, in practice, all those born in the same territory were considered a kin, forming a group which he termed 'sib' or 'extended family', as mentioned above.[31] It should be noted at this point that the Selk'nam counting system did not utilize numbers greater than ten, so Gusinde's Selk'nam-speaking informants could not have cited thirty-nine as the total number of *haruwens*, nor did this number have any mythological connotations.

K'aux, the Owl, did divide the island among the Selk'nam (or Haush) but very probably not into thirty-nine *haruwens*. My suggestion is that Gusinde counted the *haruwens* about which he had information, and thinking his data complete, he deduced that in the myth K'aux had divided the island into these territories. He compounded the error by appending to the K'aux myth other data on the *haruwens*, thus giving the impression that these extraneous data form part of the myth. He does not mention the names of the informants who told him the K'aux myth and merely notes that 'with the help of several men I mapped the districts [*haruwens*] in the south. For the northern half of the Isla Grande old Catalina Alamsharke determined the boundaries. This precise territorial division remained valid until very recently.'[32]

An attentive reader could note in Gusinde's text concerning these thirty-nine *haruwens*, that all of the northern ones (north or west of the Río Grande), his numbers 22 to 39, lack mythological references, while territories 1 to 21, which lie south of the river, are accompanied by such references. Old Catalina Alamsharke gave Gusinde the data on the northern *haruwens* and it appears that she misunderstood his questions and he misinterpreted her answers. Of the eighteen names of the supposed mythological founders of the northern territories, seven (numbers 22, 23, 24, 30, 32, 36 and 37) are names of men noted in my genealogies as members of the corresponding *haruwen* groups. Another three (31, 35, 39) also appear in the genealogies though not in the corresponding territorial group. Many of the proper names are repeated at least twice so this is not surprising. Of the remaining nine names, six can be partly translated and are similar to other proper names.[33] The remaining two names are unknown to me. The lack of complete correspondence is not surprising given the limitations of my data and the problems of transcribing Selk'nam words. It can therefore be deduced that the names which Catalina Alamsharke cited to Gusinde were not mythological ancestors, as he assumed, but rather those of individuals she knew or had heard about from those territories; men and women who lived during or shortly before the colonization of the island by the Whites.

Even the genuine mythical personages cited in Gusinde's list (numbers 1 to 21), from the southern territories, were not conceived of as ancestors of the land-owning groups; they were primarily associated with the *haruwens*, with certain localities on the island, and only secondarily with the groups which inhabited the territories. There are a great number of mythological ancestors of the sort that Gusinde cites as founders of the southern territories; they are the heroes and villains of the *hoowin* epoch. At this remote 'time', before the advent of death, according to one myth, or before the matriarchy was destroyed, according to another, these supernatural beings inhabited the earth (the island). Some became transformed into mountains, hills, cliffs and huge rocks, while others became animals and celestial bodies. Many of these personages are associated in one way or another with the *haruwens*, some with only one and others with several. According to my data, one territory had ten *hoowins*, another nine, though the majority had just one, and for some no *hoowin* was recalled by my informants, but these data are far from complete.

This level of the mythology corresponds to what Lévi-Strauss terms a 'totemic system of classification'.[34] It may be said that the lineages (the territorial or *haruwen* groups) gained prestige through the importance of their 'totemic affiliations', that is by the association of their *haruwen* with outstanding *hoowin* personages. These mythological heroes were traditionally linked to certain localities and their adventures (the myths) were interpreted differently by the sages in order to heighten the prestige of their respective territories, and hence of their lineages. The claims based on the mythology were dynamic and flexible, though not arbitrary. They were subject to discussion and even disputes among the sages and perhaps also among those who were less familiar with the finer points of the oral tradition. The association of the mythological ancestors with the *haruwens* was certainly not given for all time, as Gusinde thought. Nor were these heroes considered founders of the *haruwen* group, as Gusinde wrote.

Some previous writers regarded the territorial groups of the Selk'nam as bands. Steward wrote: 'The Ona of Tierra del Fuego fall strictly into the patrilineal band pattern ... The band was patrilineal because it was exogamous and patrilocal. Local exogamy was required even among the large bands in which relationship between members was not traceable, for native theory held that each band was a male lineage.'[35] So the lineage, according to Steward, is simply a function of exogamy and patrilocal residence, and could not be called a 'lineage' in the anthropological sense. Service, on the other hand, characterizes the 'Ona' as having a patrilocal band which he defines as a group which is exogamous, virilocal and patrilineal.[36] It is patrilineal because the members of the group are kin through the masculine line given the rule of residence. Service gives greater weight to the factor of residence, but according to both authors the principles of patrilocal residence and exogamy somehow generate that of patrilineality. These authors misinterpreted Gusinde's data, perhaps because he does occasionally employ the term 'band', as synonymous for his sib, extended family and kin group.[37] Lothrop also used this term. One might, moreover, be confused by the indigenous terminology. To my knowledge there is no Selk'nam word for lineage; *sos haruwen* (one earth) was the term used to indicate members of the same exogamous group. This expression cannot be found in the literature on the Selk'nam, but my informants used it frequently when we were discussing exogamy of the *haruwen* group. The term 'one earth' might lead one to assume that exogamy and residence did determine membership in a territory, but the genealogies I collected reveal that the people who inhabited the same *haruwen* were (with the exception of the wives) descendants of the same male line. The data also show that such lineages, like the territories themselves, were by no means static units (see chapter 1).[38]

The *haruwen* group cannot be considered a band for several reasons. First, residence did not, in itself, determine the membership in such a group. People who, for any reason, did not live in the territory corresponding to their *haruwen* group did not forfeit their affiliation with the group. Though usually a person was born in his or her father's *haruwen*, he or she would still belong to that group even if they did not have this qualification. Membership in the *haruwen* group lasted throughout life, except when the lineage divided. Normally membership was not a variable of residence. A married woman lived in her husband's territory without losing her rights over her father's territory. A widow, or a woman who separated from her husband, could return to her territory, in some cases with her children, depending on their age and the specific circumstances. If she did return with her young children, the male children had the option of either remaining there or of living in their father's territory upon reaching adulthood.[39] Offspring of both sexes could not marry anyone of either their mother's or their father's *haruwen*. This brings us to the second reason.

Since the *haruwen* group was bilaterally exogamic, residence and exogamy were obviously not coincident. Exogamy was not a function of residence but rather of certain kinship ties. The kin group, in this case the lineage, claimed rights over a certain territory but this was only one of its attributes, as will become clearer later.

A third factor which makes it evident that residence and exogamy did not generate patrilineality, as is the case with Steward's patrilineal band and Service's patrilocal band, is the fact that, as we have seen, the kindred, that is the consanguineous kin, was quite independent of the *haruwen* group. That is, kinship ties were expressed not only in terms of the lineages (the *haruwen* groups) but also in the kindreds.

Selk'nam society did not have a cell-like band configuration in which kin was only an epiphenomenon. It was a kin society, though kin ties by no means determined or patterned all the relationships. Nor can the society be characterized exclusively by its lineage structure. This entity was only one level of a more complex social organization which included the kindreds and the divisions as well as the family groups. Such complexity is not unusual for a hunting–gathering society. Australian social organization was of the same order, though even more complex.

The *haruwen* group may be termed a lineage in that it consisted of a patrilineal kin group which traced its kinship back over several generations. It was relatively unstable through time and lacked a common fictitious or mythological ancestor. Marriage was forbidden with members of the mother's as well as the father's lineage. It was virilocal, but it was not matri-patrilocal (uxori-virilocal) as has been argued by some anthropologists.[40] There is no indication that a newly married couple took up residence even temporarily in the wife's *haruwen*, although the couple did visit the latter on occasion. A divorced woman or widow had the right to return to her territory. There are several cases in the genealogies of sons of such widows who remained in their mother's territory and brought their wives there to live instead of returning to their deceased father's *haruwen*. Yet a widow sometimes married a brother of her deceased husband and remained in his *haruwen*. A man maintained a certain relationship with his mother's territory group, which could be important to him if it had greater prestige than his father's *haruwen* group or lineage, especially during the Hain ceremony, as will be explained later. There is very little data on the relationship which a woman might have maintained with her mother's lineage.

The family

The fourth and smallest kinship entity was termed *aska*, signifying 'close family', according to Angela and Federico. They did not define it precisely but it certainly embraced the nuclear family and adjacent kin. Polygyny (usually sororal) was quite common and five children for a couple was more or less average, so a 'close family' consisted of quite a number of individuals. In the large and populous territories the land was loosely subdivided into zones where the *aska* migrated and camped during the winter. But any one migrating group might be composed of more than one *aska* and almost invariably spanned three and sometimes four or even five generations.

These social institutions, the divisions, kindreds, lineages and families, formed a system in the sense that they were inter-functional. The 'system' was well suited to a hunting–gathering economy; it compensated for the necessary dispersion and isolation of the rather small migrating units (the families and lineages) by motivating people to gather from distant territories (partly because of kindred and division ties). At the same time it was flexible enough to adapt to changes in the land holdings and the demography, given the ease with which the lineage could be fractioned or divided and the possibility of changing divisions.

9. Selk'nam family.

All the structures described here were exogamic with the exception of the 'mother's brother's daughter' category of the kindreds. Each, in its own way, obliged people to seek a mate beyond the kin with whom they were associated on a day-to-day basis, and young people were encouraged to look for a spouse among distant kin who were not usually neighbours. Even the exogamy of the divisions, which were not kinship entities, had a centrifugal effect, because the territories belonging to the same sky or division were more or less concentrated in certain regions of the island. People gathered together not only in search of spouses, but also to exchange goods, information and knowledge; for economic and ceremonial purposes as well as for competitions of various sorts. Social visiting, communal hunts, feasting and large reunions were common. People were vitally interested in each other and their respective kin ties; so much so that many decades after the culture had been destroyed, the few survivors still recalled kinship and personal details concerning nearly 3,000 individuals.

Land tenure

The Selk'nam had a keen sense of territoriality. As described briefly earlier (see chapter 1) the different lineages or factions thereof claimed rights to specific tracts of land. All the habitable island was occupied; there were no free lands or waterways. Trespassing probably occurred when the owners were not in the vicinity. Although there was no way in which the boundaries of the *haruwens* could be guarded, the Indians were such keen observers and had such fine eyesight that the owners could probably detect the traces of footsteps of an intruder and identify him even some days after he had departed. Trespassing could motivate violent aggression on the part of the offended party and in addition a few *haruwens* were known to have been forcibly seized by neighbours who killed the male occupants and abducted the women and children. The Selk'nam were more successful as warriors than the Haush, and it is important to distinguish between these two groups even though they had a great many traits in common in their final period.

Land tenure was considered vital by the Selk'nam. The reason for this, and for their being so adamant about land rights that they sometimes fought over the land, was undoubtedly that, in general, the larger the tract of land the greater the resources of fauna and flora. Despite the mobility of the game, its whereabouts could be relatively easily located. The drinking places of the guanaco were well known and their trails could usually be distinguished without difficulty. Moreover the guanaco did not migrate at random and the hunters knew when and where they were likely to be found during the different seasons. The burrows of the rodents were virtually permanent. The migratory habits of the seals and birds were quite stable, certain stretches of the coast were famous for their large quantities of shellfish, and there were regions where useful plants were particularly copious and the lakes and rivers abounded in fish.

In common with all hunting–gathering peoples, the Selk'nam tended to concentrate in larger groups during the times when food was more abundant and easier to acquire, that is during the late spring, summer and autumn, and to disperse in smaller groups to pass the more trying winter season. Exceptions to this spatial contraction and expansion of the population arose when there was a windfall such a stranded whale, or when large numbers of people gathered to participate in the ceremonies and ranged further afield than usual in the quest for food.

The right of the lineage to its tract of land was modified under a number of circumstances. If permission were asked to hunt, gather or fish in a neighbouring *haruwen*, it was accepted procedure for this to be granted. The lineages which shared their lands from time to time usually did so because of kin and friendship ties. Collective hunts took place when large quantities of birds were nesting near a lagoon. The owners of the coast where a whale had been beached signalled with fires to distant groups to partake of the meat, and the guest might well remain in the territory for many months on end. The proprietors of the land on which the Hain ceremony was performed allowed the participants to live off their resources for as long as the directors of the ceremony chose to remain there and the same is true of other large gatherings. Thus although the *haruwens* were strictly limited by recognized boundaries and the land jealously claimed, they were by no means restrictive units or 'cells', as some anthropologists have described the patrilocal hunting band. The Selk'nam and Haush were not at all 'encapsulated' within their territories.[41]

The social position of women

Gusinde had an idyllic view of the male–female relationship among the Selk'nam and Haush, perhaps because he found equality between the sexes difficult to conceive. While he was adamant in pointing out that the women suffered humiliations and punishments while the Hain ceremony was being enacted,[42] he considered that the Indians enjoyed a well-balanced domestic life, that the sexual division of labour permitted the work to be shared and that the men were respectful and affectionate husbands.[43] How can one therefore explain the abuses of the women during the ceremony? Gusinde replied that the ceremony was of mixed origin; composed of a boy's initiation rite and a secret men's ceremony and that it was in the context of the latter that the men exhibited antagonism towards the women. According to Gusinde, the boy's initiation rite was very ancient, while the men's secret ceremony had been acquired from the Tehuelche of southern Patagonia. He was aware that the Selk'nam were a branch of the Tehuelche and that they had similar cultures. But he did not discuss why the status of women should be significantly different in the two groups.

Lucas Bridges, who knew the Selk'nam well either as workers on his sheep farm or as friends, wrote:

> A wife of long standing, if she obstinately refused to do her husband's will, was just as likely to be thrashed or arrowed.[44]

> I had seen many Ona women with numerous scars (principally on their heads) said to have been inflicted by irate husbands, and two or three times during my years with them I heard cries and the sounds of blows, but whatever my inclinations, I did not think it wise to interfere between husband and wife.[45]

> Children were much valued by their parents. When the men grew too old to hunt, their sons could be depended upon to supply them with food and to defend them. They might always get another wife, but children were not so easy to replace. Even brothers were far more greatly valued than wives; a brother would fight by a man's side and avenge him if he were killed.[46]

Gallardo, who lived in Tierra del Fuego at the turn of the century, writes:

> all the wives have the same rights and the same obligations – the latter can be summarized in a few words: serve the man – and her rights can be said with even fewer words: none . . .

> Among the Ona, until the woman marries she remains under the tutelage of her parents, above all of her mother who treats her affectionately. When she leaves her parents' home, a life of slavery begins for her: she follows her husband to the hut that he had built, she will be his companion, the mother of his children and his servant, and in spite of this a woman rarely remains unmarried . . .

> The submission of the woman to the man is unconditional and the bonds of solidarity that exist among the men are so strong, founded as they are on the idea of a common defence against the female sex, that if an Indian arrives at a hut where there is a woman alone and orders her to follow him, she must obey him, and if she doesn't he has the right to punish her. When her husband learns of what has happened he does not reproach his wife for having gone off with another man: she has done her duty and the offender is the man, and the husband will seek vengeance.

> We find in the physical appearance of these women the most obvious proof that their husbands do not torment them . . . the woman [Ona] is tall, robust, strong, healthy, plump. She walks with energy and does hard labour without her organism being impaired

61

because of her admirable constitution and because she is well fed
and taken care of . . .

Sometimes a wrathful Indian punishes his wives with his bow,
beating them all over until they are covered with bruises or wounds
that are more or less serious. In spite of being treated brutally by her
husband when she is punished, in normal life she receives affection
and many signs of esteem. The Indian, whose almost exclusive concern is the hunt, never fails to supply his wife with food. Sometimes
he is even gallant with her . . . [47]

It is very difficult to obtain quantitative data on the husband—wife
relationship in a culture which ceased to exist so many decades ago. As residence was virilocal, the wife was surrounded by her affines and constrained
to obey them, especially her husband. Moreover, women were often abducted
in combats and obliged to live with their captors. A wife could abandon a husband who mistreated her, escape from him and return to her own *haruwen*,
but she might also have to abandon her children and if her husband overtook
her before she reached her destination he might beat her severely. Federico
once commented: 'A man can beat his first wife. This is his right, but he
should not strike his other wives because they were [usually] married before.'

While the social position of the woman was undoubtedly inferior to that
of the man, she was neither a slave nor a bond-servant. She did exercise certain rights, but she had little power. She shared with the men the right to
attain such positions of prestige as shaman and sage, though only in a ratio of
about one to four (see table 1). The Selk'nam men generally exercised power
over the women but individually they did not necessarily have superior prestige. Achievement of the highest status (shaman, sage and prophet) required,
above all, mystical propensities, long training and specific knowledge. Most,
though not all, shamans received their spiritual power (*wáiuwin*) from a
deceased shaman with whom a kin relationship existed. But prestige and
power are phenomena of a different order. Though they may overlap and be
mutually supporting, they are often, in any society, quite independent of
each other.[48] Knowledge of the tradition might bring prestige, but 'knowledge itself breeds little power', as Sahlins remarked.[49]

One of the most appealing traits of the women in this society is their
sophistication. If I am correct in assuming that they recognized the men's
need to dominate them and humiliate them during the Hain celebration, they
were not for all that victims of the 'system'. In any event, they had great
dignity and were capable at times of defying the men's authority; of aban-
doning an obnoxious husband, of challenging a male shaman in power competitions, of hunting guanacos, if only with dogs. If need be, a woman could
feed her family with fish, rodents, shellfish and plants. The women were not
passive reproducers nor submissive wives and workers.

Was Selk'nam society egalitarian?

The search for universals concerning hunting–gathering societies has recently produced some daring models and sweeping generalizations. Theoretical discussions among ethnologists and archaeologists have tended to concentrate on an option between a patrilineal, patrilocal band or horde and a flexible, bilateral, non-territorial group.[50] The latter dovetails nicely into an egalitarian model and can be contrasted neatly with capitalism.[51]

Societies may well have existed and still exist which are definable in terms of a flux–bilateral–egalitarian model, the utility of which I am not contesting. I do, however, disagree with the propensity to limit the typological spectrum of hunter–gatherer cultures to an option between this sort of model and a band model, or to broaden the latter and label almost any hunter–gatherer local group a band.[52]

Much has been written recently to substantiate the vital importance of gathering, and of women's role in general, in societies which had previously been regarded as essentially hunting- and male-dominated. This tendency is very positive. Male bias permeates anthropology because it permeates our society. In social studies equal value must be accorded to both sexes and the roles of women awarded the same attention as those of men. If women's activities and status are assumed to be inconsequential, or are inadequately described and analysed, the study of social processes is falsified. But the feminist movements will be poorly served by anthropologists, however well meaning, if they insist that equality of the sexes was the norm in a pristine world of gatherers and hunters.

The Selk'nam society has been labelled a band-type society but, if my analyses are correct, this is an error. Given this society's emphasis on patrilineality and patrilocality, the pre-eminence of territoriality, the predominance of hunting as a male occupation over gathering as women's work, and the inequality of the sexes, it would be difficult to class it as a flexible–bilateral–non-territorial–egalitarian society. So neither model applies to this society.

A new reading of the literature and the material which I have gathered reveals that the 'Ona bands' were localized lineages, and that they were only one instance of a social organization which included families, kindreds and divisions. Though the lineages were the territory-owning groups, they by no means institutionalized the entire society. Selk'nam society does not conform to the band model used by Service when he wrote:

> From the point of view of cultural evolution this rudimentary society [the patrilocal band society] could be called, adopting Steward's phraseology, the Band Level of Sociocultural Integration. With this phrase it is possible to go somewhat beyond social organiz-

ation as such and to use the basic social features to characterize and name the whole culture as a type. The salient feature of the type is simply that *all the functions of the culture are organized, practised or partaken of by no more than a few associated bands made up of related nuclear families.* The economy, for example, is organized by

10. Two Selk'nam women, about 1914.

and takes place entirely within these units . . . The same is true of other cultural functions . . . Likewise, there is no religious organization standing apart from family and band; and the congregation is the camp itself.

The fact that family and band are simultaneously the sole economic, political, and religious organization greatly influences the character of these activities. The economy, polity, and ideology of the culture of bands is unprofessionalized and unformalized; in short, it is familistic only.[53]

Though this society was neither flexible, nor bilateral, nor egalitarian in its overall configuration, it had all three of these qualities. It was flexible in that the ownership of the *haruwens* varied over time, both in number and in extent, and that the many exceptions to the ownership principle testify that the territories were often shared by neighbours and by the community at large. It was bilateral in the sense that the mother's *haruwen* and lineage were an alternative residence and group into which the men, under certain circumstances, could incorporate themselves and their families.[54] The role of the woman's mother's *haruwen* lineage is not clear. Given the patriarchal character of the society it cannot be considered egalitarian; the women were largely economically dependent on the men, the society was ruled by men and wives were governed by their husbands. However, it did have egalitarian traits. Despite the fact that some *haruwens* were richer and larger than others, food was shared among the members of hunting parties and of one or more lineage groups. Moreover, all able-bodied adults contributed to the subsistence economy, and leadership, when it did exist, was spontaneous and not oppressive. The status of shaman, which afforded great prestige, was accessible to the majority of men, and in general status depended more on individual ability and achievement than on hereditary rights. However, among the Selk'nam, only a relatively small number of women attained high status. This society was at once patriarchal, keen on land-property rights, status-conscious, individualistic, competitive, egalitarian, and 'flexible'. As it reveals elements of both the patri-band and the egalitarian–flexible models, it cannot be considered an exception to either. This suggests that this dichotomy is logically inadequate. The substantive error in these models lies in their simplicity, in the selection of their diagnostic traits. Ecological, ethological and evolutionary criteria are advanced at the expense of sociological, economic and religious factors.

There are many problems concerning hunting–gathering or gathering–hunting societies which the social scientists may never be able to resolve. But knowledge will not be increased by excessive selectivity of typological criteria. On the contrary, comprehensive research may be discouraged by the assumption that the essential features of these societies can be expressed satisfactorily in terms of a few simple principles.

3 The ideology[1]

One of the major concerns of this study is the ideological foundation of the Selk'nam society. This ideology was perhaps most clearly expressed in the myths of the Hain. This chapter first presents two of the principal Hain myths, and then brings together dispersed mythological data under the general title 'Moon, the vengeful woman'. In order not to confuse the reader of Gusinde, his titles for the first two myths are quoted in parenthesis. The Selk'nam themselves did not give titles to their myths.[2]

The myth of matriarchy (The origin of the women's kloketen)

In the epoch of *hoowin* (mythical time) women ruled over men without mercy. They obliged the men not only to hunt and to procure all the necessities of life, but also to tend the children and do the domestic chores.

> The men lived in abject fear and subjection. Certainly they had bows and arrows with which to supply the camp with meat, yet, they asked, what use were such weapons against witchcraft and sickness?[3]

> If there was anything to discuss, the women got together privately, leaving their men behind in the huts. Men were not allowed to sit in the circle of the women when they were considering or discussing things. Only women made decisions and gave orders. Men had to do what they were told. They were completely dependent upon the women.
>
> But as the men were strong and numerous, the smartest among the women feared that some day they might rebel and refuse to obey. So they sat down together to ponder and consider how they might keep the men subjected; they did not want them to rebel and to disobey . . . The women continued to think and ponder the question for a long time. Finally the women initiated this secret meeting, very much like the one men have today.[4]

While the men were busy labouring from sunrise to sunset, the women lounged in the big hut, the Hain, which the men were forbidden to approach, let alone enter. If they dared to do so they would be killed. But such an idea

66

would never occur to them, overwhelmed as they were by the women's threats.

The most extraordinary figure was Moon (Kreeh). Not only was she a shaman of incredible ascendency, and the undisputed leader of the women and hence of the men, but she also directed and determined all that went on during the Hain celebration. She was so powerful that even today, after the phenomenal victory of the men, she alone among the women of *hoowin* still demands respect and evokes fear, especially when she enters into an eclipse. During her reign, her husband, Sun (Krren), performed the humble tasks that were the lot of his sex.[5] He too was a shaman as were his brother Wind (Shénu), Moon's brother Snow (Hosh), Sea (Kox) and the latter's brother Rain (Chálu).

From time to time, Moon would decide that a Hain be enacted so that the young women be initiated into adulthood. Moon was a stern mistress and she was known even to kill girls who, after being initiated, proved to be lazy, insolent or disobedient.[6] The Hain was also performed to deceive the men into believing that the spirits were arbitrary, capricious and so powerful that everyone was at their mercy, including the women themselves. 'With all this, the cunning women had the evil intent of terrorizing and intimidating the men, so as to keep them subordinate forever.'[7]

Women made the preparation for the ceremony in the utmost secrecy, as the men do today. Moon determined which of the women were to play the roles of the different spirits. When the paint and masks were prepared, those who were to perform spent long days practising the stance, gait, and gestures of the spirits they were to impersonate in order to beguile the men. Some of the spirits (the men were told) arose from the depth of the earth into the big hut to take part in the ceremony, while others descended from the heavens, entering the hut during the night. The purpose of the spectacle was to evoke admiration and fear in the men, to excite their imagination and impress them with the power of the spirits. The men whose behaviour left something to be desired, or who now and again rebelled slightly against the female tyranny, were sought out and punished by a spirit, named Shoort, who daily visited the camp where the men lived. The ceremony over-awed and strained the men to the limits of their endurance. They would never dare rise in rebellion knowing as they did that the powers ruling the universe had forever ordained that women be their masters.

> Every woman gave her husband the chores that Moon—Woman had mentioned, and the men took care of them all. The women spent almost the entire year in the Big Hut. During the day this or that woman would return to the camp, where she would stay for a short while to order her husband to new tasks. She would also eat the roasted meat that he had prepared for her, for she was always very

hungry. Sometimes she slept with her husband. But as a rule the women slept together in the Big Hut and seldom came to pass a night in camp.[8]

A terrible female spirit, named Xalpen, rose from the entrails of the earth into the big hut during the ceremony, and she delighted in the occasion for she was very gluttonous and anticipated assuaging her phenomenal appetite with the meat the men would bring to her (which was in fact eaten by the women). She was also dangerously capricious even with respect to the women, so the men were led to believe, and at any moment might turn her wrath against those gathered in the Hain hut and massacre them all. Thus the men were doubly harassed, obliged as they were to hunt incessantly in order to satiate Xalpen's voracious appetite and threatened that, despite all their efforts, Xalpen might slaughter the women in a tantrum. Meanwhile, in the big hut, the women would be feasting on the meat brought for Xalpen and laughing with malice at the men's incredible naïveté and stupidity.

Xalpen was rarely shown to the men, but they knew when she emerged into the Hain from her earthly abode, for they heard the women's terrifying screams and Xalpen's thudding, threatening voice. And at the same time the men saw the wall of the big hut shaking and flames flying from its summit. The other spirits appeared with less fanfare and were announced by the chanting of the women within the Hain to call the men to attention.

So it had always been, until one day Sun unknowingly passed close to the Hain carrying a guanaco he had just killed. Suddenly he heard the voices of two young women. He stealthily laid aside his burden and crept nearer to spy on them. They were practising the parts they were to play in the ceremony, giggling and merrily commenting on the fun they would have fooling the men into believing the spirits were real. Sun was aghast, for he had not only seen them, but he also had heard their cynical remarks. He was dumbfounded and perplexed. But soon he realized the truth, that the entire ceremony was a hoax perpetrated by the women in order to keep the men subservient to them. He stepped out of his hiding place and shouted: 'You false women! So that is how you've been deceiving the men! Now I know everything!'[9]

Back in camp when the men heard the news they were outraged. But like Sun they contained their indignation and together they set about making a plan to overthrow the women. They pondered for a long while until finally, advised by Sun, they decided upon the action to be taken. Several of the smallest men, who were very swift runners, were sent to spy on the women in the Hain hut. One after the other scooted through the grass and when they reached the hut they raced in one side and out the other, along the inner walls, without being seen by the women. Later these spies were transformed into little prairie birds. Each returned excitedly telling the same story. 'I only saw our wives and girls! . . . Apart from that there was nobody there in the Big Hut! . . . There really are only women and girls there! Each one has a mask standing behind her! . . . There are only women sitting there!'[10]

The men discussed at length what to do next. Another little man, who later became the oyster-catcher bird, was dispatched to sneak up very close to the Hain, watch what the women were up to and, at the most opportune moment, whistle as a signal for the men to attack.

Meanwhile the women were growing more and more anxious. Under the pretext of demanding meat for Xalpen, Moon sent her daughter Tamtam (canary) with some other women to camp to see what the men were contriving. The women were aghast when Tamtam's father, Sun, confronted her, saying: 'Go ahead, take this meat; it's all I found today! Take it to your mother and the other women; after all, it is they alone who eat and enjoy it! It will be plenty for all the women there in the Big Hut!'

Tamtam and her companions dragged the meat back to the Hain. Pale with fear she related what had happened and her fear spread to all the women. Then Moon gave an order: 'A *shoórte* is to go through the camp at once! It must carefully observe the men, listen closely to what they say and whether they are planning anything. Fast action is important!' Immediately other women went close to camp to report on the comments the men might make about the Shoort. One woman heard a man say: 'Who knows if that's really a *shoórte*?' Another man shouted: 'Perhaps one of our women has painted herself, and we believe that she's a *shoórte*!'[11]

The wisest women trembled with alarm and foreboding as they discussed what was to be done. Finally Moon ordered that Xalpen was to massacre all the women. She shouted to the men in camp: ' "Keep quiet; Xálpen is very angry and incensed!" But these words did not quiet the men. Completely at a loss, Moon—Woman now admitted to the women: "We are in serious trouble! Let's make one more attempt to frighten the men . . . " '[12] They hurriedly formed two lines and filed out, around each side of the Hain, onto the prairie, where Moon took her position in front, facing the men. 'In a loud voice she bid the men come closer, for now Xálpen was going to call one woman after the other into the hut to devour them. This was supposed to terrify the men.'[13] But instead of being terrified, the men were arming themselves with thick cudgels and bows and arrows. Suddenly the signal for attack was heard; Oyster-catcher whistled from his hide-out near the big hut and the men began moving slowly across the prairie towards the women. In desperation Moon shouted defiantly: 'Not too close, men; stay away from the hut! . . . Not so close, men, or Xálpen will jump out!'[14] But on they came, pushing Moon and all the other women back in the Hain hut. Then Sun roared at the top of his voice: 'Strike down the women!'[15]

Amidst the confusion the women hurriedly extinguished the fire in the Hain, though the embers kept on burning. The men rushed at the women, swinging their clubs and stabbing them with arrows. Each man throttled the first woman he could lay his hands on. A massacre ensued; husband killing wife, father slaughtering daughter. Sun even killed his beautiful daughter Tamtam but some of the men could not bear to kill their kin. One tried to defend his daughter who was clinging to his legs entreating him but she too was finally slain. Another man even fought with a companion in a vain attempt to save his daughter. One man disgraced himself by abusing the dead bodies, but when the men saw what he was doing they were so incensed that they killed him. The culprit was transformed into the ibis bird with a red patch on his throat looking like an open sore. Thus he wears forever the mark of the fatal wound he received in punishment for his outrageous act.[16] The massacre ended only when all but one of the women and girls were prostrated, covered with blood, dead on the floor of the Hain hut.

Sun had even dared attack Moon, his indomitable wife, the master mind. He drew a long brand from the smouldering fire and struck her three times. But while he was assaulting her the heavens trembled violently and fearing that the sky would crash down and crush the earth, he ceased beating her. Under his massive blows, Moon had fallen face forward into the embers of the hearth. It was said that Sun's brother, Wind, also struck Moon with a burning torch,[17] although neither he nor the other men dared slay her. With her face badly burnt, she rose into the heavens pursued in hot anger by her husband. Sun will pursue Moon for all eternity though he will never capture her and Moon will forever look down upon the earth, her face tarnished and scarred from the wounds inflicted upon her during the great revolt. She will never forgive her enemies, the men; and for all time to come she will seek to revenge herself upon them.

But the men had won the great battle. All the women, young and old, had been slaughtered or banished. Some of the children were so terrorized that they fled into the woods and became lost, surviving only by feeding on mushrooms, roots and berries. As time passed hair grew all over their bodies, finally they lost the faculty of speech, and became those dreaded creatures, the Joshils, which haunt the forests to this day.[18] Of the female sex, only the innocent little girls and babies remained, ignorant of the perfidy of their mothers and sisters.[19]

The first men's Hain (The origin of the men's kloketen)

The men and children then began the great trek to Maaj-kum, to reach the very limits of the universe, and all the while they mourned the women. They travelled to the east, *Wintek*, from where they circled a long way around until they came to *Kámuk*, the north, from where they passed on to *Kenénik*, the west, and finally by way of *Kéi-kruk*, the south, they arrived back on earth. It was winter when they returned.[20] Then a great question arose: 'How could the men keep the upper hand now they had it? One day, when these girl children reached maturity, they might band together and regain their old ascendancy. To forestall this, the men inaugurated a secret society of their own.'[21]

Many clever strong men gathered in the region of Máustas (the southeastern part of the island) and there they erected a tremendous construction entirely of rock, the first Hain hut of the men. 'The entire mountain [Máustas], especially the soaring cliffs standing close together like pillars of stone, appears . . . as a huge conical hut.'[22] Seven very powerful, tall, handsome men, the great shamans of *hoowin*, each dragged a huge rock post from the region where he lived.

> Next the rest of the men, in turn, brought forward additional posts and closed the spaces between one main post and the other. Each worked in the space that represented his home territory, and here each man was assigned his place. All those posts were of stone, just as we use tree trunks now. The first hut was built the same way [conical] as it is done today. It was a tremendous construction.[23]

The greatest shaman among them, who was to direct the Hain, and the other renowned men gathered at the hut came to an agreement about all that was to occur during the Hain. They pondered for a long time about which men were to disguise themselves as the different Hain spirits. These were the very same spirits with which the women had deceived and terrorized the men when they controlled the Hain. Thus the men's Hain was founded and so it has been ever since.

All this and many other events concerning the Hain of the *hoowin* epoch were to be guarded with great vigilance in the memory of men for all time to come; the women were never to learn about them.

Moon: the vengeful woman

Every month Moon relives her terrible defeat. Her rage and her hunger increase as she waxes. She is said to devour human beings, especially children, in order to avenge herself. When she appears full, she is the undisputed mistress of the nocturnal heavens, as she had been of the earth in the epoch of her ancient dominion. But her face remains forever streaked with the scars of the inexpiable offence committed by her husband.[24]

One autumn evening when I was with Lola, she pointed to the huge red moon glowing low on the horizon and said '*Kreeh háaten*' ('Moon is in a rage'). This same expression means that the moon is in eclipse. The men told Gusinde that Moon appeared to be satiated when she was full, but that this was a deception to lull the fear she creates, so that she might consume humans, especially children, who are off their guard. The men also told him that children should not stare at Moon, above all when she is full, for if they did they might lose consciousness and fall dead, such is her wickedness. He once observed a mother, whose child had been sitting in front of a hut staring at the moon, grasp her child firmly by the arm and hurry him inside the family hut while shouting with alarm, 'Moon is looking at you!'[25]

And when Moon is waning the men said she is also pretending, lulling the people into believing she is old, weak and near death. Then too they become less cautious and she can easily seize a child who is running about outside and devour it, but nevertheless she is thinner then because she eats fewer humans.[26]

One moonlit night the elderly shaman Tenenésk shook his fists at the moon, saying to Gusinde: 'How it hurts me that the men of old did not kill that deceitful woman . . . Do you see the scars on her face? She deserves them! . . . Moon is man's worst enemy!'[27] When I was with Lola and the moon disappeared from the sky, she commented: 'She [Moon] is now hiding from her husband [Krren, Sun] but he is still pursuing her!'

Just as Moon is despised so Sun is highly esteemed. He is affectionately called *tul-ulichen* ('beautiful heart') for the warmth he gives to the inhabitants of the earth.[28]

Since the world has become what it is, the memory of Moon's humiliation infuriates her beyond all measure, and at times she will suddenly go into an eclipse. Her face is then flushed with the blood of the men whom she condemns to perish in coming battles, and her red tainted shadows cover the land as a foreboding of their destiny. Lola and Angela said that when the Whites first came to the island, Moon predicted who would be their victims. A man signalled out by her was *chin Kreeh* ('seized by Moon') and in this manner she avenged herself against all men. Shamans were in particular danger of being 'seized', for they had been the cause of her disgrace.[29] The shamans knew by their dreams just when an eclipse would occur, and visited Moon when she was in that state.[30] If there was no shaman in the camp during an eclipse, the people let the fires in their huts die out and huddled under their guanaco capes until the danger had passed, and they remained silent or at most spoke in whispers.[31] But when a shaman was in the camp during an eclipse he gathered the people who lived near his dwellings, everyone having extinguished their fires. The women then painted their bodies red and drew a white stripe across their face, from ear to ear under the nose, and the shaman painted one red circle on each cheek to represent the Moon. Then he donned a special head-dress (*pòòr*), made of feathers of the *kex* eagle (*Buteo polyosoma*). The women made sweeping movements towards the moon, with long sticks or with their guanaco capes, 'to clear' the moon, to drive away the eclipse.[32] Angela told me they chanted in unison, as they did to Xalpen during the Hain ceremony, in order to appease Moon, so that she would not condemn the men.

Beautiful heart *tul-ulichen*,
Ample face *koosh háxitin.*

Then the shaman sang to prepare his spirit (*wáiuwin*) to soar into the heavens, to Moon's abode. He began by imitating the call of the *kex* eagle when it flies high into the sky, just as the shaman's spirit travels through the nocturnal heaven to the presence of Moon. As he felt his spirit soaring to its destiny, he chanted repeatedly,

Let us go to the daughter of the sky,
Wiirik keené shó'on tam on mai. [33]

Moon was in her abode, awaiting the shamans' spirits, within an area marked out by four long poles (*laki*). Like the space of the Hain ceremonial hut on earth, her space also symbolized the universe, but it was square or diamond shaped and the poles were laid out horizontally, whereas the Hain hut was circular and its poles upright. Moon was seated in the far corner of her abode, the corner of the south sky which was the sky of her ancient homeland on earth (the island), and all four skies were represented, one at each intersection, as they are in the Hain. Like the director of the men's Hain on earth, Moon in the heavens determined where the participants in the ceremony were to place themselves. When a spirit arrived and she assigned it a seat in the corner which corresponded to the sky of the real shaman on earth, he realized that he had been favoured by her and that he would not be killed in battle in the near future. He was gladdened, though still fearful, because the poles of Moon's abode were very unsteady.

But if Moon disdained the shaman, his spirit fell into her shadow, beneath her knees. The shaman on earth knew this had occurred if he saw the feathers of his head-dress in her shadow beneath her knees and he knew then that he was doomed to perish in an approaching combat. He lamented his fate, chanting:

[Moon] has my head-dress beneath her knees.
Ja póòr jiman k'nooch káin.

And the women insulted her by singing:

Moon burnt face,
Kreeh koosh áixten,
Face full of rage,
Koosh háàten. [34]

Angela stated that if the shaman was 'sentenced to death by Moon', he would probably die within two or three months.

These texts portray Moon as hating men, but for all that not as loving

73

women. She is a lone, vengeful, indomitable, denatured female. She devours children to appease the fury caused by her ignominious downfall. She is the enemy of all human beings. Xalpen, the 'earth monster' (my term) may be considered complementary to Moon, the 'sky monster' (also my term) (see below and chapter 10).

The 'secret'

Esteban said to me: 'If a woman thought something of the truth about the Hain, she wouldn't let on because if she did a shaman would kill her.' During the 1923 Hain, Tenenésk, the head counsellor, warned the *kloketens*, including Gusinde: 'No woman must learn what the men do in the [ceremonial] hut. The last of us must carry the secret to his grave.'[35]

Gusinde commented that the women were conscious of their inferior position and that they were wracked with anxiety because they feared the incalculable power of the men.[36] It was absolutely forbidden for a woman or child to approach the Hain hut where the men spent most of their days and nights throughout the long ceremony. It was never left empty. When the men were hunting one at least would remain in the Hain to keep the fire burning, above all to guard against the possibility of a woman or child coming near it and to make sure that dogs did not damage the masks or devour the meat. All the meat that was sent there from the camp was supposedly to feed the spirits, so from time to time the men would go to camp pretending to be very hungry, asking for meat which they themselves or other hunters had procured for family consumption.

The camp where the women and children lived was about two hundred metres from the Hain hut. Usually a few men remained in the camp, attentive to the conversations and observant of the attitudes of the women, particularly with respect to the Hain spirits. The women were said to ignore the fact that the spirits, which appeared daily, were simply men in disguise, and were told that the spirits had arisen from the earth or descended from the sky to participate in the ceremony. But as Bridges commented:

> As women may be less foolish than they would like the other sex to imagine, I often suspected, while watching the antics of these grotesque and comic personifications, that those Ona women were not so deceived and terrified by their men's crude make-up as they pretended to be. When I once ventured to suggest to the men that the women only did it to please them, their reaction left me under no misapprehension as to their firm conviction of the women's blind credulity. To me it seemed impossible that the women were utterly deceived . . . One thing is certain: that if any woman had been indis-

creet enough to mention her doubts, even to another woman, and word of it had reached the ears of the men, the renegade would have been killed — and most likely others with her. Maybe the women suspected; if they did, they kept their suspicions to themselves.[37]

Halimink, a very well known Selk'nam shaman, told Bridges not only that a woman or uninitiated lad would be killed if they learned the 'secret', but also that the same fate would befall the man who revealed it, even if the person assigned to do the killing were the father or a brother of the offender.[38] Gusinde was also told this many times.

It should be noted, of course, that in this culture the verb 'to kill' has a double connotation: homicide and the 'killing' power of the shaman. If a shaman were determined to destroy someone and went through the necessary procedure, his victim sometimes died in the near future, without any physical contact whatsoever with the shaman. In the latter cases, judging from my data, death seems to have been psychically induced. This complex subject cannot be treated here but it should be made clear that the shamanistic threat 'to kill' only implied the use of his power (*wáiuwin*) and not physical aggression.

During the final days of the Hain in 1923, Gusinde himself was accused by one of the men of having revealed the 'secret' to one of the women. He passed some very tense moments but finally convinced the men of his innocence.[39]

Lola told me that she had never gone near the places where she knew a Hain hut had once stood. It is my impression that even during the last year of her life, when we lived together, she still firmly believed in the Hain spirits, even though she knew that those which appeared in the ceremony were only men in disguise. I never queried her directly on the subject because I thought I might offend her if I did. Angela did confide in me that she had never believed at all in the Hain spirits, but this disbelief notwithstanding she never approached a site where a ceremonial hut was known to have existed. She told me that when she was younger and rode on horseback through the countryside, she would avoid such places.

On one occasion, when Angela was participating in a ceremony, she whispered to a woman friend that one of the spirits looked human. A man overheard her comment and later repeated it to the men in the Hain hut. After telling me this, Angela commented in earnest, 'In old times a shaman would have killed me.'

One day while Angela and Federico were telling me about the Hain, Angela left the room for a minute and Federico said to me, 'Even though everything is finished, Angela is a Selk'nam woman and I shouldn't speak of these things in her presence.' This was forty years after the last Hain had been held.

75

Mythology as ideology

The myths presented here may be considered to be an ideology because they provide not only an explanation of, but also a justification for the existing power structure, as well as a technique for maintaining it. This is exemplified by the comments of the men that 'When the women had the Hain (in mythical times) they did the same as we are doing now.'[40] No matter how badly the women may have been treated, the men possessed a completely plausible construct by means of which they could exonerate themselves in their own eyes. Moreover, the ideology solicited the sympathy, support and allegiance of the women through the man-eating females, Xalpen and Moon. In the Hain ceremony the female 'earth monster' Xalpen threatens to harm and even consume the men rather than the women; likewise the 'sky monster', Moon, defies only the men. Paradoxically, the women are *not* threatened by these terribly potent creatures.

But the paradox is only on a formal level and there is a latent level at which it does not apply. The seeming contradiction disappears once its function is comprehended. I suggest that it functions to compromise the women, precisely because they are *not* in danger and because the 'monsters' are both female. Thus the ideology plays an effective role, not only by providing the men with a foolproof, tightly reasoned rationale for their dominant position in society, but also by allying master and subject in a struggle against supernatural threats, which provide a scapegoat. An outside enemy unites society on a common front. This is a strategy frequently employed for asserting dominance in almost any society and certainly in our own. However, for the Selk'nam themselves the struggle was not perceived as a strategy. The men were not manipulators of power; they were as convinced as the women that the dangers were real. I will return to this crucial point several times.

This ideology appears to be a closed system. The existing social order, the patriarchy, is opposed to a hypothetical (mythical) antithesis, the matriarchy which is totally opposed by all men and concerning which the women are supposedly ignorant. The women are compelled to defend a social order which negates their realization as equal members of society. Ideologically they are confronted with the society's most threatening symbols: the man-eating female monsters (Moon and Xalpen) which they also oppose as there can be no society without men. Through the interplay of these factors, the ideology constitutes itself as a monolithic block, as an obstacle to any basic rearrangement or modification of its power structure. Any fundamental alteration of the structure would logically (in terms of the ideology) expose the society to the imminent danger of a re-establishment of the ancient (mythical) matriarchy; no other alternative is formulated. The implication here is not that the society is (was) frozen, that is it is without history, nor that it has no internal dynamics,[41] but rather that the ideology expressed the notion of absolute status quo. The socio-economic reality could be analysed as a dynamic entity.

This may seem quite clear. However, there is a hidden factor in this ideology which only a detailed knowledge of the Hain celebration reveals with full force. The 'hidden factor' lies in the treatment of the masks. It provides, I believe, a clue to the answer to the question of whether or not the Hain ceremony was a 'hoax'. According to Gusinde and Bridges the men were simply play acting to deceive the women. Is this true? Before discussing this question the ceremony itself will be described in further detail in the next chapter.

4 The setting and symbolism of the Hain ceremony[1]

The location and timing of the ceremony

Great care was always taken in the choice of the site for the Hain. Ideally it was in a forest clearing or on the edge of a wooded area or belt of trees (figure 11). The entrance, toward the east, always faced away from the clear area, toward the interior of the forest or at least toward a small copse. The trees served to hide the movements of the men from the audience. The Hain could be set up on an open plain, but such a locality would create added problems for the men. It was essential that there be a rather wide flat area to the west, behind the ceremonial hut. In 1923, when Gusinde witnessed the Hain, this 'meadow', 'lawn' or 'prairie' as he called it, was 200 paces wide.[2] Bridges stated that the 'lodge' (the Hain hut) was 440 yards from the 'village' (the camp).[3] In my description this treeless space is referred to as the 'stage', because this was its function in the ceremony. The living quarters of the women and children, which will be called the camp, were located directly behind the Hain (in 1923), to the west, just beyond the stage. More prosaically, the site had to be close to a source of water and not too far from herds of guanacos. The hunters ranged over greater distances when based at the ceremonial site than they did from their usual camps. They also hunted in larger groups than was customary. During the Hain they would complement their diet as usual with rodents, birds, eggs, fish, mushrooms, berries and plants. Hains were sometimes held on the coast near a herd of seals or near a whale which had recently been beached,[4] so that the participants could be served seal or whale steaks instead of guanaco. Angela said that, after the arrival of the Whites, the Hain seldom took place on the coast because of the sheep farms which were being established there.

The best sites for the ceremony were well known and former Hain huts were repaired and used again. In pre-contact times, when the ceremony might last well over a year, the participants probably moved many times. During the last Hain in 1933, which only lasted a few months, Federico told me that the people changed sites five times. The director would simply announce to the women and children that it was necessary to move, indicating where they were to go, and everyone would pack up and be off. After the Whites settled

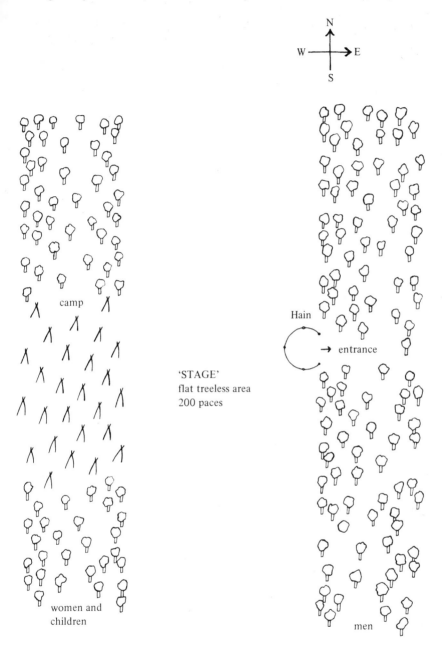

11. The setting of the Hain ceremony.

on the island, the Indians were careful to choose a locality where they were safe from intrusion, for they took every precaution against the ceremony being seen by the Whites. As far as is known, the only non-Indians to have taken part in a Hain were a shipwrecked man referred to as Jack, Lucas Bridges and his brother William, and Martin Gusinde. Some Chileans and European farm workers who lived with Indian women in the latter years may also have seen a Hain from time to time.[5] One of the main reasons why the Selk'nam hid on these occasions was to prevent the 'secret' from being revealed to the women by the outsiders.

Ideally, the Hain would begin in autumn or early winter when guanacos of all ages were at their weight peak and there was an abundance of foals; this was also the gosling season. But a Hain could start at any time of the year, as often occurred in former times when stranded whales were plentiful.

The ceremonial hut

In 1923 the ceremonial hut was built in a day, thanks to the availability of the steel axe, the knife and the horse, which the Whites had introduced, but when stone-tipped tools were used and the poles had to be dragged to the site, the construction took much longer. The ceremonial hut, like the ceremony itself, was called Hain.[6] It was conical in form, like the tipis of the Plains Indians. Once the seven principal posts had been carefully aligned and set up, smaller, thinner trunks were placed between them to fill in the spaces. About fifty of these were used in the 1923 Hain hut. Clumps of turf were then pressed all around the wall to a height of about three metres. The turf served as added shelter against the wind, rain and snow and ensured that the activities of the men inside the Hain remained completely invisible from the outside. Grass and leaves of the evergreen beech tree, which would period- ically be renewed, were placed on the floor around the wall of the hut as seats. At the beginning of the ceremony, a fire was built in the centre of the Hain and was kept burning night and day during the entire ceremony, except when the phallic dance was performed (see chapter 7). At least one man always remained on duty in the hut, as was mentioned earlier.

The Selk'nam sometimes constructed huts of a similar type for their every- day living.[7] However, guanaco hides which were used as a covering for the dwellings were not used for the Hain, which was also much larger and sturdier. The wood used was the native beech. The height and circumference varied according to the length of the tree trunks available, but every attempt would be made to build it as large as possible. The Selk'nam had no means of trans- port for objects other than their own physical strength. Thus a site in close proximity to trees would be chosen. According to Gusinde, the Hain of 1923 measured eight metres in diameter on the inside and six metres in height at the centre. The entrance was very wide, four metres and thirty-five centimetres, in order to allow the men wearing high conical masks to leave and enter the hut without difficulty.

The Hain was always constructed according to a set plan, with the entrance facing east (figure 12). The framework consisted of seven large posts (called *élin*), which were carefully oriented. Four of them represented the cardinal points, the four skies (*shó'on*); these were placed in the 'centres' (*oishka*) of their respective direction. The remaining three posts were located between the central posts and each was considered 'peripheral' (*shixka*) to one of the *oishka* posts. The names given to the posts reflect the heterogeneity of the ceremony, at least during the latter period when the more recently arrived Selk'nam had added certain elements to the ancient Haush

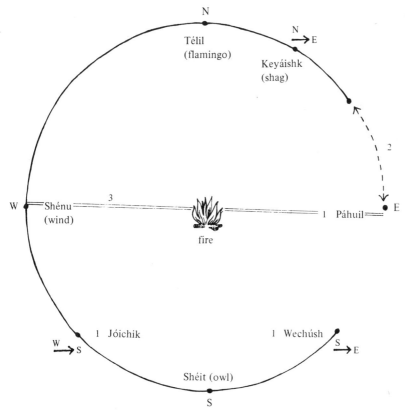

12. The seven principal posts of the Hain ceremonial hut. 1. Haush words, meaning unknown. The other four names are Selk'nam. 2. In ancient times Páhuil was at the exact east, creating a double entrance. In 1923 it was placed to the north, on the edge of the entrance. 3. Imaginary crevice.

81

ceremony. Three of the posts had Haush names, Páhuil, Wechúsh and Jóichik. Neither Gusinde's informants, several of whom were Haush,[8] nor my own knew the meaning of these words. The other four posts were designated by the common Selk'nam words, Télil — flamingo (*Phoenicopterus chilensis*), Shéit — owl (*Speotyto cunicularia*), Keyáishk — shag or cormorant (*Phalacrocorax olivaceus*) and Shénu — the wind. The myth of the first masculine Hain (chapter 3) relates that the seven great *hoowin* shamans hewed the seven posts from rock, and that the posts were named for the seven great shamans. The relationship between post and name should not be taken literally, even though the *hoowin* ancestor derived his name from the animal or natural phenomenon into which he was later transformed. For example, the flamingo post was in no real way associated with the living bird.

The relationship between posts was hierarchical, with the east post most pre-eminent. There is no doubt that the entrance to the Hain was placed in this direction because of the supreme significance of the eastern sky, and not, as some authors have suggested, for protection against the predominant west winds.[9] According to Federico, the east and west posts were the first to be set up and were considered brothers-in-law. They were mutually supporting, he explained. The north and south posts were referred to in the same manner. As the skies, or sections, were exogamous the brother-in-laws were from different skies (see chapter 2). These four posts were located in *oishka* (the centre of each side), also called *háiyen* (the womb), and symbolized the places of creation. They were thus considered superior to the three *shixka* (peripheral) posts (see figure 12). Although all the seven posts were *élin* (principal posts), the *oishka* posts had greater prestige than the *shixka* posts.[10]

The ceremonial hut symbolized the cosmos whose four wombs (*háiyen*) were situated in the four skies of infinity. The skies were conceived of as 'invisible cordilleras of infinity', in Angela's words. First was the most magnificent yet treacherous of all, the great slippery cordillera of the east (*Wintek*), womb of the east wind. This cordillera was surrounded by a sea of boiling water. In the infinity beyond was Pémaulk, the most abstract and aloof of all the divinities, whose very name signifies the heavens.[11] The beautiful cordillera of the west (*Kenénik*) was the centre or womb of the west wind. This was the cordillera of the great shamans of *hoowin* Wind (Shénu) and his brother Sun (Krren).[12] The prevailing wind of Tierra del Fuego originates in the west. In the beautiful cordillera of the south (*Kéikruk*), womb of the south wind, lived Owl (Shéit) and his mighty brother Snow (Hosh). Their sister, the great and once sovereign shaman Moon (Kreeh), was also of the south sky. Finally, the slippery cordillera of the north (*Kámuk*) was the home of Sea (Kox) and his sister Rain (Chálu). Here the mystical Flamingo (Télil) existed and this was the womb of the north wind, the wind of the sea.[13] The cordilleras were the skies (*shó'on*) where the 'souls' (*kaspi* or *mehn*) of humans returned at death, not to exist as entities in an afterlife but rather to be reunited with the eternal forces of the universe.[14]

The configuration of the imagined cordilleras may be partially explained by the actual geomorphology of the island. The north coast is limited by the horizon of the Atlantic ocean, and there are no mountains at all in this direction, while the southern and western horizons are mostly bordered by cordilleras. The mythical northern cordillera is described as slippery, water-shrouded, and as rising from a sea. The southern cordillera, toward the Antarctic, is realistically conceptualized as snow-bound, while the western cordillera is portrayed as being at the origin of the most relentless of all winds. The east is quite different. The tip of the island, in the Haush area, is on a strait (Le Maire) beyond which lies another island, called Jáius (Staten Island). If one gazes across the strait from this most extreme eastern point, one rarely sees the huge ridge of barren jagged rocky mountains which nearly fill the horizon, because they are almost always shrouded in clouds or haze. Angela told me that this island was reputed never to have been inhabited, and has remained uninhabited since the White man first saw it in 1616 until the end of the last century when it was deemed an ideal setting for a prison. But the Selk'nam thought quite differently. They named this mountain ridge the 'Cordillera of the Roots' (Kéoin Hurr). Far into infinity beyond it was the centre (*háiyen*) of *Wintek*, of the east, the 'womb of all that exists'.

These mythical cordilleras beyond the world were the sources of shaman-istic power. While in a trance the shaman's *wáiuwin* (power) would struggle to reach the summit of one of these four cordilleras. If the shaman's *wáiuwin* were extraordinarily endowed it might at times attain the summit of the east-ern cordillera. But to do so it would have to traverse a sea of boiling water and then ascend the terribly slippery 'Cordillera of the Roots', near or beyond which lay the greatest source of all power of the universe, Pémaulk. Angela said that when a shaman felt he was entering into a trance he would name the 'Cordillera of the Roots'. This name was probably thought to irradiate a power of its own.

Although the great mythical personage, Wind, was of the west sky, each of the other skies were conceived as the womb of the wind that originated at that cardinal point. Similarly Rainbow, the sister of Moon and Snow, was of the south sky, yet she was also associated with the other three skies. The storms were coded by their particular characteristics: the wind storm was of the west sky, the snow storm of the south sky, the rain storm of the north sky, while a great outburst combining these elements was deemed to originate in the east sky. Yet the moon and the snow were exclusively associated with the south, just as the sea was linked with the north and the sun with the west. These mythological ancestors had married according to the role of exogamy which forbade marriage between members of the same sky. Moon was married to Sun (south to west), Snow was the husband of Rain (south to north) while the great shaman, Wind of the west, had a wife of the north. The seasons were also identified with the four skies: autumn to the west, winter to the south, spring and summer to the north while the east symbolized all of the seasons and possibly even Time itself.

The colours, which the Indians reproduced in their paints, were also linked to the skies: red with the sunset and the west, white with snow and the south, and black with the sea and the north. I never heard, however, that the east was thought to represent either all the colours or any particular colour.

The elements of nature such as the mountains, lakes, rivers, valleys, bluffs and boulders were personified as mythological heroes (as *hoowins*) and assigned to one of the four skies, with the exception of the east sky. When my informants knew the name of a topographical feature in the Selk'nam language, they usually recalled the sky to which it belonged. I recorded some 650 toponyms, many of which are so identified. Angela insisted that nearly all the natural features had a mythical history although many could not be recalled. Sometimes Angela would narrate the myths, like the one in which a *hoowin* hero had been metamorphosed into a species of bird that nests in the bluffs, just at the same time as the girl he was courting was changed into a bluff by the sea. This story explains why this species of bird nests in bluffs. Gusinde also was told some of these myths. In one he relates the story of a dreadful giant cannibal, named Cháskilts, who was transformed into a huge boulder when he was slaughtered by the culture hero, Kuanip. As Cháskilts was of the south sky, the boulder named after him was also located in a *haruwen* assigned to the south. Kuanip, who was of the north sky, was eventually transformed into a star. Animals were likewise identified with the skies; for example, the guanaco and the canary belonged to the west, the whale, the sea lion, the flamingo and the parakeet to the north, and the albatross, the condor and certain species of owls to the south.

At least in late Indian times the four Indian groups which inhabited the island were also represented in the Selk'nam symbolic system. The Selk'nam themselves contended that they were of the north, *Kámuka*, the termination *ka* meaning 'people'. When I asked Angela to explain this to me, she replied: 'Because we came from the north.' The Haush were *Winteka*, people of the east, because they lived in that part of the island and perhaps too because it was thought that they originated in the east. The Alakaluf (whom the Selk'nam called Airu) were *Kenénika*, people of the west, while the Yámana (the Woo) were *Kéi-kruka*, people of the south. These four groups spoke different languages and each occupied the appropriate part of the island, although the Selk'nam inhabited by far the largest area of the island (see chapter 1). However, this notion is only expressed in the Hain plan in so far as the east post, Páhuil, was assigned to the Haush.

The individual was also classified in the system. Upon birth a person was automatically associated with the exogamous entity of the sky (*shó'on*) assigned by tradition to the *haruwen* of his or her father (termed 'division' in this text). As suggested in chapter 2, this symbolic system appears to be an example of what Lévi-Strauss terms 'totemic classification'. For instance, Lola once said to me: 'I am Snow [Snow being classified as south as was her territory]. My mother is Wind [classified as west as was her mother's territory] and my husband Rain [classified as north as his territory].' Federico was considered north because, although his father was White, his mother was of the north sky. He said, 'My *hoowins* are the sea lion, the whale, the shag and the flamingo. They are all *Kámuk* [north].'

The seven posts of the Hain had social significance because they represented the eighty *haruwens* into which the island was subdivided. Men took their place in the Hain according to the sky or division to which they belonged, which was associated with their respective *haruwens*. Just as the four centre posts were superior to the three peripheral posts, so the *haruwens* represented by the centre skies claimed more prestige than those represented by the peripheral skies. The three posts considered to be on the periphery (*shixka*) were the Shag post corresponding to the northeast, the Wechúsh post to the southeast and the Jóichik post to the southwest (see figure 12). However, the peripheral position northwest lacked a post. I was unable to discover why this was so. The men whose *haruwens* belonged to this peripheral sky were assigned to this section of the hut even though there was no post there representing their sky.[15]

As each man entered the Hain the counsellors assigned him to a specific place under or near the post representing the sky of his *haruwen*. If there were too many men belonging to a particular sky in a given ceremony and the area near that post became overcrowded, the counsellors might decide that some of them take their positions under the post (sky) of their mother's *haruwen*. Moreover, if a man's mother's sky were more prestigious than his father's it would be advantageous for him to arrange to be seated there.

When the Selk'nam performed the Hain among themselves there was no one who represented the east sky. Federico and Angela told me that, in the Hains they attended, it was customary for some of the men of the northeast (Shag) or even the north (Flamingo) to be seated under the east post. In the nineteenth century when the Haush performed the Hain without the Selk'nam, they might similarly have designated men of any one of the three posts situated to the south (Jóichik, Shéit or Wechúsh) to occupy the west post. These arrangements to fill the empty space under the east or under the west posts conform to the logic of the Hain symbolism for, as we shall see, the ceremonial hut was divided into two hemispheres, with the north and east posts on one side and the south and west posts on the other. All the seven skies had to be represented so that the men were located in a full circle, which was essential for the correct performance of the ceremony.

Although the location of men within the Hain hut was supposed to have been ordained during the epoch of *hoowin*, lengthy disputes might arise over which men had the right to the most prestigious posts. I was told that at times there would be arguments over access to the centre posts, even though Gusinde stated that there was no ranking order within the ceremonial hut.[16]

The Hain was divided into hemispheres by an imaginary line running from east to west, starting at the entrance and passing through the fire to the back of the hut. This line was considered very dangerous for it indicated a vastly profound crevice or chasm, which eventually led to a sea far below, which was called, according to Federico, *chali koxain*. Upon entering the Hain a man took great care not to step on or across the 'crevice'. If he entered on the right side, toward the north, he could not walk to the south of the hut except by leaving and re-entering on the left side. This explains why, as Federico told me, there was a double entrance, one on each side of the east post. He also said that those of the west post had to enter on the south side of the Hain while those of the east post entered on the north side. Gusinde describes the two paths which led from the entrance of the Hain onto the stage around each side of the hut. Men took the path which corresponded to their assigned post and the spirits who were associated with the different skies or posts did the same.[17]

The masks

The masks used in the Hain were carefully fashioned of guanaco hide or bark, adorned with painted symbolic designs; some were stuffed with leaves and grass. There were two types of masks. The first, called *tolon*, was conical in form, about seventy centimetres high and held on by the performer with both hands at ear level. It had long slits for the eyes because the actors often walked or danced sideways. The other type, called *asl*, was a simple leather hood stuffed with leaves or dry grass to give it body. It was pulled down over the head and tied at the back. Small holes were cut out for the eyes and mouth. Bridges saw a mask of this type which was folded over on the front thus forming a monstrous drooping nose.[18] The spirits always wore either one or the other type of mask. The colours and patterns of the paint varied, depending on which sky or post they represented.

The masks were treated with a veneration which puzzled Gusinde. He thought that the men were disguising themselves as spirits simply to make the women believe they were supernatural, so he could not understand why the men themselves venerated and respected the masks. I would suggest that they did so because they were not really acting, putting on a show or farce to fool the women, but that by the spirit impersonation they felt they became closely identified with the supernatural. This is a crucial point, for it concerns the subjective significance of the Hain ceremony (see chapter 5). I will return to this argument in the final chapter.

When not in use, the masks were propped carefully against the interior wall of the ceremonial hut and great precaution was taken that they did not topple over on to the ground. If a mask were damaged, it was thought that its user would fall and injure or even kill himself 'accidentally' during the next performance. If a mask fell off a performer's head, even while he was out of sight of the women, the performer was thought to be in great danger. Gusinde had difficulty obtaining masks for the museums. The older men simply refused to give or sell him any but he did finally persuade one of the younger men to let him have two.

The masks were never burned at the end of a ceremony but hidden in the hollows of trees near the Hain. This was a secure place because the women never approached the site of a former Hain. They did not have to be watched or warned in this respect for they themselves were convinced of its importance. If a Hain began in the location of a recent ceremonial hut, the old masks would be brought from their hiding places and repaired and reused if they had not disintegrated.

The paint

Women were responsible for supplying the men and the emissaries of the spirits with paint throughout the ceremony. The body paint consisted mostly of clays, the colours ranging from black through grey to white and from dark red to yellow (see chapter 1). Usually the entire body was painted in from one to three colours. For instance, the designs might be applied against a red or black background, or the lower arms and legs might be painted white and the rest of the body another colour, or each half of the thorax in a contrasting colour. The designs were painted over these backgrounds in a great variety of motifs, all of which could easily be interpreted by the audience. As a general rule a predominance of red paint denoted the west sky, white the south sky, and black the north sky. A cloud effect produced with a chalk-like powder also signified the west sky. Apparently there was no one colour associated with the east sky although it may have had a distinctive design referent. The designs which the participants in the Hain ceremony painted on their faces were different from those on the body. However the Hain spirits were painted as a unit, that is, the face (the mask) and the body were decorated with one or more continuous motifs.

When the design was rather large and the outlines did not need to be very carefully traced, the paint was applied with the fingers or palm of the hand and retouched with the fingernails. To achieve roughly parallel lines the palm of the left hand was covered with paint and lines scraped on the palm then pressed against the body. When a finer design was desired, the point of a stick or a wooden spatula was used. For drawing very thin parallel lines the jaw of a dolphin was used. To achieve a cloud-like effect, the paint was ground and the powder blown onto the body through the teeth. To sprinkle the paint on, someone would clap the powder between his hands very close to the person being painted.

Before the arrival of the Whites, the women painted their entire body with designs (*tari*) representing their sky and earth and appeared naked (weather permitting) during certain scenes of the Hain ceremony. During the 1923 Hain, the women painted only the upper body and wore their everyday woollen skirts; it is thus that they appear in the photographs taken by Gusinde. Only the initiates (the *kloketens*) were obliged to paint themselves every day. They and the spirits were the greatest consumers of paint.

Gusinde commented on the extraordinary variety of forms and colours and the highly developed personality of each spirit. He added that there was a great unity in the style and ornament, which could never be surmised if one only observed Selk'nam everyday life. The designs could not be modified. Each spirit could be identified by the patterns and colours of his paint and mask or costume, as well as by his particular body movements or dance. Angela told me that 'the spirits didn't look like men. You could never tell they were!'

5 Girls' puberty rite and the organization of the Hain ceremony

Girls' puberty rite[1]

By contrast with the male initiation rite, the girls' puberty rite was very simple. At menarche a girl was confined to her home for five or six days, during which time she was instructed and admonished by older women as she sat silently in front of the fire. She was not allowed to speak, play or laugh nor go far from home, and she was told to listen attentively to the advice given her. She was never left alone; her mother and neighbouring women, who were usually kin, kept her company and were very attentive. The children were not allowed in her hut. Every morning during the first five days, her mother or a neighbour painted her face in a design consisting of fine white lines radiating from under the eyes over the cheeks. On the first day, she was forbidden to eat and only allowed to drink a little water. The following day she was offered a few small mushrooms or bits of fish or fat. By the third day, she began to eat meat again and by the fourth or fifth day she would be eating a normal diet. Although her seclusion only lasted five or six days, she was expected to remain quiet and to show particular diligence in her work during the following three or four weeks.

Her mother, or another kinswoman, counselled her at length concerning the conduct expected of her as an adult. She was admonished above all to be swift and assiduous in the performance of such tasks as gathering fire-wood, fetching water, keeping the fire burning, preparing animal hides, sewing capes and weaving baskets. Every morning she should wash herself, arrange her hair and paint her body with red clay (*ákel*). She was, in other words, counselled to be attractive, busy and silent. As she would marry soon, she was told to obey her husband willingly and avoid quarrelling. After marriage she should also remain obedient to her father and maintain good relations with her family. She should be generous with visitors, help those in need without being asked, and not seek the attention of men other than her husband. Angela said that the mother advised her daughter not to abandon her husband if he treated her well, but if he abused her and she tried to escape and return to her family she should be very careful that he did not catch her, for if he did he might kill her. The mother and other women informed her about birth and the care of infants, about all that concerned her coming life as a wife and mother. She was warned not to be flattered by the attention of other men for, if she had a child out of wedlock, the child would be fatherless. After the arrival of the Whites she was told above all to avoid White men because they afterwards abandoned both mother and child. This was true in the great majority of cases. Rape, kidnapping and seduction of Selk'nam women by White men occurred frequently at the turn of the century during the disintegration of the culture. One rare exception was a White man who was disinherited by his older sisters from his portion of one of the larger sheep farms because he refused to abandon his Indian wife and two children.

The male initiates[2]

For the young man the Hain ceremony was not only a rite of passage but also a prolonged learning experience. While being initiated, he was called a *kloketen*, but afterwards he would be a *maars*, an adult man. Every male youth had to be a *kloketen*; there were no exceptions. A recalcitrant youth might be obliged to go through a Hain ceremony twice or even three times if the elders were not satisfied with his achievements after a first or second Hain. In the extreme case three Hains might take five years or more, depending on how often the ceremonies were held and how long they lasted, but a man could not marry until he had 'graduated'. It is not without reason that the last generation of Selk'nam spoke of the Hain as a *colegio* ('college' in Spanish).

In the past, the *kloketen* would have been between seventeen and twenty-two years old when he entered the Hain,[3] as physical stamina and mental alertness were demanded of the novice, and a certain maturity required. The two counsellors at the 1923 Hain, Tenenésk and Halimink, commented to Gusinde on the cruelty and severity of the torture they had endured as *kloketens*. Gusinde observed that in 1923 the men were especially considerate towards the two *kloketens* who were being initiated, because of their lack of physical development and their youth. One was fourteen years old and the other sixteen.[4]

Considerable discussion probably took place between the elders about whether or not a young man was sufficiently mature to become a *kloketen*. Gusinde cites the kinds of questions that were asked about a candidate. 'Can he keep quiet? Does he still play with the children? Does he spend his free time at work? Can he oppose the women? Does he associate with girls? Does he have the capacity to value what our secret means?'[5]

Once the candidates had been chosen they would be sent into the forest alone or together before the ceremony began. Bridges wrote that they were given instructions by the men to go to a certain place in the woods where they would find a recently killed guanaco, hanging in a tree out of the reach of the foxes or on the bottom of a pond in a leather bag weighed down with rocks. If the guanaco was too heavy for them to carry they were not obliged to bring the entire animal back, but they did have to follow a specific route which was neither short nor easy. Bridges stated that to make certain that these commands were obeyed, one of the men would shadow them all the way, without allowing himself to be seen. The candidates were warned just before they set out that, if they encountered the spirit Shoort, they were not to shoot at him with their bows and arrows for he was invulnerable and, if they raised their weapons against him, he might kill them. If they met such a creature they were to take refuge in a tree, for the spirit was not accustomed to climbing trees. Bridges observed: 'The real object of these expeditions was to reduce the kloketen to such a condition of fear that it needed real courage to go on through the haunted woods.'[6]

Each candidate was also sent on a hunting expedition alone for several days or even weeks. Again he was warned that he might run into the dreadful Shoort. The youth lived off the forest as best he could, sleeping, making fire and hunting in solitude. Meanwhile, one of the men disguised himself as Shoort and set out in pursuit of the novice, surprising him at the moment when he could appear most terrifying. He further frightened the candidate by threatening him, or even striking him with a burning torch. When the youth returned to camp and told his story the men would react, pretending to be horrified and terribly scared too, with the intention of increasing the candidate's fears.[7]

When the young man entered the Hain hut and became a *kloketen* his separation from the world of the women and children was virtually complete for the duration of the ceremony. He was ordered to keep out of their sight. A mother would grieve when her son departed from camp to intern himself in the Hain for she was not to see him again for many months or perhaps a year or more, except on very few occasions. When the ceremony had ended and he did return he would, in a sense, no longer be her child. He would not only have learned the 'secret' which propelled him into the closed quarters of a masculine world and deprived him of his spontaneity, he would also have suffered humiliation, hunger and fatigue. He would no longer feel like a child. This transition to adulthood can perhaps be more fully appreciated in the light of the demands which were made on the male population, particularly with respect to hunting guanacos. It was, without doubt, an arduous and exhausting task even though it excited great passion. The guanaco is a very swift runner, and is known to attack an aggressor. Muscle power and much skill were necessary to make the Selk'nam bow and stone-tipped arrow effective against a guanaco. The hunter himself had to be a fast runner as he often had to track the prey for long hours. He prided himself on losing neither his prey nor his arrows.

In pre-contact times the men organizing the Hain ceremony endeavoured to prepare at least three *kloketens* associated with the three skies (north, south and west). Angela told me that each was advised to seek a special friend, a *hopin*, among the *kloketens* belonging to a different sky and that the elders counselled them to become good friends and eventually to marry each other's sisters.

The kloketen mothers[8]

The mothers of the *kloketens* (*kai kloketen*) played an outstanding role in the ceremony.[9] Gusinde related that the mother of the oldest *kloketen* had special duties, and she also had the privilege of wearing the men's head band, the *kóchil*, although hers was a larger version. The *kóchil* was part of the men's everyday dress, but it was also the symbol or badge of manhood which was tied to the *kloketen*'s head after the rite of passage. During the entire ceremony the mother of the oldest *kloketen* was expected to devote her time and energy working for the other families in camp and to do so without being asked. It was assumed that she was constantly grieving for her lost son, and she was expected to foster this impression. She was also responsible for initiating the singing every day, before dawn and at noon. She was required to begin the welcoming song for Shoort when he emerged from the Hain to visit camp, which he did daily if the weather permitted. Of all the spirits, Shoort was the most aggressive towards the women. All the *kloketen* mothers stood in front of their homes, with their heads shrouded in guanaco capes, while Shoort rampaged through camp. The other women hid under cover, inside the huts or tents, as they were ordered by the men.

The *kloketen* mothers had similar duties towards the most dreaded of all the spirits, Xalpen. When this spirit became outrageously violent against the men, as she invariably did during the ceremony, the mothers would be blamed for causing her rage. The other women would scold the mothers for arousing Xalpen's anger by their laxness in the performance of their ritual duties. The mothers were also required to supply their sons with meat every day, though they were told that Xalpen consumed most of it.

The supervisors[10]

Each *kloketen* was assigned a supervisor, called *k'pin*. Federico said that he was usually a patrilineal kinsman, often a cousin or an uncle who was a few years older than his charge. He was chosen by the influential men and/or the counsellors of the Hain and was under their orders. The *k'pin* was constantly at his *kloketen*'s side; helping, directing and disciplining him.

The Hain counsellor[11]

Gusinde wrote that the Hain director (his term was *Vorsteher*) was a 'father of the word' (*ch'anha'in* or *chan-ain*), or, in other words, a prophet. Traditionally the counsellor was chosen from among the prophets. But Federico stated that the term used for the counsellor was *ai-órien*, which referred to the function rather than the status. He translated *ai-órien* into Spanish as *consejero del Hain*, counsellor of the Hain.[12] This seems a more appropriate term than 'director' because, as Gusinde himself pointed out, no one man really managed the Hain. All the men participated in decisions and they were only advised by the *ai-órien*. Federico explained that in pre-contact times there was an *ai-órien* for each of the four central posts. The counsellors were chosen from among a number of respected men who had knowledge of the Hain lore and experience of the ceremony.[13] In pre-contact times, the *ai-órien* was probably always a prophet, but in 1923 the counsellors Tenenésk and Halimink (figures 13 and 14) were both shamans (*xo'on*) and sages (*lailuka-ain*) but not prophets, for by then no prophets remained.

The shaman was obliged to rid himself of his mystical power (*wáiuwin*) for the duration of the ceremony. This was done simply by concentrating on the problem while shaking the body violently, before entering the Hain hut at the very beginning of the ceremony. All the male shamans did this, even those who were not counsellors, for it acted as a precaution against the eventuality that the female shamans' *wáiuwins* might contact the men's *wáiuwins* during the ceremony, and thus acquire the forbidden knowledge. For instance, Federico told me that the older male shamans could interpret the spirits Shoort and Halaháches. If chosen for one of these roles, before performing the shaman had to 'turn off his shamanistic power' (*wirik me shójen*), otherwise the female shaman could identify the impersonator by means of her *wáiuwin* and discover that the spirit was not supernatural.

The counsellor had a very extensive knowledge of the *hoowin* tradition; not only was he familiar with the myths, as were all of the men, but also he was a gifted raconteur and had mastered the numerous details concerning the Hain spirits. He had to be assured that the performers were disguised according to regulations, knew exactly what they were to do and understood the limits within which they might improvise. He was well-versed in the entire symbolic system concerning not only the spirits but also the *hoowin* ancestors. Each man had a place in the system, a claim on certain symbols, including the right to paint them on his body and to a specific place in the ceremonial hut. The counsellor also had to recognize any abuses in the use of these symbols which might be committed by the women, for they too painted themselves quite frequently during the ceremony and took positions in the camp which corresponded to their respective skies.

The counsellor was the main instructor of the *kloketens* with respect both to the *hoowin* tradition and to the moral code. When necessary, he solicited the collaboration of the men (especially the *kloketens*) for such work as hunting, fetching water and fire-wood, and cleaning the hut. Gusinde remarked

93

that all such tasks were performed cheerfully with good humour and without the slightest resentment. The same may well have applied to the women who were responsible for supplying great quantities of painting materials.

In consultation with the other men the counsellor decided the day the ceremony was to begin, and if and when the participants should move to a new site to continue the 'show', and he announced the termination of the ceremony to the women and children once the men had reached a common agreement.

Moreover, the counsellor had to know when the rules could be modified; how much liberty could be taken with the age-old tradition. Rather than give orders he persuaded, taught and explained in an effort to prevail upon dissident opinions or projects which might jeopardize the objectives of the

13. Tenenésk, Haush shaman and sage, principal counsellor at the 1923 Hain ceremony and Gusinde's informant.

ceremony. The wheels of society had to be kept turning, an equilibrium maintained between the forces of the universe and the discrepant centrifugal actions or attitudes of the members of society. In short, the counsellor had to be a tactful and convincing diplomat. Gusinde remarked that 'the formless, in any case impassionate choice of the leader for this meaningful ceremony [is] a proof of the clear view these simple [sic] people had, of their sharp judgement, of their pedagogical sensitivity and of their far reaching knowledge of human weakness'.[14]

At times the ceremonial hut must have looked like a communal work shop or a happy get-together. Many of the men would be engaged in making or repairing the hunting weapons, mixing paint, preparing feathers for ornaments, making the masks and roasting meat, while the rest might be simply

14. Halimink, Selk'nam shaman and sage, second counsellor at the 1923 Hain ceremony.

relaxing. According to Gusinde, the men, particularly the older ones, spent long hours chatting, happy to find themselves again among male friends and kin whom they might not have seen since a previous Hain.

The younger men would often wrestle in the ceremonial hut, while the elders offered criticism or encouragement. They would go into the forest to practise arrow shooting under the direction of the expert bowmen. The lack of restraint, the freedom from coercion, the enjoyment of the men and their willingness to cooperate partly explains the enthusiasm this gathering generated among the men and why it drew people from distant parts of the island.

The 'actors'[15]

I use the term 'actor' in quotation marks because the performers were not simply enacting roles; they were not just impersonating the spirits in order to control and terrorize the women in an objective calculation of their own interests. The 'actors' were somehow imbued with the supernatural personality of their prototypes. This is revealed, for example, in the treatment of the masks. These were not props, they were objects which emanated power and accordingly had to be handled with respect. This attitude toward the masks implicitly contradicts Gusinde's statement that the men knew that if the spirits had a strong personality they would be even more credible to the women but that the men by no means believed in the existence of the spirits. Gusinde understood that the men wanted to reaffirm the present social order 'by which they obtained a certain superiority',[16] and he assumed that this was why they used the deceptive appearance of the spirits. I will return to this point in the final chapter.

Long training was required to represent most of the spirits. While the easier roles were given to the younger men, even the experienced 'actors' had to practise body tension, the steps, leaps and pantomimes they were to perform. A few men gained great fame by their personification of the spirits and played the same role time and again in successive Hains. They were the models to which the elders pointed when younger men were trying out the roles for the first time. A man who was especially gifted at representing one of the spirits would take pains to teach one or several of the younger men. If the Hain were too confining or crowded to demonstrate and practise the different movements of the spirit, the master would take his pupils into the forest and drill them for hours at a time, or alternatively they might practise while out hunting.

The order of events[17]

The ceremony itself was organized informally. In 1923, the rite of passage took place on the first day, though there was no rule stipulating that it had to take place then. For the sake of convenience it always occurred quite soon after the inauguration of the ceremony, because of the difficulty of keeping the 'secret' from the *kloketens* for very long. They could be sent on a hunting expedition during the first few days or weeks and be initiated upon their return, but they could not be kept in the woods for months at a time after the Hain had begun.

Shoort was the only spirit to appear daily in the camp, if the weather permitted. Under different guises, this spirit was often presented several times during the day. The men had to verify that those who assumed these roles appeared approximately at the correct time, were painted with the symbols corresponding to that period of the day and knew what they were expected to do on stage or in the camp. There were scenes which had to follow in a certain order, but with these exceptions, the men decided a day or two beforehand which spirits would be presented. The fabrication of the costumes for certain spirits required long hours of work, so their presentation had to be well planned. The women were able to influence the programme through their singing. A woman would be proud if her singing brought forth a particularly beautiful Shoort, painted with the designs of her sky, and the men were very attentive to the women's chanting.

The weather was a limiting factor. The theatre closed down for the duration of a snow or rain storm and the performances were postponed because the make-up would run, the masks would become soggy and the 'secret' would be no more. However, the men did perform without paint or masks during a storm in a rite called 'stop the water' (see chapter 7).

The Hain terminated when the men, for one reason or another, decided that it should. Shoort made his final visit to the camp and later one of the counsellors would simply announce to the women and children that the ceremony had come to an end.

6 The first day

The beginning[1]

The day of the inauguration has arrived. It is probably autumn or early winter and with luck, a crisp sunny day. Everyone is excited.

The last preparations are being completed throughout the morning. Inside the Hain hut, two Shoorts, the only spirits who are to appear on this day, paint themselves. First they rub red *ákel* all over their bodies, and then they whiten their lower legs and chalk a number of large white circles on the rest of their bodies in honour of K'tétu, the *hoowin* who was transformed into a small white owl (*Speotyto cunicularia*). The principal Shoorts decorate themselves with the designs (*tari*) of the mythological K'tétu shaman who played the part of Shoort to perfection in the first men's Hain. He was *hauwitpin* (perfectly formed) and of the west sky, like Krren (Sun).

The masks for each of the principal Shoorts had been made by a man with the title of Ténin-nin. Each person who acts the part of Shoort has a Ténin-nin companion. The two must be kinsmen and belong to the same sky. As Ténin-nin ties the mask over the performer's head and neck, he asks his Shoort, affectionately yet ponderously: 'Are you the same [being] as you were?' Ténin-nin does not wait for an answer but continues: 'Come sit here. You are the same as me. We are grandsons of the Hain. You are now transformed. The *hoowin* K'tétu has penetrated you and you are now the image of him . . .'[2] Ténin-nin speaks further words while Shoort listens silently, unable to speak for he has ceased to be human. The content of Ténin-nin's discourse is fixed by custom, although it may vary according to the *hoowin* ancestors incarnated by the principal Shoorts.

Gradually and inconspicuously, most of the men leave the camp and gather in the Hain where they paint themselves with the markings which symbolize their respective skies. In camp meanwhile the mothers of the young men to be initiated are fretting over their sons, spending the final few hours with them as if to bid them farewell forever. They are troubled, sad and anxious. The other women accompany them trying to console them. The *kloketens* are bewildered and taut; fearful of what awaits them in the secret hut. The children are sensitive to the atmosphere and less playful.

By early afternoon, the men in the Hain have prepared themselves. They are painted and composed. The Hain counsellors indicate to the men exactly where they are to take their positions with respect to the seven principal posts. Cautious not to step over the 'crevice', they stand rigidly in a circle against the inner wall of the hut. The fire burns brightly. Suddenly they begin chanting in strong, rhythmic and emphatic voices, *ho?ho?ho?*[3] The Hain has begun. They chant for a half an hour, or more. When the people in camp first hear the singing they cease all activity and remain quiet. The atmosphere is so hushed, so expectant that it creates a feeling of being transported to a different level of existence.

Slowly the people in camp being to move again, for the *kloketens* have to be painted. The supervisors (*k'pins*) come to fetch them at their mothers' huts and escort them out holding them by the left forearm, while the mothers accompany their sons on the right-hand side, sobbing and crying loudly. They proceed to a hut which has been assigned for cleaning and painting the *kloketens.*

A *kloketen*'s cape is removed and his supervisor tells him to stand facing the wall of the hut with his arms stretched high over his head. The other *kloketens* in the hut are asked to do the same by their supervisors. The mothers are present as well as other women and several men. The supervisors rub down the bodies of their *kloketens* with stringy fungi, while the women chant a rhythmic wordless measure, *hoshócherikó.*[4]

Then each supervisor paints his candidate with red *ákel* clay mixed with guanaco fat. Red is considered to be particularly beautiful and pleasing to the spirits. Soon all the women sing *kot te hepé*, 'his body is dry',[5] and the *kloketen* mothers paint their sons' faces with three stripes; one down the centre of the nose and one on either side of the face. The singing continues as the mothers' faces are painted with the same design. Today they wear the men's head-dress, the *kochil*, as a special privilege.

Just before the painting is completed the two Shoorts make their first appearance on stage; one emerges from the north side of the ceremonial hut and the other from the south side. As they leave the Hain the men chant *ho?ho?ho?* from within. The Shoorts have come to show that they are impatient to receive the *kloketens* and the men who are still in the hut where the initiates are being painted call upon all present to look at the Shoorts.

Meanwhile the girls and young women have painted their upper bodies with red *ákel*. After the Shoorts have returned to the Hain, the women line up together and run on stage shouting cheerfully, swinging their arms in wide circles while swaying their bodies from side to side. They stop in the centre of the stage, turn around to face the camp and run back, still shouting. This is their welcome to the Shoorts. In 1923 one of the girls became terror stricken while rushing back and fell down on the stage. This was taken to be an ominous warning of some kind. In past days she would have been 'killed' by a shaman but in 1923 she was only confined to her hut for four days, until the danger had passed.[6]

Shoort[7]

Shoort is the most dynamic and active spirit of the Hain and certainly the one most feared by the women and children. It is he who tortures the *kloketens* during the initiation rite. Shoort dwells under the earth with his wife, the dreadful Xalpen, and, like her, he emerges into the Hain hut through the fire. He begins the ceremony and is the last to appear on the final day. He is the only spirit who performs every day (weather permitting) and the only one to go daily into camp among the women and children. Above all Shoort synthesizes the complex symbolism of the Hain. He is both transcendent and pragmatic and I suggest that, since he directs the Hain by assuring the succession of diurnal time, he represents the Sun. He also controls the nocturnal female Moon power which threatens to reinstate the tyranny of the matriarchy. Should women regain power, Moon (night) would suppress Sun (day) and annihilate the patriarchal forces in society. In everyday language, *krren* signifies both the sun and the day and Shoort symbolizes both. As the husband of Xalpen (the earth monster whose counterpart is the sky monster Moon) he epitomizes that dauntless male, the great *hoowin* shaman Krren; he who discovered the secret of women's power in the female Hain, he who led the great revolt during which nearly all the women of *hoowin* were massacred, he who caused the instauration of the male Hain and founded the patriarchal society.

There are more Shoorts than any other Hain spirit even without counting the servants of Shoort, the Hayílans (see chapter 7). While they all appear to be manifestations of the same symbol, Sun (Krren), they have different attributes. But there is a prototype Shoort who represents the *k'tétu* owl mentioned in the beginning of the chapter. As a mythological being, K'tétu belongs to the west sky, the sky of Sun. Federico and Gusinde both identified K'tétu as a *hoowin* of the first men's Hain who played the part of a subordinate Shoort particularly well. K'tétu was 'very perfect', handsome and muscular, *hauwitpin*. Federico insisted that all the Shoorts imitate the movements of this owl, especially by short jerky movements of the head, that the mask also represents him by white bands around the eyes, and that the white knees and white splotches of paint depict the pattern of his feathers.[8]

While all the Shoorts probably embody the 'perfect' mythological K'tétu, each type of Shoort has a specific role in the Hain.[9] There are seven principal Shoorts, a number of subordinate Shoorts (the helpers), and eight others who represent the course of the sun through the heavens from dawn to dusk. Given the considerable number of Shoorts which appear in any one Hain celebration, the same men would play one or more roles. Despite the basic patterns of the K'tétu designs, each individual Shoort could be distinguished by the combination of colours (red, black and white), the designs and their positioning on the body and the masks. Bridges wrote that there was a wide variation in the colouring and pattern of the make-up for this spirit. One arm and the opposite leg might be white or red, with spots or stripes of another colour superimposed, to which feather down might be added. In 1923 Shoort's mask resembled a pointed cap pulled tightly down over the head and neck.[10] This is the *asl* mask (see chapter 4) which was probably preferred to the cumbersome conical mask, because Shoort often went into the camp within close proximity to the women and because at times his movements were very energetic.

The seven principal Shoorts were associated with the seven main posts of the Hain and were known by the names of the posts: Télil Shoort of the north post and sky, Páhuil Shoort of the east post and sky and so on (figure 15; see chapter 4). The seven mythological ancestors represented by each post were the founders of the men's Hain: each had brought a rock post with which to construct the first men's ceremonial hut and each played the part of Shoort during the original men's ceremony (see chapter 3). Ever since, these seven *hoowin* Shoorts have been presented, although the Shoort which appears most frequently during any one Hain represents the sky of the *haruwen* where the Hain is taking place. In 1923 the Shéit Shoort of the south sky was presented most frequently because the ceremony took place in a territory associated with the south sky. The 'actors' belonged to the same sky as the Shoort they represented.

There are at least seven and perhaps more subordinate Shoorts (figure 16). They are the helpers and messengers of the principal Shoorts. They come on stage singly or in twos and threes and occasionally go into camp. Although K'tétu played the part of a subordinate Shoort in the first men's Hain, he was reputed to have performed with such perfection because (it may be surmised) he symbolized Krren, Sun. Be that as it may, in the real Hain the seven principal Shoorts all represent K'tétu as well as the seven founders of the male Hain. The mythical identity of only two other subordinate Shoorts are documented. One was K'héu of the south sky, who became transformed into the cormorant *k'héu* (*Phalacrocorax magellanicus*) and the other was Kapre, the large albatross *kapre* (*Diomedea exulans*) of the north sky. Gusinde remarked that the subordinate Shoorts were less graceful than the principal ones.

Eight different Shoorts symbolize the passage of time through the day. In 1923 one or more of these Shoorts appeared each day, although when the culture was still fully functioning they probably all acted. The terms by which they are designated undoubtedly signify the periods into which the day was divided. Gusinde did not give their names. According to the Salesian document the name of the first one to appear, Kuan Koseca (or Wánkoška according to Gusinde), means 'low tide of dawn'. He presents himself in camp before sunrise when the women sing their chant welcoming the dawn (see chapter 7). The second one, called Koxó, comes when the pale light of dawn breaks on the horizon. The third (Yáro), whose appearance coincides with sunrise, is followed by the fourth (Yarárix), who is presented when the sun is above the horizon. According to Gusinde, the fifth (Ak'éu) is shown when the morning star is half way to its zenith. Then comes a Shoort whose name includes the word for sun or day (Krankénuk) and, as it appears at noon, the term probably signified 'mid-day'. The seventh (Krankáishk) is defined in Beauvoir's dictionary as 'sun fall', though Gusinde wrote that it is presented early in the afternoon between one and two o'clock. The last (Sanenke-páuwen) is seen between two and three o'clock, which during the shortest

15. Two principal Shoorts of the 1923 Hain. *Left*, north sky. *Right*, south sky.

winter days is close to dusk. The women believed that he remained in the Hain hut until late at night. Gusinde remarked that, in 1923, the sixth and seventh were presented most frequently and that the women were very pleased to see them.[11]

The men who were handsome (*hauwitpin*) and played the Shoort roles exceptionally well were long remembered. The women especially appreciated a beautiful Shoort among those who paraded on the stage — not those who went to camp daily to intimidate or punish the women. When they were lax about singing, for example, the counsellor sent a Shoort to camp, to 'harm them', as Federico said.

Shoort's movements are very stereotyped. As he is said to be made of rock, the performer has to have a very hard, muscular body[12] and give no sign

16. A subordinate Shoort of the 1923 Hain.

of breathing. He moves with very small steps, suddenly leaping and unexpectedly stopping dead, his body trembling. While advancing, he jerks his head from side to side, his hand folded into fists, the upper part of which are turned to the front, his arms arched. When he emerges from the Hain and upon re-entering it, he lifts both arms up, still arched, holding his fists upwards as if flexing his biceps. Like all the other spirits he cannot talk. All of his movements are stiff and decisive as if to fascinate or to create panic in those who observe him.

Great training and aptitude are required of the Shoort who goes into the camp. This is perhaps the most difficult of all the spirit roles, for the representation must not lapse among the women and children. Any gesture which reveals the real identity of the performer would betray the 'secret'. Esteban, who was *kloketen* with Federico, told me that a child had once recognized the true identity of a Shoort by his manner of walking.[13]

The rite of passage[14]

We return to our account of the first day. When the *kloketens* are fully painted, the two Shoorts appear once more from the opposite sides of the Hain while the men again chant *ho?ho?ho?* A woman in camp whispers to another while pointing to one of the Shoorts:

> That one seems to be happy! How slowly they move. How joyful they are! They are pleased that both *kloketens* will soon be in their power. Let us hope they treat them gently – the poor lads. We have painted them beautifully and prepared them well so that Xalpen will have mercy on them and so that the poor boys will not suffer.[15]

In camp the supervisors have finished painting the youths and now place a guanaco cape, fur side inward, over the shoulders of each *kloketen*. The women continue chanting 'the body is dry'[16] as each *kloketen* is led out of the hut, the supervisor on his left side, the mother on his right side, sobbing. They walk solemnly onto the stage toward the two Shoorts and the Hain. The *kloketens*' faces show increased anxiety as the mothers cry and scream ever louder while making compassionate gestures. On the camp side of the stage the young women draw up into a line, and dance toward the two Shoorts, shouting in joyful unison. Gusinde was struck by the contrast between the young women and the mothers. Having greeted the Shoorts again, the girls return to the camp. Meanwhile the little group continues approaching the Hain, the mothers bewailing the fate of their sons. 'My poor child! How sad you must be! We have painted you beautifully so that Xalpen be pleased. How I grieve for you!'[17]

The final moment of separation has arrived as the mothers, the *kloketens* and the supervisors come to a halt in the centre of the stage. By now the two

Shoorts have returned to the Hain. Led by their supervisors, the *kloketens* step away from their mothers, walking slowly ahead. As they disappear into the Hain, the women return to the camp. Shortly afterwards the women throw ashes toward the Hain. The mothers' sobbing gradually subsides. The camp is silent, and the atmosphere one of foreboding. The women know that the *kloketens* are about to endure the most trying and painful moments of the entire ceremony, the rite of passage, which is performed for each *kloketen* separately.

As the first *kloketen* is ushered into the Hain he sees the men standing in a tight circle against the inner wall of the hut staring at the fire and hears them chanting *ho?ho?ho?* Each man is painted with the design of his sky and has his cape slung over his shoulder. The men do not look at the *kloketen* but continue singing. When the women hear this chant they know that the rite of passage has begun and they run into their huts to hide. As the *kloketen* enters the ceremonial hut he peers around at the men's faces but fails to see the Shoort who squats somewhere behind the men, between them and the walls, waiting for his cue. One of the counsellors stands near the fire to receive the *kloketen*. He motions to the supervisor and the initiate to take their positions in the rear of the hut, facing the fire. The supervisor removes the *kloketen*'s cape and the youth stands naked, waiting, motionless and firmly held in place by his supervisor to prevent him from escaping. Suddenly heavy thuds are heard as if the earth were trembling, for behind the circle of men, Shoort is pounding the floor with all his strength. A counsellor shouts at the novice: 'Look upwards!'[18] Thereupon the supervisor, who is standing behind the *kloketen*, takes his head in both hands and jerks it upwards, holding it in this position. At this moment Shoort springs in front of the *kloketen*, as if he were rising out of the fire, his arms arched downward and his fists tight. The *kloketen*'s head is freed and he trembles violently, terrified of the red and white spotted being squatting in front of him whom he has feared all through his childhood and who has probably attacked him recently in the woods. An instant later Shoort fiercely clasps the *kloketen*'s knees, clinging to them and struggling to throw him. The *kloketen* desperately tries to keep his balance, his arms pressed against his sides, as he was ordered. A counsellor shouts at him to place his hands on his head with his fingers interlaced, elbows stretched out. The *kloketen* obeys automatically and Shoort moves excitedly around this naked youth, grunting and puffing through his nose and mouth as if panting with sexual urge, body swaying, pushing and bending his head. Suddenly he grasps the *kloketen*'s genitals, pressing them hard and panting in agitation. The *kloketen* endures the acute pain without resistance, his hands folded on his head while his supervisor tightens his hold on him. Shoort forcefully tugs and squeezes the initiate's genitals for some time. He finally pulls them violently with both hands, giving out a shrill yell and releases them.[19] The *kloketen* is allowed to let his arms drop. He is shaking, shocked from the intense pain and terrified of what may follow. After a few moments Shoort squats once more and again grasps the *kloketen*'s knees, this time making him fall. The men shout at the *kloketen*: 'Fight! Grab Shoort!'[20] and a wrestling match begins. Shoort circles round, still squatting, now dodging his opponent, now attacking him, threatening to bite his genitals. The *kloketen*, infuriated by the torture he has endured, plunges at Shoort, but he is strictly forbidden to touch his enemy's head or neck (the mask). He has been warned that Shoort would ram him with his head of rock if he so much as brushes against it. Shoort pushes him toward the fire, as if he were trying to draw him through it into the underworld. If Shoort loses control of himself he may bite the *kloketen*'s genitals or seize a stick from the fire and burn him. The odds are against the *kloketen*, for if he gains on Shoort, the supervisor intervenes; a *kloketen* must never triumph over Shoort.[21] When the youth has reached a state of frantic despair, when both he and Shoort are panting heavily and sweating from exhaustion, the counsellor orders the fight to stop and the men chant *ho?ho?ho?* again.

Shoort relaxes, sitting on his haunches, hands between his legs, head sinking a little, trying not to breathe hard. The *kloketen* may faint, or nearly do so, not only because of the physical strain but also because he is bewildered as to why Shoort attacked him so ferociously and why all the men are against him. Before he has time to recover his supervisor, pointing to Shoort's head, gives him a startling command: 'Grasp it!'[22] And a counsellor shouts at him: 'Touch Shoort! Is he of rock or of flesh?'[23]

Shoort remains in the same position, impassive. The *kloketen* approaches him cautiously and, touching him timorously, replies with incredulity: 'He's of flesh!'[24] The men pretend to be bewildered and one ventures: 'Where could such a man come from?'[25] Encouraged by his supervisor, the *kloketen* passes his fingers over Shoort's head and neck. Urged on, he finally grasps the head, feels the mask and starts pulling it off. As he does so, the performer covers his face with his hands. A counsellor then orders the *kloketen* to pull Shoort's hands away from his face. He obeys and stares in amazement at the unmasked face. One of the elders shouts at him: 'Who is he? Could he be a *hoowin* [a mythical ancestor]?' Another joins in: 'Who could he be? Maybe an Airu? A Woo [both neighbouring groups: the Alakaluf and the Yámana]? Perhaps a Joshe [a killing spirit of the forest]?' Others question: 'Don't you know him?' 'Name him if you do.' 'Don't you recognize the face?'[26]

Some minutes pass before the *kloketen* finally identifies the impostor. The identification may take a while because the *kloketen* is staring at a blackened face with contracted muscles and tightly closed eyes. When he does call out the actor's name, one of the men shouts: 'Push him!'[27] As the false Shoort tumbles to the ground the men roar with laughter and the *kloketen* relaxes, drained but exhilarated, though a second later he may flare up indignantly and furiously attack the 'spirit'.[28]

With the crisis over, the *kloketen* grabs Shoort's mask and presses it against his navel while jumping around, laughing and shouting: 'I am not afraid of Shoort any more! Now I know who he is! I am so happy!'[29] Sometime later a counsellor will tie a triangular head band (*kochil*) around the *kloketen*'s head as a symbol of his manhood.

The rite has come to an end. The supervisor wraps a cape around the youth's shoulders while everyone sits down, the supervisor behind his *kloketen*. A counsellor turns to the *kloketen* and says: 'This was all contrived to frighten you. This is how we men play. The women must never discover what goes on here in the hut.'[30]

The initiate now knows that Shoort is only a man and he may have guessed already that all the other spirits are the same. Garibaldi once told me that the aim of this scene is to wear down the *kloketen* so that he becomes willing and disposed to follow the orders of the men.

Sometime afterwards the *kloketen* will be made to confess: if he had misbehaved by stealing, being disrespectful to the old people, or having sexual relations (though he would not be required to name the woman or women involved).[31] Later on the first day and at times throughout the long months of the ceremony the counsellors and other knowledgeable men will relate to the assembled company, paying special attention to the *kloketen*, how the Hain came into existence, dwelling on the perfidy of the *hoowin* women and their outrageous mistreatment of the *hoowin* forefathers. The *kloketen* will be told many stories which explain how the world and present society originated. He will be taught the mysteries of nature and the animals, the wind and the sea, the stars and the sun and most especially the moon. His attention and intelligence will be tested with such questions as: 'When Sun lived on the earth where did the light of day come from?'[32]

If his attention wanders, the counsellor or other wise man will stop talking, thereby insinuating that the *kloketen* is *tul-láken*, meaning disrespectful. Federico insisted that if he continued to be *tul-láken*, he would be obliged to go through the entire ceremony once more.

The *kloketen* will be repeatedly admonished never to tell the women the 'secret', nor ever mention what transpires in the Hain. He will be warned time and again that he will be spied upon when he returns to normal life, and that if he lets out the slightest hint of the forbidden knowledge to the women or the children, he will immediately be killed and the person in whom he confided also will instantly be put to death.[33]

Bridges commented that a good reason usually accompanied the wisdom of the Hain. Here are some examples from various sources.

> Do not be frivolous with the women of your own *haruwen* so as not to excite the jealousy of the other men, and so that no one may say of you, 'He wants to marry his sister' (a very injurious imputation).

To avoid both dangers you should choose a wife from a distant *haruwen* which also has the advantage, in case of a matrimonial dispute, that her kin will not be nearby to take her side and therefore she will be more submissive to you.[34]

Respect all women because all are mothers, even the old woman for she too, as any other woman, is the mother of us all.[35]

Be affectionate with your wives but never let them know your intimate thoughts, for if you do they might regain the power they had in the past.[36]

Do not be gluttonous because if you are you will become corpulent and lazy and not be a good hunter, and then your wives will have to feed you with the fish they catch. Your wife should be fat to show that you are a good hunter.[37]

Do not throw food away because you may go hungry later.[38]

When you cut a piece of meat, divide it into about twenty pieces and give one to everyone, taking the last for yourself, then you will be treated the same way when you are old.[39]

Do not laugh at the old people, be generous with them and with those who are invalid so that when you are old or if you become invalid, the young will have the same regard for you.[40]

Do not get angry before a meal because your food will sit badly.[41]

Do not pardon offences. Always take vengeance, not only with your enemies but even with the members of your family and 'tribe'.[42]

Be courageous and do not give much importance to food and comforts.[43]

Be generous with friends.[44]

Be physically fit for battle.[45]

Work without being asked.[46]

Be a useful member of society.[47]

In the 1923 Hain, Halimink, one of the counsellors, also warned his *kloketen* son: 'Do not have anything to do with the Whites.'[48]

Although the *kloketen*'s most trying time was the anguished encounter with Shoort, he was subject to severe discipline throughout the long ceremony. Here are some of the rules he had to obey:

Listen intently to all that is said and never talk except to answer questions.[49]

Keep out of the women's sight, except on rare occasions, because Xalpen is very jealous of the women.[50]

Only laugh after unmasking Shoort.[51]

Stretch out your legs in front of you when you sit, although you may raise your left leg and rest your chin in your left hand, supporting the left arm on the raised knee (figure 17).[52]

Stand up while drinking water and do not spill it (water was served in a leather bag held by his supervisor).[53]

Only scratch yourself with a little stick given to you for the purpose (he carried it over an ear like a pencil or dangling from his head band, secured by a string made of guanaco nerve).[54]

Do not yawn or stretch in the Hain.[55]

While he was in the Hain the *kloketen* was assigned the tasks of gathering firewood, keeping the fire lit while the others were asleep, sweeping out the Hain, burning the rubbish, keeping the meat from the dogs, etc. In short he was to do all the unpleasant work.[56]

If an initiate gave any cause for complaint while he was in the Hain, the man next to him would hit him with a stick.[57] Moreover he could only eat sparingly and was not permitted to consume any of the delicacies such as liver, heart, brains, marrow or guanaco blood. Federico explained the latter taboo in terms of the belief that men menstruate invisible blood and that guanaco blood is the same as human blood. He said that this is why neither *kloketens* nor pregnant women were allowed to eat it. When the Hain was terminated the *kloketens* had to purify themselves before consuming guanaco blood again, by painting their bodies with white chalk and lighting fires in all the huts, just as a man did when his wife gave birth to their first child.

The initiate would sleep little and was kept busy all day and late into the night. He might be woken before dawn and sent to fetch fire-wood or ordered to set out on a hunting expedition. He was taken hunting almost every day.[58] The supervisor was charged with preventing him from relaxing, but care was taken not to anger the *kloketen* for otherwise he might acquire a mean temper.[59] Every day, the *kloketen* had to paint himself from neck to feet, with white stripes on his face.[60] He was expected always to appear diffident, but after the rite of passage he would not be tortured again.

In the past the intensive training of the *kloketen* began on the first night with a three to four day hunting expedition. He was drilled to be constant and fearless, to have endurance, to be an accurate bowman and to be skilled in tracking game. He was taught how to survive without meat, how to shelter himself in a snow storm and how to build a fire in the rain. All the men were his teachers but his supervisor and the counsellors had particular responsibility for him. The men endeavoured to harden him both morally and physically and to give him self-confidence as well. On the hunt, the party moved at a trot; crossing prairies and valleys, running over sandy and rocky beaches and scaling bluffs, hills and mountains. They waded through marshes, sank knee-deep into bogs, forded fast-flowing rivers and marched through rain or snow braced against the furious winds.

The hunting party might travel for many hours the first night. When the elders decided to make camp the *kloketen* was ordered to halt, to fetch wood, and to build a fire which he had to keep burning all night. The men would take meat along for the first meal, but afterwards the *kloketen* had to carry any freshly killed guanaco and to roast it, although he was given very little to eat. If he was asked if he were hungry he was expected to reply negatively. Every morning he was obliged to paint himself white just as he did in the Hain hut. For relaxation, the men would practise shooting arrows into a cape with him, or race and wrestle with him.[61]

The *kloketen* was kept busy all the time both in the Hain and while out hunting. The women were aware of this but they thought he was under the despotic orders of Xalpen and that she might at any moment emerge into the

17. The two *kloketens* initiated during the 1923 Hain, in the *kloketen* sitting position.

110

Hain from her earthly abode, demanding meat. If she were not given enough she might kill a *kloketen*, or some of the other men, and even eat them if she was not offered guanaco meat. The women imagined that the *kloketen* had to hunt indefatigably to save his own life. When Xalpen's presence in the Hain was made known to the women, the mothers would sometimes sing *màà tóni* (now far away) *tília k'óchen* (ankles tired from hunting) in order to console and strengthen their sons. To appease Xalpen they chanted *tul-ulichen* (beautiful heart) in her praise.[62]

7 Daily and frequent scenes of the Hain

Some of the Hain scenes, such as the women's dawn singing and the visits of Shoort, were enacted every day for the duration of the ceremony. Others took place at different intervals. As was indicated in chapter 5, apart from a few scenes which had to follow a particular order, there was no prescribed sequence for the performance of the occasional scenes, which could occur at any time as decided by the men.

The women's dawn singing

Every day during the Hain, long before daybreak, the *kloketen* mothers take up positions outside the entrance to their dwellings and begin singing the *haichula* chant[1] which Gusinde described as 'dreadful, unpleasant and anxious'.[2] The other women join in and the chant continues for about half an hour. Lola told me it brings the dawn, and this is confirmed by one of the Hain myths:

> The *kloketen* from the north had a sister. She noticed how long the darkness lasted, and stepped in front of the hut to sing. While she was singing it grew lighter and lighter. The day was now much longer. During the day the girl sang a few more times so that the light would not dim.[3]

A few hours later, they reassemble to chant repeatedly the word *yóroheu* (dawn), as a greeting for the sun.[4]

The daily visits of Shoort[5]

As a warning that Shoort is about to begin his daily visit to camp, the men chant, *ho?ho?ho?* Upon hearing this all the women, except the *kloketen* mothers, make themselves ready to receive him, by lying motionless in their huts, completely covered by guanaco furs, for they have orders not to set eyes upon Shoort while he is in camp. Only the *kloketen* mothers may stand in front of the huts, but their heads must be shrouded in capes, for they too are forbidden to look at Shoort.

The mother of the oldest *kloketen* has a very special relation to Shoort, as he exerts the same power over her as he does over the *kloketens*. She therefore has to demonstrate full submission to him while he is in the camp. During these visits all the women have to chant *ho?ho?ho?* from beneath their guanaco capes.

Shoort is always accompanied to camp by a shaman, who remains at his side, probably in order to give him added authority. If snow is on the ground, the shaman discreetly covers Shoort's footprints as they approach the camp by sweeping snow over them with his own foot, for spirits do not leave footprints.

These daily visits are a time of grave anxiety for all the women apart from a favoured few, the wives and affines of the shamans.[6] Shoort is invariably in a tyrannical, solemn mood; he comes to make his presence felt and to select for punishment those women whose behaviour has not conformed to the model of subservient wife, those who have failed to work diligently, who have not given an acceptable rendering of the chants or who have not donated sufficient paint and meat to Xalpen. If a man is not satisfied with the conduct of his wife, he confides in the Shoort who is scheduled to visit the camp. At the next opportunity Shoort seeks her out. He may only frighten her by shaking her hut violently, stirring up her hearth, throwing her belongings out of her hut or flinging a basket at her as she huddles under a guanaco cape. But he may also stab her with a stick, or even beat her and tear down her dwelling (with the help of other men). The action taken depends on what her husband has said, her reputation among the other men or even Shoort's feelings and mood. Shoort begins to demolish a hut with great caution, as if he were afraid of it. First he touches one of the hides which partially covers the hut or tent, then slowly grasps it and finally jerks it forcefully off the wooden frame and throws it to the ground, continuing until only the posts remain. These he seizes one by one, scattering them until the entire structure is demolished; but he is very careful to avoid the water bags while tearing down a dwelling, for spilt water might wash off his paint.

If at any time Shoort notices a woman or older child peering at him he might strike them with intent to kill. Bridges related that he saw a Shoort throw a hot piece of fire-wood at a woman cowering under her cape, even though she was a renowned shaman. Later the performer told Bridges that he had done so because she had not been well covered and was spying on him.[7] Children either hide under their capes or flee to the edge of camp to escape Shoort because he occasionally whips them.

Gusinde mentioned that in 1923 the men secretly removed all the firearms from the dwellings in the camp and hid them in the ceremonial hut for fear that a woman might fire at a Shoort.[8]

When Shoort is about to leave camp one of the men hollers to the women: 'Get up. Shoort is leaving.'[9] At this the *kloketen* mothers rush to the edge of the stage, where they sing while moving their forearms up and down to pay him homage as he returns to the Hain. Their chant is a repetition of the words *ho kreek* which Lola and Federico told me is another name for Shoort.[10] As he nears the Hain he stops and flexes his biceps once again. Then he stands in front of the post with which he is associated (corresponding to the performer's sky) and jerks his head from right to left while simultaneously making his whole body tremble. Finally he takes a great leap, disappearing head first into the Hain as if he were plunging into the underworld.

Throughout the duration of the ceremony, the women and children often go into the nearby forest, looking for fire-wood and food such as berries and mushrooms. Occasionally they rush back to camp terribly frightened because they have seen a Shoort hidden in the forest who they believe might kill them.[11] The men tell the women that Shoort will punish them if they are negligent wives or mothers. It was said that he might even kill a man. When Shoort is in a murderous fury, the women hear screams coming from the Hain followed by a terrifying thud which signifies that a man has been killed. The thud is produced by beating a rolled-up guanaco hide on the earthen floor of the Hain. But soon the women hear soft hand clapping, which announces that a good little shaman, called Olum, has emerged from the underworld to restore life to the victim. Frequently men come into camp, their faces covered with blood, and tell the women that they have been wounded by Shoort in retaliation for some female misbehaviour. The women do their best to take care of them, without however being allowed to inspect the wounds too closely, for they were self inflicted, made by jabbing the lips, nose or ears with a pointed stick, and adding guanaco blood to achieve the desired effect.

Quite often a high-ranking Shoort presents himself on the stage simply to be admired by the women. He comes in response to a special type of chant called *k'méyu*. Each woman knows one or more of these personal chants which she has either inherited from a kin or received as a gift. According to Angela such chants remained unchanged 'for centuries'. I recorded fifteen of them from Lola, only one of which was her own. She could sing the others because the owners were dead; if they had been alive she would not have had the right to sing them.[12]

Sometimes several women competed in singing their *k'méyus*, in the hope of making a principal Shoort appear. When a Shoort did come on stage his paint design indicated the sky to which he belonged, and any woman associated with that sky would consider that her chant had lured the Shoort from beneath the earth. Federico told me that once during a Hain celebration his mother had said: 'I brought out a very beautiful Shoort.'

Every day at noon the women take their positions in front of their dwellings. The mother of the oldest *kloketen* starts singing her *k'méyu*, and the other mothers join in, until often all the women are singing their different chants simultaneously hoping to please the spirits so that they treat their *kloketen* sons kindly.

The offensive clowns[13]

Shoort's servants, called Hayílans, contrast vividly with their master. There are several Hayílans, and often they appear as pairs of old and young. Although they are completely disguised with hooded masks and paint which make them resemble Shoort, they are undoubtedly recognized as humans by the audience. They are comical yet often offensive. At times they perform an extremely erotic homosexual show and on occasions behave roughly towards the women. They rarely emerge from the ceremonial hut and usually come directly from the woods to perform. Like all the spirits they are mute but unlike most of the others, they are left-handed. The women shout and jeer to express amusement or disgust at these ridiculous, unfriendly spirits.

The *kloketens* are known as the 'sons of Hayílan', and they are expected to work for them. Shoort sometimes takes the *kloketens* underground to satisfy his wife's lust. On such occasions a Hayílan is supposed to lead them back but there is always a danger that the Hayílan may abandon a *kloketen* underground and that he may never return. Another task of these servants of Shoort is the supervision of the *kloketens* when they are out hunting. But the Hayílans frequently lose their charges and wander back to the proximity of camp. When this happens the women see a pair of Hayílans, one carrying the other on his back, both covered with mud. The carrier stumbles, slips and both finally slide on the ground rolling over each other as if utterly exhausted. Leaning heavily on crooked sticks, they signify their discontent at having let the *kloketens* escape from them. The *kloketen* mothers gather at the edge of the camp and sing the *ho kreek* chant to them. As this word is another name for Shoort, it is meant as a mocking comparison and succeeds in further infuriating the Hayílans. Then the mothers chant:

> My friend is angry? *Aimere j'hópin?*
> Where did you leave them (the *kloketens*)? *Kishmá táishtr?*
> Bad hearts. *Tul jippen.*[14]

This is all the Hayílans need to fall into a tantrum. They threaten the women with their fists, pantomime their intentions of whipping the *kloketens* once they lay hands on them and then trudge back into the forest. A while later one may be seen riding to the Hain on the back of a *kloketen*. If thudding noises issue from the ceremonial hut, this means that the Hayílans are thrashing their charges, whereupon the mothers implore them to have mercy on their sons by intoning the *ho kreek* chant again.

On another day an old hunch-back Hayílan appears, limping along, falling hard on his bottom and struggling to his feet. Suddenly he begins scratching

115

in the snow or on the earth with his stick. After a while he stoops down and scratches more vigorously with his fingernails as if he were intent upon finding something he has lost, persisting until he sinks down helplessly as if utterly defeated. A *kloketen* mother calls to him:

> You miserable old man – go back quickly to the Hain. We are all laughing a lot at you. You are so very clumsy. Why indeed do you come here and bother all the people? You are an odd fellow. Where is your son [his *kloketen*]? You certainly make our children work too hard. Why is my son plagued by you?[15]

Hayílan manages to pull himself to his feet, bracing his body on his stick. Then he makes a dumb show that he wishes to race with the women, an idea which is met with hilarity. Crestfallen, he sinks down into the snow again. Soon a young Hayílan appears, proud and vigorous. He attempts to help the old one to his feet and finally after a great effort succeeds, but having done so, he attacks him with a vengeance, pounding his hunch back with his fists, until the infuriated victim retaliates by beating the aggressor with his stick. Then they wrestle; tripping, tottering and falling over each other, dragging one another around by the head. Suddenly they fraternalize, swooning into each other's arms. The audience laughs heartily, calling them names: 'Go you and your bad companion! Trouble us no more! Aren't you ashamed to show yourself here? You dirty riffraff!'[16] Showered with curses, the pair limps back to the Hain.

Gusinde wrote that at times the sensuality and 'sexual lust' of these spirits beggared description. They spread out their legs and make violent pelvic thrusts, while the women bellow their indignation. Amid all the excitement, the young one may suddenly give in and let himself be manhandled by the other, like a limp dummy. The old one stands him up, rolls him over on the ground like a cylinder, kicks him on the buttocks, beats his head, and then carries him pick-a-back while striking him on the bottom with both fists. The old Hayílan may carry the young one on his head. While the latter attempts to balance himself, his genitals fall over the carrier's eyes, obstructing his view and causing him to stumble with every step. But this does not stop the old Hayílan performing a grotesque dance to show sexual excitement. Finally he lays his companion on the ground who remains motionless and helpless, and what Gusinde called the 'impure play' begins. The young Hayílan springs to his feet and kicks the old one, who wheels around from the shock, and falls flat on the ground. The young one then pulls him to his feet again, lugs and drags him around until he is in a crouching position. Then they mime anal intercourse, to the disgust of the women who shout: 'Go away quickly, you and your unclean companion. You old fellow, aren't you ashamed to do such things, here in front of us all. You other, let him go. How disgusting to take advantage of an old man in this bad way! You repulsive creature.'[17] Responding to the accusations of the women, the old Hayílan slowly regains his feet, waves his arms and nods toward the Hain. A bent and ancient third Hayílan then makes his entrance, and on this frail body the first two perform what Gusinde referred to as a 'most contemptible manifestation'. Hardly has the newcomer dragged himself into their presence when they both kick him, causing him to swoon awkwardly. Thereupon the others turn somersaults over him and treat him like a ball, to the great amusement of the audience. As the erotic play continues the women shout incriminations at the performers. After a while they tire, and pushing and dragging each other they circle into the Hain while making threatening gestures at the women.

In 1923 Hayílans came into camp at about six-day intervals, always at night. Lola said that in her time they used to bother the women every day. Gusinde related that one might suddenly present himself near the camp beside a fire, brandishing his stick. The women and children who are still outside flee into their huts or tents, although they are not obliged to hide as they are during Shoort's visits. They sit around the fire inside their homes and peek through the walls to see where he is, or they get into bed and pull the covers over their heads.[18] At other times Hayílan may dash into camp without any notice, while everyone is asleep, striking the huts with his stick. Whether he announces himself or not, he bangs on the walls of the huts with his fists, tearing and pulling at the leather covers, throwing them into the nearby forest, and scattering the branches which form the walls. He jabs at the women with his stick through the walls of the hut, or even dashes into the hut to kick and strike the women who are squatting around the fire. Hayílan is a creator of disorder. He is very careful to keep his identity concealed and always comes into camp to attack the women at night. The women hear him gasping as if in a state of great sexual excitement while he gropes around the walls of their dwellings, seeking an entrance. Gusinde remarked that if there was a husband or other kinsman present, he would bar the entrance to Hayílan and strenuously forbid him passage. Once thwarted the spirit capered toward other huts. When Gusinde observed him, Hayílan finally gave up and returned in ill humour to the dark forest. I consider this scene very significant because it demonstrates the way in which the men were aggressors while pretending to be protectors of the women.

My interpretation differs from that of Gusinde who said that Hayílan represented the insertion of a comic figure in the long line of dull enemy spirits. He thought that Hayílan relieved the strain which the women endured, eased the psychological damage and brought equilibrium to their oppressed minds.[19] Hayílan certainly provided comic relief, but he was never the women's ally. The ambivalent nature of this spirit is obvious. He was funny, erotic and ridiculous, but at the same time created havoc in the woman's world by destroying her home; he was a woman-beater and a menacing rapist.

117

The rumpus makers[20]

Frequent night-time visits are made to camp by a couple, Hashé and his wife, Wakús, who is of course played by a man. They are believed to be emissaries of the dreaded Xalpen but, in fact, they are sent by the counsellor when the men run out of meat and paint, especially *ákel* (ochre). They are not really spirits for they are maskless, although their faces are covered with charcoal. Their hair is ruffled and surmounted with a crown of twigs and leaves and they wear their guanaco capes with the fur turned inside. Hashé carries a staff. When the couple is about to depart from the Hain, the men sing *hú ku hú*,[21] another name for Hashé.[22] The other words of the chant, 'Women give *ákel*', are sung in the Haush language, undoubtedly because the emissaries are of Haush origin although the performers may be Selk'nam. Hashé and Wakús cross the stage on their knees, chanting louder and louder as they near the camp. Federico said that they looked and sounded as if they were drunk. Once they arrive in camp they rise to their feet and gambol around, entering one hut after the other, where they make a pantomime of beating the women, especially Hashé who pretends to strike them with his staff. Wakús is less wild but more comical than her husband. He stabs at the fires and she nearly falls in. They pretend to set fire to the huts and throw themselves on the bedding amid the laughter of the women and children. But all the while they make mute gestures demanding gifts. If they are not given anything in a hut, Hashé steals a piece of meat or ochre or throws ashes at the women. The women tease them all the while. One may proffer a piece of meat to Hashé, then snatch it away before he can grab it, and another may mime feeding his penis with meat and ochre. The women also throw ochre at Wakús who gently picks it up with her left hand and stores it under her cape. He receives the gifts of meat and ochre, while she carries the goods, as befits a woman. Both are considered *chiteré* (gluttonous) and eat much of the meat, only saving the remains to take back to Xalpen. Hashé also performs tricks for the women, such as pretending to swallow hot chunks of meat or burning charcoal. After all the rumpus, they walk solemnly away. Hashé with his staff and Wakús bearing the gifts for Xalpen.

Xalpen[23]

Xalpen is the central figure of the ceremony: the most sinister, nefarious and heinous of all the Hain creations. All the earth spirits, with the exception of a spirit called Halaháches (see chapter 8), are at her command. Although she is Shoort's wife, all the men, and especially the *kloketens*, are considered to be her husbands. Thus she has a particular hatred for women, because, according to Federico, they are her mothers-in-law. She is *chiteré* (gluttonous) and even cannibalistic. It was said that she sometimes devours the *kloketens* and might do the same to any woman or child who goes too close to the ceremonial hut. If not given enough meat she threatens to eat human flesh. She is unpredictable, irascible, the ally of no one. At any moment she may turn her fury on the men and kill them, and so, as we shall see, the women aid and abet the men in the moment of great crises. Paradoxically, the terrible Xalpen is herself the mother of a most charming spirit, the baby K'terrnen, who is said to have been fathered by one of the *kloketens*.

During the 1923 Hain, Xalpen 'appeared' inside the ceremonial hut on eight occasions, raging, demanding food, indulging in sexual intercourse with the men and threatening to slaughter them.[24] Unrelenting repetition of this highly dramatic scene contributes greatly toward sustaining the intensity of the long ceremony. When Xalpen is in a frenzy of hunger a shaman, painted with a black line from ear to ear across his upper lip, cape with the fur turned inside, goes to the camp accompanied by several other men, to demand meat for Xalpen. Angela said that after they depart the women take up position in the camp area at their respective skies and sing in praise to Xalpen.

Xalpen arises from out of the earth passing through the fire into the Hain. She arrives carrying a large leather bag, adorned with red and white painted stripes, which she intends to fill with food to take back and feast upon. The women know the moment of her arrival because the men cry *wā* from within the Hain. If Xalpen is hungry, her food bag flies out of the Hain, indicating that she expects it to be filled. Then the women run toward the Hain bearing baskets full of mushrooms, berries, fish or any other food, for Xalpen accepts anything edible. As they run they chant *ha?ha?ha?*[25] in a playful mood, and approach as close to the Hain as they are permitted, sometimes competing in races. The baskets are set on the centre of the stage and the women return to camp, probably pleased that they have fed the monster, for when she has food in her bag she usually calms down for a while.

If Xalpen is not given sufficient quantities of food, particularly meat, she might eat the *kloketens* and other men, though she would not devour a counsellor or a shaman. But apparently she never 'really' consumes anyone, for if she did the victim would have to disappear forever.[26] But in a paroxysm of ravenous rage Xalpen does kill some of the men, although not the *kloketens* whose turn to die comes later in the ceremony. Federico insisted that she might slaughter the other men at almost any time. When this happens the Hain trembles and the terrifying *wā* cries are heard by the women who identify the individual voices and lament 'Xalpen has killed so-and-so'. Each woman then sings her *k'méyu* chant in an attempt to calm Xalpen's fury. A while later the women hear the soft hand-clapping which announces the arrival of the little shaman, Olum, and the women rejoice in the knowledge that he will restore life.

When Xalpen arrives at night she invariably shows sexual hunger. Once again she is announced by the frightful cries of *wā*. Then the women intone a chant calling Xalpen 'forehead of rock',[27] an expression which refers to her upper body being made of rock while her lower parts are of flesh. I understand this expression to carry a double meaning; that the singers secretly wished to insult Xalpen, while appearing to offer her adulation. In any case such a subtlety was lost on Xalpen, because upon hearing the chant she becomes all the more furious, *aimer-ré*.[28] As the women chant, the Hain begins to shake as if there were an earthquake, the effect being produced by the men pushing the structure of the hut back and forth from within. Great thuds are heard from the swaying hut, as the floor is being pounded with rolled-up guanaco hides, to imitate the hollow screams of Xalpen.[29] Then fire flies out of the apex of the Hain. The men even set fire to a long pole and project it through the top making the hut appear to be in flames. Amid the turmoil, Xalpen continues screaming and the men cry out in terror. Suddenly several men rush on stage brandishing burning torches as if they are fleeing the monster. They are followed by another man carrying a victim of her lust on his back. The victim clutches his own knees and his head flops as if he had fainted, while a third man brandishes a torch. Several similar groups then appear on stage and dash around near the ceremonial hut in broad circles as the fire grows menacingly and Xalpen's screams of sexual excitement, coupled with the pitiful cries of the men, become almost intolerable. The women approach the Hain as near as they dare, still chanting 'forehead of rock', imploring Xalpen to have pity on the men, or at least to spare the young *kloketens*. As the naked men scurry around the stage, the burning hut in the background throws long shadows on the glimmering snow.

When all the men return to the Hain, five others emerge slowly. Naked, with their arms linked and holding hands, they form a semi-circle facing the women. The man at the centre walks painfully with his legs apart because of the large inflated skin bag tied to his penis and reaching below his knees. After he takes his position in full view of the women, he cries out as if he is in extreme pain. The women can see the incredible damage that Xalpen has inflicted on her mate, causing his scrotum to become so overwhelmingly swollen that he can scarcely move.

This scene sometimes terminates by the men dragging themselves to the camp pretending to be utterly exhausted and drained by Xalpen. There they are surrounded by the loving solicitudes of the women. Alternatively the scene might end with the appearance of the horned male spirit, Halaháches, whose presence makes Xalpen sink immediately into the earth (see chapter 8). When she does depart, two female spirits, the Wáàsh-héuwan (foxes of *héuwan*) are heard barking and whining. These are Xalpen's companions, but they never appear and only bark and whine from within the Hain hut, to calm their raging mistress.

Xalpen's aggression against the men may be aroused if they do not submit to her sexual demands, if her hunger is not appeased or if the *kloketen* mothers do not sing long or loudly enough. If she does attack the men, they appear afterwards in the camp, their faces smeared with blood from self-inflicted wounds, to evoke the pity of their womenfolk.

When Xalpen has been raging with special fury, the women sometimes turn on the mother of the eldest *kloketen* and insult her noisily. They scream reproaches at her for her misconduct:

> Why don't you behave better? Why don't you work? Why do you give Xalpen the excuse to get all stirred up, to torment our men? You lazy, idle woman! You are to blame that Xalpen vents her anger on our men! How the *kloketens* must be suffering now! When are you going to change your conduct? It had better be soon, so we can have peace from that woman over there![30]

One afternoon in 1923, when the men were screaming terribly and Xalpen was at the height of her rage, the mother of the eldest *kloketen* went to the edge of the stage and called to Xalpen in a loud voice:

> Be kind to the men. Treat them gently. Don't make them suffer so much. You get excited so quickly and then you torture our men. Let them be. Then we all will be very peaceful here in camp. Trouble us no more. Then we will be calm. Be more friendly with us women. We have done you no harm. I hope you will treat our men and the *kloketens* in a friendly manner. You seize upon any little thing and go into a rage. Why do you get yourself all stirred up? Be more indulgent and treat my son more tenderly.[31]

After this plea, Xalpen's screaming did calm down somewhat.

The *kloketen* mothers do their utmost to provide meat for their sons every day. They entrust it to a shaman, to their husbands or to an elder brother of the *kloketen*. On one occasion, a mother gave a particularly large chunk of meat, so large that the emissary who received it asked, 'Why give so much? Xalpen will take most of it and leave just a little mouthful for your son.' To this the mother replied, 'Take it anyway. Then maybe Xalpen will be more friendly with my son and perhaps she will leave him a larger portion.'[32] When a mother only had a small piece of meat to offer, she would worry lest her son go hungry, and the men would increase her anxiety by commenting that she had given so little that Xalpen had taken it all and had left nothing for her son.

Xalpen was rarely shown in public and sometimes did not appear at all during a ceremony. In 1923 she was displayed only once, on the thirty-first day of the ceremony. Xalpen was the only spirit to be represented by an effigy, although on some occasions there was one man or more inside the structure to move it. The frame was constructed of long Selk'nam bows tied firmly together with guanaco nerve strings, and was about six metres in length

121

(in 1923). It was partially stuffed with branches, twigs, leaves and grass and half covered with guanaco hides. Bridges wrote that when he saw Xalpen conducted to the stage by a naked shaman, the man inside staggered slowly along, often pausing under the great weight of the object, until he manoeuvred it into position facing the women from a distance. Lola told me that she had heard tales of a Xalpen with three men inside.

The surface of the effigy (the guanaco hides) was either painted entirely with white chalk or with red *ákel* clay decorated with long white stripes.[33] Once when Lola saw the effigy it had a long drooping nose, and she commented that it was as big as a house (a hut). As the limbs were not represented, there was no sign of Xalpen's index finger with its long, sharp nail. Gusinde wrote that the effigy resembled a whale and Bridges that it looked like a fish, but there is no evidence that Xalpen was associated with any aquatic creature. Its bulky shape can be attributed to the fact that the spirit's upper half was supposed to be made of rock. In any case, the audience of nervously waiting women was only permitted a brief view of her upper body (the portion covered with guanaco hides) as the man (or men) slowly carried or pushed the effigy on to the stage.

According to Gusinde, there were seven Xalpens to correspond to the principal posts and Shoorts of the Hain.[34] Angela insisted that there were only four, representing each of the four skies. But only one ever appeared, and her orientation with respect to the skies and posts was not specified.

The Kulpush dances[35]

Kulpush, a female earth spirit, is never shown to the public. There are said to be four manifestations of this spirit, one for each principal sky. Kulpush is unmarried and emerges frequently into the Hain to have sex with the men. She is not spoken of as having any characteristic physical or personality traits and I found no clue as to her symbolic significance. When she ascends from the underworld into the Hain hut she is announced by male voices chanting an unaspirated *hohoho*, progressively faster. Four performances are commanded by her or presented in her honour, but to my knowledge they are not associated with the four skies which she represents. For the sake of convenience I have named them the Hopping, the Undulating, the Penguin, and the Pushing dances. They all delight and amuse everyone, particularly the young people who perform them.

The Hopping dance begins with the men chanting *hohoho* in short intervals, a chant which is taken up by the women in camp as they gather to view the dance. Then they all repeatedly chant *kulpush*.[36] Meanwhile the dancers in the Hain have painted their bodies red and their faces black. Two men, one with his arm around the other's neck or shoulder, hop lightly and rapidly on their right feet out of the Hain, facing the audience and singing the same word. They circle in the centre of the stage, letting their arms swing freely to the beat of the chant. Then they hop back to the Hain, reappear with two more men and repeat the steps until there might be eighteen or more men dancing in the centre of the stage. As the chanting becomes wilder, the men, still dancing, form a large circle, which finally breaks into a line and traces its way back to the Hain. In 1923 this dance lasted for about an hour.

The Undulating dance was called the Snake dance by Bridges. He was unfamiliar with the Kulpush spirit, although he knew there are (or were) no snakes in Tierra del Fuego with which this dance can be identified. Nor did the Selk'nam call it by this name. Nevertheless his description of it is well worth quoting.

> There were certain ritualistic performances in which the monsters played no part at all. They took place outside the *Hain*, and in some of them the women participated. Sometimes the men and lads, their bodies, arms and legs encircled with clear horizontal stripes of white paint on a deep red background, would gather stealthily in a clump of trees near the village. They would stand side by side in a line, each with his arms round his neighbours' shoulders, as in a Rugby scrum. Care was taken that there should be a clear open space between the trees and the village, so that the women, who would be on the look-out, would have a good view of the line's snake-like progression from the tree-clump to the *Hain*. When all were in position and ready to emerge into the open, the line was set in motion by the man at the end. He would give a little jump sideways and forward. This action would be immediately copied by the man next to him, and so on right to the end. In a row of thirty men, there would be at least three waves or ripples running from the head to the tail, as the whole body slowly advanced sideways towards the *Hain*. From a distance, this gave the exact impression of a huge caterpillar's laborious motion. When the leaders had proceeded far enough to be out of sight of the village, they broke off one by one, until the lonely end of the tail gave its last wriggle and disappeared from view into the *Hain*.
>
> The whole performance, if I remember rightly, was carried on in silence and greatly enjoyed by the actors.[37]

Gusinde and Bridges both called the next dance the Frog dance, although again there are no frogs on the island. Angela and Federico described the movements as those of a penguin. The dance takes place by day or night. In day-time the men put on their make-up with considerable care, applying red, white and black diagonal stripes to their torsos or entire bodies, as they do for the Undulating dance. But when they perform it at night they simply blacken their faces and paint their bodies red. A row of men emerge from the

Hain in a squatting posture, jumping alternately on their fists and their feet, while chanting *hohoho húkush kulpush*. Or they might emerge en masse from the hut and proceed to jump over the entire stage 'like penguins' chanting and producing what Bridges called 'the most infernal hubbub'. He added that 'Boys too young to become members of the Lodge [the Hain] joined in this prank, which was greatly enjoyed by the participants.'[38]

After this dance Bridges saw several men still squatting and making ugly faces and 'jaculations of disgust . . . to show their hatred and scorn of the women, who, unfortunately, were too far away to appreciate the efforts of their menfolk'.[39] They had inserted bits of wood in their mouths and under their eyelids to make themselves look hideous. Federico, who mentioned this, said that the women laughed at them a great deal.

The Pushing dance is often played at night around a huge fire built in the centre of the stage. Like the two previous dances, if it occurs during the day the men paint themselves with coloured stripes, but for the night they simply blacken their faces. They dance out of the Hain in a line formation, stooped as if carrying a heavy load and taking short steps, left foot forward, chanting *hohoho húkush kulpush*. The leader places his hands on his hips with the elbows stretched out, the others put their hands on the shoulder of the man in front. Meanwhile the young women, having painted their faces with stripes and spots of red and white, form a compact row with their arms around each other's hips. They are led by an older woman, who holds a two and a half metre pole, one end of which rests on her shoulder and the other on the ground. In this position, with the girls behind her, she waits defiantly for the men to dislodge her. Some of them stumble over her pole while others try to pull it away from her. As the male line gyrates around the female line, a girl might give a chosen man what Gusinde called 'a highly significant push' with her elbows.[40] The men jostle the girls with their shoulders, endeavouring to break their line, but they hold on tightly to each other, taking the strain by rocking back and forth with each onslaught. If the men succeed in making all the girls fall at once, like ninepins, then they win. The girls can win if they make just one man fall, in which case they return gleefully to camp. Gusinde commented that everyone enjoyed this teasing dance game.

The game of female vengeance[41]

Hóshtan is another earth spirit[42] who is never shown, although she is repre-sented by male dancers who imitate her movements. When she comes up from the interior of the earth into the Hain hut the men chant *héhéhé*[43] and the women approach the edge of the stage to wait happily for what is probably one of their favourite dance games. Angela called it *Hóshtan wáixten*, which can be literally translated as 'Hóshtan falling down with her feet in the air', but I call it 'the game of female vengeance'.

124

The long drawn out *héhéhé* which precedes the dance was described by
Bridges as 'squeaky wailing'[44] and it is intended to notify the women that the
men are frightened and expecting punishment. A small group of men hop out
of the Hain, as they do for the Penguin dance. Their faces and necks might be
blackened with the rest of the body entirely naked, or their bodies might be
painted with red horizontal stripes covered over by white chalk. Their long
hair is tied into three or four bunches, using grass or thin reeds as string. The
first group hops briefly out onto the stage and then returns to the Hain to
bring forth several more Hóshtans, and so on. When all the dancers are in the
centre of the stage, they scatter and sit quietly on their haunches, thorax
slightly forward, ankles not touching their buttocks, fists on the ground,
chanting *héhéhé* once again. Then they begin to bounce up and down on the
same spot. Suddenly the women, particularly the girls, charge them, each one
aiming for a special man – her husband or a likely bachelor. When a woman
is almost upon a man he tries to dodge her, jumping sideways, forwards and
backwards, jerking his head away from her as she attempts to grab one of the
bunches of his hair. If she succeeds, she tugs at it using both hands, pulling
with all her strength and trying to topple him, laughing all the while. He
resists as best he can, screaming and finally giving up, falling prostrate on the
ground. The victor scans the stage for another potential target and the game
continues until nearly all the men are 'killed', at which point the women
return triumphantly to camp. Lola vividly recalled how a Selk'nam named
Kankot was not daunted by his attackers, and never fell. Her husband, Anik,
was also very difficult to topple.[45] Gusinde commented that 'For once the
women had the possibility to triumph over the men . . . The women delight in
this game and "kill" many men in a short while. They enjoy it immensely.'[46]
After the women leave the field of battle, the dead spring to their feet and
run back to the Hain as though in fear.

La femme terrible[47]

Kulan is *la femme terrible* of the Hain. Unlike Xalpen she is entirely formed
of flesh and bones. The men announce her descent from the heavens, where
she normally dwells, by chanting *yoyoyoyo* very fast in the same key.[48]
Although she does not always appear when expected, she does come often
and always at night. When they hear her chant, the women and children hide
under their capes in the huts, particularly if she comes into camp, which,
however, she rarely does. The Salesian document tells of one occasion when
she did, and an old woman peeked out from under her cape and noticed that
Kulan had legs just like a man.

Only one Kulan is presented at a time and the spirit is not known for
representing any of the skies. She wears a conical mask which is painted red
and bears a broad white stripe from the tip of her head to her crotch, which is

125

concealed by a pubic covering. Other stripes are painted across her thorax, and her dainty breasts (formed from leather bags) bulge slightly. Kulan, who is young and slim, is impersonated by a *kloketen*,[49] and as she is constantly surrounded by her lovers, past, present and future, naturally the women do not like her. Even so, at times they sing to her calling her *mak chian* (lovely woman). When Kulan is thought to have absconded to heaven with one or more of her admirers the women sing the *maukel* chant[50] to entreat her to return and liberate their men. She often keeps her lovers for a week or more, and they come staggering back to camp suffering from the effects of Kulan's excesses, their hair strewn with the excrement of the emperor penguin. For some reason, the lovers eat only the eggs of this bird while in heaven, and as the birds abound there some of their excrement inevitably gets into their hair. The wives greet their faithless husbands with solicitude, knowing that Kulan has abducted them against their will. They do not inquire about exactly what has taken place in heaven with Kulan, for they have been told that the men never remember where they have been when they return.

Kulan also makes love in the forest, not far from the camp, and even in the Hain hut itself, but despite all this activity, she moves exceedingly slowly. In 1923 she only covered ten metres in an hour, by taking short lateral steps, pausing for a long time between each.

Sometimes a young, newly initiated *kloketen* returns from a long sojourn in heaven, beautifully painted and adorned with an elegant head-dress. Upon arrival several men escort him to the front of the stage, in full view of the women. The purpose of this exhibition is to arouse the sexual desires of the women, and Kulan may also parade around the stage with two such lovers, to excite the women's jealousy.

The cuckold[51]

Kulan has a husband, Koshménk, who is represented under four guises, his body paint and design differing to symbolize each of the four skies. But like Kulan his basic design and colours are red with broad vertical white bands and he too wears the large conical mask. At times two Koshménks appear together (figure 18) kicking and fighting for the wife's favour. One night in 1923 all four Koshménks presented themselves near the bonfire in the centre of the stage. They remained quiet for a time then chased one another into the woods, while the women yelled at them, mocking and teasing them for losing their wife. Koshménk is a cuckold by any standard and his performances cause much hilarity among the women, who greet him chanting *húp ke kep*.[52] This spirit is forever frantically searching for his faithless companion and falls into a rage if he discovers her in action. If she is making love in the Hain, he pounds on the wall outside, throwing himself against it as if to batter it down. Failing this, he jumps all around it furiously, much to the delight of the women who view his antics from a distance. He is tireless and rampages for hours at a time. When Kulan is taking on one lover after another in the centre of a circle of candidates, he peeps between the men's legs and mimes a jealous frenzy. Sometimes he remains immobile for ten minutes at a time, which, as Gusinde noted, makes him seem all the more stupid. But when Koshménk appears alone he is calm and consoled.

One afternoon in 1923, the women in camp suddenly heard the Kulan chant and rushed into their huts to hide. Then they heard a man scream and they ran out of their huts to the edge of the stage, where to their great amazement they saw Koshménk standing, trembling, on the apex of the Hain, peering over the countryside. Kulan had passed him by with a lover and in his

18. Two Koshménks of the 1923 Hain.

desperation he had climbed the wall of the Hain to scan the forest for her hide-out. He remained in that precarious position for two hours.

The men who interpret this spirit have to be very agile, capable of making high, buttock-kicking leaps while grasping the mask with both hands. Only Matan, the great dancer, excels Koshménk in leaping. The resemblances between Koshménk, Kulan and Matan may well be due to the fact that they all descend from the sky.

The ballet dancer[53]

Matan is the great dancer of the Hain, whom I call 'the ballet dancer'. Lola and Angela insisted that Matan is a female spirit while Gusinde's male inform-ants said the opposite.[54] In the description which follows I assume Matan to be female. She arrives from the sky during the day, perhaps in contrast to Kulan who always descends at night. Sometimes two or three manifestations appear together but only one dances at a time. Lola said that Matan is 'like a beautiful day'. She is acclaimed by the audience who greatly appreciate her amazing balletic vertical leaps. Between each leap she moves by springing laterally, always grasping the mask firmly with both hands at ear level, like Koshménk. She is usually painted red with broad white stripes or elongated ovals, with a white band around the waist and a similar pattern on the conical mask. In the past, according to Federico, the mask was painted half white and half black to recall the black-necked swan, *kohmen*. In the *hoowin* days of the women's Hain one of the girls, a perfectly beautiful person (*hauwitpin*), was practising the role of Matan when Sun discovered her and her com-panions. The girl instantly became transformed into the black-necked swan of the west sky.[55] Like Koshménk, Matan's disguise varies slightly, according to which of the four skies she is representing.

The men sing the *hohoho* chant for several minutes to call Matan from the heavens into the Hain. The chorus chanting is followed by two voices singing on different scales as a duet. Then the chorus joins in once more and may continue for a half an hour or more. A shaman precedes Matan to announce her arrival to the women, who rush to the edge of camp to greet her, chanting *Matan Matan Matan.*[56] The spirit enters by taking one great leap on to the stage as the shaman moves to one side to watch her movements intently, to make sure that her mask remains secure. The women continue chanting to lure her closer to them. Matan delights everyone and performs frequently. Gusinde described a particularly beautiful scene, when Matan appeared at night under a pale moon, whose reflection glimmered on newly fallen snow. Long, moving shadows of her dancing figure were cast across the stage by the light of the fire in the ceremonial hut. He commented that Matan seemed to be independent of the tyranny of Xalpen.[57]

The sister of Xalpen[58]

Tanu, the sister of Xalpen, presents an extraordinary figure (figure 19).[59] Bridges remarked that she is cruel and malignant though not to the same degree as her sister, but Gusinde said that Tanu is agreeable, harmless and causes no sorrow.[60] According to Gusinde all the richness and creativity of the Selk'nam's fantasy is manifested in this spirit.

Like other spirits Tanu is displayed at different times with four variants of painted design on her costume, each of which symbolizes one of the four skies.[61] Tanu is broad and tall (in 1923 Tanu's frame extended ninety centimetres above the actor's head) and has a conical head. Despite a protruding

19. Tanu of the west sky, 1923 Hain.

stomach, her shape is almost rectangular. Only the lower legs and feet of the performer are exposed and they are daubed with feather down. Like the other spirits she is almost faceless. The costume frame is constructed of Selk'nam bows tied together. Over these are stretched guanaco hides, which are painted with different combinations of white, black and red lines and stripes, with down sometimes glued over the black stripes. This structure is stuffed with reeds, grass and leaves to fill it out. It is strapped on to the performer who supports it on his back. He therefore has to face away from the audience and walk sideways, and also moves slowly because of the great weight of the costume. She is always accompanied by an old man who guides her and prevents her from stumbling. Federico said that this spirit carries a red pointed stick about the size of an arrow, tied to the front of the costume, with which she is said to jab the men in the nose and ears so that they bleed for the ceremony.

This spirit was presented at the first men's Hain in *hoowin* times after they had massacred the women and adopted the Hain for themselves. The *hoowin* who played the role of Tanu was subsequently transformed into the earth creeper bird, called *shocits*, which is of the south sky.[62] This bird is reputed to be very filthy because it eats excrement. This 'dirt' is metaphorically compared to the performer's perspiration as he supports the weight of the heavy costume. Tanu also represents a small female whale (*ochen*) of the north sky, who in the *hoowin* epoch played the part in the woman's Hain before she was transformed into a whale. She is symbolized in the bands of dark paint on Tanu's costume.

Tanu is a presiding spirit who merely walks onto the stage, remains there to witness a scene and then returns to the Hain. In a sense she represents Xalpen's authority. The scene described below is called *Tanu tien* or *Héuwan tien*, the term *tien* (to ask for) signifying that Tanu had requested the performance in her role of Xalpen's emissary.[63]

It is night and a large fire burns in the centre of the stage, while in the Hain the *kloketens* and other bachelors paint themselves red in preparation for the Tanu scene. The one who is to lead the dance adds a white stripe from his neck to his genitals and they all jab their noses until blood flows on their chests. If they are not satisfied with the quantity thus obtained they smear their faces and chests with guanaco blood. Just before they leave, they begin the *hu? ku?* chant,[64] yelling the phrase loudly as they step out of the Hain. The leader puts his hands on his hips while the others place theirs on the shoulders of the man in front. Their pace is very short, slow and tiring, one foot advancing a little ahead of the other, one foot being brought up to touch the other ankle. As they dance in this fashion toward the fire, they pierce their noses again with the pointed sticks they carry. Meanwhile Tanu slowly emerges from the Hain accompanied by an old man, and moves downstage to one side, quite close to the camp. The men encircle the fire, still pounding their feet, now chanting *hush lish héuwan.*[65] The older women gather at the edge of the stage while the unmarried girls form a line on the dance floor, placing both hands on the shoulders of the girl in front or one hand on her shoulder and the other on her hip. The leader of the female line is a kinswoman of the leader of the male line. The men, panting heavily, advance with short jumps, still chanting, and close in on the woman's line. Each girl carries a piece of guanaco fur with which she tries to wipe the blood from the face or chest of a favourite man, someone kinship rules would permit her to marry.[66] As she makes this gesture the man in question responds by pushing her playfully with his elbows. Finally Tanu returns to the Hain followed by the men.

Ritual to bring good weather[67]

When bad weather, a snowfall or a rain storm, is threatening to begin or become worse, the counsellor orders that the *chowh-toxen* ('water-cease') rite be performed. In the Hain a number of young men (there were eight in 1923) wind pads of dry grass around their heads to form a crown. They leave the Hain naked in a row, chanting *wa wa wa*, and dance to the centre of the stage, where a fire is either smouldering or entirely extinguished. They rotate about the embers and then move in a line to a nearby source of water. Arms entwined, they circle the source facing inwards and chanting *sh sh sh* while rotating faster and faster, alternately clockwise and anti-clockwise (figure 20). At some time during the scene, the older women begin chanting *yó shu xe é yó*[68] if it is threatening snow, or *yó te kó hu ó ru*[69] if rain is the problem. Meanwhile, the girls gleefully throw leather buckets full of water, often mixed with snow and ice, on the backs of the men. Sometimes they throw snow balls. When the girls tire of this the men join hands and dance in a line back to the Hain. The rite may be repeated several times during a day and on subsequent days until the weather does improve.

Imitation of sea lions[70]

When the women hear deep bellowings from the Hain they eagerly approach the edge of the stage to see the sea lion pantomime. According to Gusinde, Ochanhéuwan, a female earth spirit, orders the presentation of this scene, which was a favourite of the Haush, among whom it originated. Gusinde is, however, mistaken about the name of the spirit who orders the presentation of this scene. He translated *ochen* or *óchan* mistakenly as 'sea lion', although elsewhere in the same book he defined it correctly (with a different spelling, *achenk*) as a small whale.[71] The men were certainly imitating sea lions and not whales, so the name of this spirit is an error. The term for sea lion is *koori* or *keorjn* (*Otaria byronia*).

The performers cover themselves with their guanaco capes, the fur turned inwards, and form an irregular group close to the Hain. Balanced on their knees, they rotate in all directions, pivoting on their hips to mime the movements of a herd of sea lions. One male stretches out amorously towards a smaller female who, coyly sinking down, nibbles her mate's neck voluptuously. Two males feign a combat, fiercely attacking one another, recoiling, stretching their necks, lumbering around each other to gain new attack positions and all the while emitting terrifying grunts and bellows. In 1923, they were in continual movement for more than an hour. Gusinde commented that from a distance one could hardly believe that they were not really sea lions, the pantomime was so exact. The women and children were apparently equally impressed and very much delighted.

The phallic dance[72]

The phallic dance or rite is named *Oshkonháninh*. *Osh* signifies tail and evokes the costume used. But the remainder of the expression defies attempts

20. The rite to bring good weather during the 1923 Hain.

at translation. According to Gusinde this dance is not integrated into the Xalpen complex, but neither are the sky spirits Kulan, Koshménk and Matan.

An authoritative elder announces to the women that immediate preparations should be made for the presentation of the *Oshkonháninh*. Sometime later he sends several men to the camp to gather the elongated bundles made up of small twigs, reeds, grass and tiny branches with fresh leaves (one species of the native beech tree is an evergreen) which the women have made ready. The men carry the bundles from camp to the Hain, where they build up a high stack at its entrance. Finally an elder shouts to the women: 'We have enough.'

Meanwhile in the Hain the men are painting themselves black, leaving only their faces clean. When this is done they draw broad white stripes and lines of white dots on their thoraxes and limbs, except for their knees which remain black. Each man then ties about ten pads of the vegetation which has been prepared on different parts of his body: wreathing the front of his head, encircling his neck, girding his loins, winding around his legs above and below his knees and stretching over his shoulder and down his back. An especially long pad is tied on the chest and attached to the one around his neck at the upper end and around his loins at the lower end. This represents the *osh* (tail). Another long thick bundle is fastened over his genitals and hangs between his legs to the level of his knees to symbolize his penis.

During this scene the women are allowed to approach the Hain, and stand in the entrance, to observe the ritual dance. Gusinde explained that this is the reason why this scene had to be performed soon after the ceremony began. In 1923 it was presented only once, on the fourth day. During the preparations the Hain was carefully cleared of all food debris. Recall that the women are led to believe that most of the food they donate is packed up by Xalpen in her bag, and that only titbits are left for the *kloketens*. The masks, paints and all other paraphernalia are hidden in the nearby forest. Were the dance to be held later, considerable work would be necessary to rid the ceremonial hut of all signs of the men's meals and theatrics.

Just before the ritual dance commences, the fire in the Hain is extinguished, for the only time during the ceremony, and the embers are swept away. The men, decorated with the bundles of vegetation, form a circle around the fire site ready to perform. Facing inwards, arms around their neighbours' neck, they take short stamping steps as the circle rotates and soon begin chanting *xas xas xas*, increasing the intensity of their singing as they gyrate alternately clockwise and anti-clockwise. When their greatest speed coincides with the full volume and shrillness of their chant, they sink their heads down, thrusting out their loins so that their pad phalli fly up as if erected. The release follows as the movement ceases and the men, still yelling, throw themselves against the wall of the hut, bracing themselves with their heads which are bent backwards. At this moment the women scream and flee back to the camp. Quiet descends, the dance has ended and the men are exhausted.

133

Further clowning[73]

Ulen is a male spirit of the northern section of the island, and is thus of Selk'nam rather than Haush origin. Apparently he was seldom presented in the southern part of the island. He is an extremely dexterous clown and is characterized by a formidable, slightly pointed head, represented by a bulky bark mask filled with dry grass and leaves and decorated with a row of three stripes across the apex. His body is dark red, overlaid with white horizontal stripes from his neck to his feet and wrists.

A man goes to camp and tells the women and children to observe the Hain closely. A while later they see Ulen's huge head protruding from the north side of the Hain and his right arm bent over his head. He stares fixedly at the audience for several minutes and then suddenly vanishes, but reappears a fraction of a second later on the south side, with his left arm arched over his head, still staring. The women and children marvel at the speed with which he apparently covers a distance of some eight metres. 'Backstage' of course there are two rigorously identical Ulens, posed on either side of the Hain. A third man between them gives them signals as to the exact moment at which they should poke out their heads and arms. The performers practise a great deal in order to be able to coordinate their movements with precision and remain immobile for several minutes.

Gusinde did not obtain data on the significance of this spirit, perhaps because very few men from the northern part of the island participated in the 1923 Hain; by then most of them had been killed or had died of diseases.[74] In so far as is known, this spirit was presented simply to amuse the audience.

The dance of the painted men and women[75]

Everyone anticipates with pleasure the scene called Kewánix,[76] in which nearly all the adults participate. It was presented only once in 1923, on 4 June, the fourteenth day of the ceremony. It had originally been planned to be repeated on 27 June. On this day people were painted and were about to begin to perform, when snow fell at about 11 a.m. The scene had to be cancelled because the designs would be spoiled and it would therefore be deprived of its meaning. Almost everyone was disappointed, including, of course, Gusinde.

He reported that the only masked figure which appears in this scene is Hainxo, but there are reliable indications that this spirit is in fact Tanu, the sister of Xalpen, Hainxo being simply another name for Tanu.[77] Gusinde described Hainxo's costume as similar to although simpler than Tanu's, consisting of a large rectangular structure which terminates in a conical mask. The scene is commanded by Hainxo (Tanu) who witnesses it from the side of the stage.

Gusinde considered that the Selk'nam attained their highest artistic expression in this scene and stated that both men and women judged it to be the most beautiful and enjoyable part of the entire ceremony. I imagine this would be because of the symbolism expressed in the body designs and the sensual dancing of the naked painted bodies. The presentation was probably enhanced on 4 June 1923 because it was a clear day and the sun glistened on the snow and reflected on the decorated dancers.

In former times both sexes danced naked except for a pubic covering. But in 1923 only the girls did so and the women appeared naked only from the waist up. They explained that it was too cold to remove their fur or woollen skirts but the men did not approve of the skirts and protested that the upper part of the body was not sufficient for a correct display of the designs (*tari* in Selk'nam).

Early on the morning of 4 June, while the men were painting themselves in the Hain, the women and girls gathered in three huts in camp to do the same. First the entire body, or only the upper half in the case of the women, was rubbed with bright red ochre (*ákel*). Then a specific design was drawn on the red body. The wearing of a particular design was a matter of right, but there was a range of designs or emblems from which a person could choose. The designs, for which different coloured paint was used (see chapter 4), consisted of combinations of vertical and horizontal forms (from fine lines to wide bands and from dashes to solid lines) and round forms (from dots to quite large circles).

The parts of the body which did not have a design were painted again with other colours, over the red paint. These basic elements were sufficient to compose a great variety of motifs.

By 9 a.m. all who were to participate in the scene were painted with their personal emblems. First the men emerged from the Hain forming a horizontal line on the stage, and holding hands at about arm's length from one another. Then they walked downstage to about five metres from the edge, very near the camp. There they stood quietly in front of the women, who looked at them with pleasure. Everyone was silent for a moment. Then the men formed a circle, still holding hands, taking short steps by closing one foot up to the other in a dragging stride, chanting *xas xas xas*. They circled twenty times in one direction, stopped and then circled in the opposite direction, chanting continuously. Next they pressed inward, each man placing his arms on the shoulders of his neighbour. Increasing their speed, they circled and finally came to a halt with little pushes. They repeated this movement in a tight circle, going anti-clockwise and chanting all the time. The women then came on stage and encircled them, standing about three steps behind them, and moved lightly back and forth, with their hands placed on their stomachs. The women's circle was not closed, however, because it was large and because there were only about a quarter as many women performing as there were

135

men. The older unpainted women, together with the children, formed the audience at the edge of the stage. The rotating circle of chanting men, enclosed by the circle of women moving gently to and fro, created a beautiful impression. Finally the men broke their circle, took hands again and, facing the women, backed into the Hain. Gusinde commented that everyone danced in unison, very earnestly, and that no one spoke.

When the men disappeared into the Hain the women sat on their ankles in irregular groups, resting and waiting for the men. Some twenty minutes passed before the men reappeared, walking downstage again and seating themselves in the snow about fifteen metres from the women. They simply looked at them silently for a few seconds, then rose and returned to the Hain in a wide sweeping line.

Some time later, everyone in the camp came to the edge of the stage in lively anticipation. The men had begun hopping out of the Hain in penguin fashion, supporting themselves on their fists. They sprang around the stage thus with great excitement for about a quarter of an hour. Gusinde described the colourful painted forms springing on the snow in the light of the sinking sun and observed that the women seemed to take great pleasure watching them. The women advanced to the centre of the stage while the men were hopping about in every direction. Gusinde finished his account of the Kewánix scene by commenting once again on the beauty of the spectacle and the intense joy that everyone apparently experienced.

This scene was a vehicle for a particular form of symbolism. All the participants were decorated with designs representing their skies (*shó'on*) or, less frequently, their earths (*haruwen*). These designs were emblems of exogamic units; of the divisions (skies) or of the territories (earths) of the lineages (see chapter 2). The emblems, the *tari*, were symbolic manifestations of the *hoowin* tradition, and each individual had the right to claim the *hoowin* identified with their particular sky. The *hoowins* were also identified with one or more *haruwens*, corresponding to the individual's lineage affiliation. These elements form a complex system of classification which, I suggest, can be termed 'totemic', in the sense used by Lévi-Strauss.

The referents of the emblems or designs were elements of the sky and the earth: natural phenomena, animals and plants into which the divinities, the *hoowins*, had been metamorphosed. However, not all the divinities had a *tari*; for example neither Sun nor Moon had one.

The divinities were identified with one of the four skies in terms of premises which are too complex to describe here. The association with the earth (territories or *haruwens*) is more obvious as it is a function of the localities on the earth (the island) where an adventure or a metamorphosis had occurred. Divinities which were transformed into particular mountains, hills, cliffs or boulders represented the *haruwens* where these natural features were located. However, the *hoowins* were quite often associated with more

than one *haruwen* because of the adventures (events as related in the myths)
which they had had in different parts of the island. Most, if not all, of the
hoowin divinities had two names; one by which they were known in the
hoowin epoch before they were metamorphosed, and their common names
which were part of the Selk'nam's everyday language and comprise the
lexicons of the toponyms, fauna, flora and other natural phenomena.

A few examples should suffice to explain the system in terms of the choice
of emblems available to a given individual. Here I will mention those which
are illustrated in the photographs published by Gusinde (1931) concerning
which I have confirming data, so that the reader may refer to them. The
emblems for everyone affiliated to the south sky represented the rainbow
(*akainink*) of the south[78] and the lagoon bird (*ko'oklol*).[79] In addition to
these, members of two southern *haruwens* could use the designs of the
buzzard eagle (*kuárje*) and a species of albatross (*chalné*).[80] People of the
north sky might use the emblem for the rainbow of the north,[81] a small
whale (*ochen*)[82] (see figure 21) and the sea lion (*koori*).[83] Also, members of
certain northern territories could paint themselves with designs of the pejerey

21. Three Selk'nam women painted for the 1923 Hain. Angela Loij, in the
centre, is painted with the design (*tari*) of the whale, a symbol of the north
sky to which she belonged.

fish (*eéksail*), a large dolphin (*ksámenk*) and a small penguin (*káste*).[84] Anyone belonging to the west sky might employ the emblem of Wind (*shénu*).[85] A few territories associated with this sky could use the designs for the young male guanaco (*klátuwen*)[86] and that of the small dolphin (*k'manta*).[87]

8 The climax and anti-climax of the Hain

Death and birth[1]

The enactment of the death and birth scenes takes place at night by the light of a huge central bonfire. Because of Xalpen's indomitable sexual urge and so much love-making with the *kloketens*, sooner or later she becomes pregnant. The birth pains drive her into an even more uncontrollable state than usual and when her suffering is most intense she throws a bow out of the Hain. This is an ominous sign, for it means that she is about to kill somebody, in order to vent the rage caused by the torments of giving birth. The Hain quakes as never before, as her ghastly thudding screams boom through its walls and flames spring through the roof as if the entire hut were on fire. Using her long, sharp fingernail, Xalpen disembowels the *kloketens*, one by one. The women hear the terrible *wa* groans of the *kloketens* as each expires, and they intone the *yó te kó ho lí* chant[2] hoping in vain to appease the murderess who is killing the fathers of her baby. Suddenly all is silent and then the women know that the baby has been born and that Xalpen has returned with it to the underworld.

The men too are overwhelmed with grief for the *kloketens*. A short while later the women, who have gathered on the edge of the stage, see two elders carrying the corpse of a *kloketen* drenched in blood. One elder supports its head and the other its legs and feet, the head flops to one side, the eyes are closed, blood seems to seep from its ears and mouth and pour from the disembowelling wound which reaches from its neck to its genitals. The procession moves slowly and silently around the stage and returns to the Hain. Soon two other elders emerge carrying another corpse, until all the dead *kloketens* are displayed. The women approach as close as they are allowed, chanting a lament *hain kojn hórsho.*[3] The oldest women step forward, waving their capes in an attempt to give breath back to the corpses. Federico, who was *kloketen* in the Hain of 1933, commented, 'I felt really sorry to see the women cry so. They really thought their sons were dead.'

Lola and Angela, as well as Federico, said that Xalpen kills only the *kloketens* in this scene and the Salesian document is in agreement with this. But according to Gusinde, 'all the men must be killed so that her [Xalpen's] child may be born'.[4] The display of the *kloketen* corpses did not take place in 1923. I suggest that it was excluded either out of consideration for Gusinde or because the Indians were worried that tales of such a scene might arouse the criticism and curiosity of other Whites. When the Selk'nam were alone, in 1933, they did enact this scene. But ten years earlier, in 1923, after Xalpen had given birth and supposedly massacred all the men in the ceremonial hut, the latter slipped out and spent one or two days and nights in the forest, hunting and amusing themselves with wrestling matches, foot races and the like.

During the fifty day duration of the Hain in 1923 the (censored) death and birth scene was played twice,[5] which illustrates the theatrical aspect of the Hain. If the Hain were just a ritual, this scene would logically be enacted only once. As a rite, what would be the necessity or justification for repeating it? But as a spectacle, as theatre, there was every reason to do so, given its highly dramatic content. In this context, we can understand the reaction of the female audience. They 'believed' the young *kloketens* were killed by Xalpen, the first time as well as the following time or times, for they were participating in a drama and not merely observing a ritual. The impact of the ceremony as drama is crucial to an understanding of the women's alleged ignorance of the 'secret'. It seems clear to me that the women were involved in the same earnest play-acting as the men (see chapter 10).

The restorer of life[6]

The restorer of life is a small creature, the beloved Olum, whom the audience rarely sees. He is such a powerful shaman that the scars vanish as he heals the wounds and brings life back to the victims of the man-killing spirits.

A day or two after the massacre of the *kloketens*, when the men have returned surreptitiously to the Hain, Olum begins his work of *wá?r skóten* which Lola translated as 'bringing the blood together'. The sign that Olum is restoring life is the sound of rapid soft applauding accompanied by a clicking vocalization,[7] both of which are heard against the background of a rhythmic beat caused by the men pounding their fists on the floor of the Hain.[8] Soon afterwards a real shaman shouts to the women: 'All is well. *Kai ko'osé*. Now you may leave. *Kai joje wi*. The *kloketens* are alive again. *Kloketen kau ko'osé*.'[9] Federico commented that the women felt very relieved.

Olum's role as life-giver appears in another context in Bridges' revealing description of a show put on for the women during a Hain shortly before 1914. A well-known shaman, called Halimink, was carried into the camp in a pitiful state, covered with blood, moaning and gasping as if each breath were his last. After he had been gently laid on the ground, the men in the camp hovered over him, inquiring what had happened, while, in the background, the women listened attentively to the explanation. A lone hunter had shot the shaman; the shaft of the arrow had been extracted, but the barbed flint arrow head remained in his flesh. Two shamans tried desperately to save his life by sucking at the wound and chanting their curing songs. But their treatment was of no avail, and they announced that Halimink was near his end. The women then began loud mourning chants and his nearest female kin scraped their legs and arms with rough stone and glass until they bled. One of Halimink's bows and several of his arrows were broken and thrown into the fire, as was the custom. Suddenly 'some bright fellow' suggested: 'Could we not summon Ohlimink [Olum]? If he would come, might he save our brother?'

Immediately several men rushed to the Hain and great activity ensued. Soon a small group of men walked rapidly toward the camp, 'for every minute is precious'. In their midst was the celebrated Olum, played by an unusually small man who was masked and painted for the part. The women drew back and the shaman doctors gave way to their illustrious colleague. Olum cannot speak but he understands. As he was told of the gravity of the prostrated man, he showed his sympathy by mime and moaning. Halimink continued to gasp as Olum set about his cure just like any other shaman. 'Then after mighty efforts of suction, he produced from his mask [his mouth] the offending arrow head.' The expiring man began to revive, supported by Olum and surrounded by his delighted companions, and he feebly made his way back to the Hain. Once the men knew they were out of sight of the women, they all gaily discussed their hoax.[10]

The baby[11]

Shortly after the men return from the forest and have been restored to life by the beloved Olum, a shaman announces to the audience: 'Soon you will see something beautiful. Get ready!'[12]

The new arrival is Xalpen's baby, K'terrnen, who is impersonated by a slim *kloketen*. The baby could be of either sex, and if it is a girl the actor presses his genitals between his legs and binds them there with a string made of guanaco nerve or tendon. Esteban said that this role was very difficult to play and that the performer was chosen among the youths who were *hauwitpin*, perfectly formed. Federico agreed, adding that the actor's body had to be so straight that there was no space between his legs when he was standing and that his chest had to be flat, without prominent nipples.

The infant is decorated with parallel rows of down, from the tip of its conical head to its fingers and toes. The tiny feathers are glued to the body paint, which is applied in the form of vertical stripes of either red and black, or multi-coloured paint. The red and black striped design was said by Federico to represent *koori*, the sea lion, a mythical ancestor (*hoowin*) of the north sky who had played this part in the first masculine Hain before his

141

transformation. The multi-coloured stripe design recalled a small colourful bird, the *ko'oklol*, a *hoowin* of the south sky who had been practising for this role when Sun discovered her and her companions. She leapt into the nearby lagoon and was changed forever into this bird which always nests on the shore of lagoons. K'terrnen may also have been painted with other designs symbolizing other *hoowin* ancestors, but only these two have been identified.

The bright paint colours seen through the soft white down produce a glimmering effect, making the baby seem all the more supernatural. According to Esteban, K'terrnen was not adorned on its back and so great care was always taken to keep its face toward the public. The entire body was held rigid with the arms flat against its sides. K'terrnen is made of rock so it does not breathe, but it sways slightly, back and forth, and looks straight ahead.

As soon as the shaman announces that 'something beautiful' will soon be seen, the women prepare themselves by painting their faces with small white dots in lines which radiate from the lower eyelids down on to the cheeks. When they hear very soft hand-clapping from the Hain, they know that K'terrnen is emerging from the earth. The women begin their welcoming *héj ká rak?* chant,[13] stretching out their bent arms to draw the baby out of the Hain so that they can rejoice in admiration of 'Xalpen's gift of life'.[14]

Lola explained that although the creature is newborn, it becomes big soon, but it can scarcely walk, so has to be supported. This is the task of two respected men, usually shamans, one of whom may be a counsellor, as was the case in 1923 (figure 22). These men appear with their faces adorned with three dots, one above the nose and one on each cheek, and they wear especially handsome feather head-dresses as well as the usual capes, the fur inside. The *Wunderkind*, to use Gusinde's term, emerges from the Hain, braced on both sides and taking very tiny steps. The elders gently push the baby forward, stamping their right heels on the ground. The baby takes one little step with the left foot, then an even smaller step with the other foot, which it draws up to the left heel while holding its legs stiffly together. The threesome advance sideways across the stage, facing the audience. Lola used to imitate K'terrnen's gait by moving her shoulders slowly to and fro while chanting *héj ká rak?*. If K'terrnen sees a woman who is the object of complaint by her husband, it stops and takes a few paces backwards. But even so, the women continue to sing their admiration and contentment during the entire scene. When the baby re-enters the Hain, the men greet it with very gentle hand-clapping, while the women shout: 'It went below! *Kau kó?him.*'[15] A shaman closes the scene by telling the women: 'Now return to your homes.'[16]

K'terrnen may appear six or seven times during a scene lasting about four hours, as occurred in 1923. On that occasion the men suddenly called out *xas xas xas* between its third and fourth appearance, using high voices and pausing between each phrase. This meant that Olum was in the ceremonial hut. He was so overjoyed at the happy event that he began to toss the men out of the Hain, one after another. Each somersaulted onto the stage and then lay inert, until there was a great heap of entangled motionless bodies. The women commented: 'How strong Olum must be! He must be a powerful *xon* [shaman] !'[17]

I was told that K'terrnen may be presented frequently during a Hain, but after the first time it is not necessarily preceded by the massacre of the *kloketen* scene. In 1923 the K'terrnen scene was played twice.[18]

22. The baby K'terrnen being presented to the women by the counsellor Tenenésk during the 1923 Hain.

The anti-climax[19]

The spirit which the women call Halaháches and the men Kótaix is anti-Xalpen and, appropriately, male. In Gusinde's words, he 'wrests supremacy from Xalpen'.[20] Although Gusinde described him as a sky spirit, Lola, Angela and Federico as well as the Salesian document associated him with the earth. Whenever he appears in the Hain hut, Xalpen immediately returns to her underground abode. When Xalpen is in an ominous fit of rage, the men may suddenly chant *ua* repeatedly, thus announcing the arrival of Halaháches (Kótaix). Upon hearing the *ua* chant, the women begin singing *Halaháches*[21] to welcome him, knowing that his presence will make Xalpen vanish. Halaháches further demonstrates his power over Xalpen by sending the *kloketens* to be viewed by the women, thus defying Xalpen who is notoriously jealous of her young lovers. This is the only time during the ceremony that the *kloketens* appear without masks before the women. They are painted red, with white stripes on either side of their bodies from the middle of the shoulders to the knees, their faces are adorned with a white dot on the outer rim of the eyes and stripes on the cheeks. They simply encircle the stage and then return to the Hain, but the women are delighted to see them and are aware that they have been sent by Halaháches. Yet the women also know that this spirit is capricious and that he may kill the adult men.

Halaháches is particularly grotesque and frightening, even though he is comical when the mood strikes him. Angela and Federico both said that he has a physical defect, a pot belly. His body is white, overlaid with broad red bands, and his white close-fitting mask is surmounted with long horns made of a bow about a metre long, which is padded and painted. The horns do not represent those of a stag or a bull as some authors assumed but rather a horned fish (*háchai*), a metamorphosed *hoowin* ancestor who was a famous wrestler and warrior of the west sky, and who played this part in the first men's Hain.[22]

Halaháches moves swiftly and aggressively, looking intently from side to side. He grasps his chin in his left hand, with the left elbow raised, while he makes sweeping semi-circular gestures with a long pointed stick held in his right hand. The movements of his right arm propel him sideways as he advances in wide lateral jumps, legs spread out, thorax bent forward, knees slightly flexed, never letting go of his chin nor relaxing his staring gaze. A few minutes before he appears for one of his scenes, guanaco capes begin to fly out of the Hain, falling on the centre of the stage. Then Halaháches leaps on to the stage, chin in hand, accompanied by two cringing naked men who jump along on either side of him, their hands clasping their knees. When the trio reach the capes, Halaháches pretends to beleaguer his stooping captives about their heads. The victims slowly sink down as they are beaten, until they lie motionless on the capes, apparently lifeless. Halaháches then springs

144

back into the Hain and brings forth two more men who undergo the same treatment, with identical results, until six or more inert bodies are heaped on the capes. Then the women start screaming and go into action by throwing volleys of mud or snow balls at the culprit from a distance of about thirty metres. Without letting go of his chin, Halaháches dodges nearly all the missiles by jumping and twisting in every direction and fending them off with his swinging stick. When he tires he leaps back toward the Hain leaving his victims prostrated on the capes and his attackers with missiles in their hands. Shortly afterwards he reappears. Striding up to the corpses, he grabs one by the hair and jerks its head up, letting it flop down again to demonstrate that the body is completely lifeless. Amid a new flurry of snow or mud balls he returns triumphantly to the Hain. Then several men emerge from the ceremonial hut and drag all the corpses back, while the women continue their attack. Very soon the women hear the *xas xas xas* chant followed by a rhythmic hand-clapping, sure signs that little Olum, the beloved restorer of life, is hard at work. In 1923 Halaháches enacted this scene twice and appeared on the stage alone five times. Thanks to Gusinde we have a description of his startling performances.[23]

Angela and Federico said that Halaháches often came on stage, prancing around, racing toward the women who, laughing all the while, did their utmost to hit him with their snow or mud balls. Even if he fell, they said, he did not let go of his chin.

Bridges related a scene involving Halaháches which recalls one of the Hayílans (the offensive clowns). When the women knew that Halaháches was to appear they gathered on the edge of the stage in anticipation. But this time he surprised them by jumping out of the bushes at some distance from the Hain, instead of performing on the stage. As he sprang up from the bushes he snorted and startled the women and rushed toward them (though he stopped before he actually reached them), while the men in camp dashed to the aid of their womenfolk. Bridges commented: 'Notwithstanding the presence of these valiant defenders, the women fled to their homes, where they threw themselves on the ground in groups, face downwards, covering their heads with skins.'[24] Halaháches entered the camp that day, escorted by several men whose duty it was to prevent the women from spying on him. Afterwards, without more ado, he returned to the Hain.

Lola always laughed a great deal when she imitated Halaháches, clutching her chin with one hand and making the sweeping gesture with the other. Peering intently at me she would mutter, 'Halaháches was very bad.' Angela once told me that the women laughed at him because they were afraid.

9 For women only

The sham Hain[1]

On the first day, while the initiates are being subjected to the terrors of the rite of passage, the women, left alone in the camp with the children, are not necessarily idle. Some are busy 'having fun',[2] but to the outsider this looks like very daring and highly significant fun.

A group of women go a short distance from the camp in the opposite direction from the Hain. They are naked to the waist and as it is the first day of the Hain they are painted with the *tari* of their respective skies. Their faces are either covered with charcoal or painted white. All wear the men's head band, the *kochil*.

One of the *kloketen* mothers pretends to be Shoort while another plays the role of a *kloketen*. They wrestle with each other,[3] in imitation of the rite of passage, while the rest of the women stand about and bait them. One of the bystanders shouts at the *'kloketen'*: 'Grab him! Grab him! Don't let him throw you down! *She-un! She-un! Mata mae kisé!'*[4]

Almost any day during the ceremony and especially after Shoort had made a particularly ominous visit, he might be caricatured by a woman who would stride through the camp stabbing the women who had remained in the huts with a stick or lambasting them with a basket, just as Shoort was in the habit of doing. The women would laugh until they could bear it no longer. Finally, the female Shoort would take her leave, flexing her biceps in the proper manner. These games were played, as Angela said, 'while the men were busy in the Hain'.

A woman or girl might also imitate a *kloketen* returning from the hunt, struggling under the load of a heavy guanaco, lugging bags full of mushrooms and the *terr* fruit.[5] Dragging her feet as if exhausted, she would limp up to one of the huts pretending it was the Hain, to offer her burdens as gifts to Xalpen.[6]

The women also imitated Hayílan, the erotic buffoon, but never Xalpen nor the scene of the procession of the dead *kloketens*, for, as Angela said, these were 'of much respect'.

146

Mother and son[7]

The mother–son relationship was obviously a factor of supreme significance in the Hain ceremony. Among its many manifestations was a playful, affectionate one, epitomized by the word *hané* which means 'good person'. In the context of the games which the women played among themselves, *hané* refers to the mother who playfully imitates her *kloketen* son who is being initiated. If the *kloketen*'s mother was dead, the *hané* was played by the same female kin who assumed the role of his mother during the ceremony.

Gusinde described two incidents of *hané* play which took place in 1923. The mother of the oldest *kloketen* had spent the greater part of the night worrying about the fate of her son. At dawn she herself behaved like a boy who had been roused from his slumbers and fights against his drowsiness. She repeated in a dull voice, 'I slept over time' (*máshenken haush ya*).[8] On another occasion she ran shouting happily to a hut to play with the neighbours, crying with cheerful excitement: 'This is how my child dawdled in the neighbour's hut. He made the whole camp joyful. Everyone was his friend.'[9]

The *kloketen* mother imitated her son's boyish expressions: the way he would sing, whistle or shout *jak hopin* (my pal); his mischievous and affectionate manners with her. Another woman would then play the role of his mother. The *kloketen* mother would also pretend to play-fight with another woman as her son had with his companions. The two women would fall over each other and push each other around as all boys do. The mother might go to one of the huts and simply stand at the entrance, staring at those inside without saying a word, as her son had done so often.

When Esteban was a *kloketen*, in the Hain of 1920, his mother, whose name was Tial, imitated him by playing with a woman who took the role of Esteban's father. She would shout at 'him': 'Papa [the affectionate term for father is *ké'é*], papa, my pal, let's go and play. *Ja ké'é, kai-né, jak hopin tireéme.*'[10] Yoimolka (a Haush woman) played *hané* for Nielson, Angela's first husband, when he was a *kloketen*. Yoimolka was Nielson's maternal grandmother and she was his *hané* because his mother was then dead.

When Federico was a *kloketen*, during the same Hain of 1920, his mother, Atl, often appeared in camp from the forest walking stiff-legged just like him and pretending to carry a load of grass, a dead duck or cormorant or several eggs. She would go directly to her sister's hut, saying on different occasions:

> I feel sorry for my mama, this is why I bring her grass [grass – *hushl* used for padding the sandals] . *Ja tájin j'ámi hushl k'é-un.*

> I feel sorry for my mama, this is why I bring her these little birds.

> I feel sorry for my mama, take these eggs for her.[11]

As a boy Federico did just that; he deposited gifts for his mother in his

147

mother's sister's hut. At other times Atl would imitate the way Federico used
to chant while playing at being a shaman. Then again she would climb a tree
and in a loud voice imitate the songs, shrieks and whistles of different birds,
like the sound of the *k'aux* owl, just as he had done when he was a child.[12]
Nicolasa (Lola's cousin), who had participated in that Hain, would laugh so
much at Atl's *hané* demonstrations that she always had to sit down when Atl
began. Sometimes she would shout at her: 'Here comes your father! *Ai-ain
mir winé!*'[13] Angela explained that Nicolasa could not climb a tree because
she was too fat, but that Atl was skinny so had no trouble and she climbed
them frequently when pretending to be her son during the 1920 Hain. Angela
added, 'We were happy in those times. We had so much fun.'

23. Angela Loij, 1923. At her request, this photograph was retouched to
remove her face paint, which was only applied for the photographer.

148

10 Concluding remarks

The richness of the Hain ceremony, and the state of knowledge about it, are such that to attempt to draw any conclusions may seem impossible. There are very important aspects of the ceremony which remain only partially documented, such as the role of the eight Shoorts which represent the passage of the sun through the sky and the identities of the female spirits Hóshtan and Kulpush. There are others, such as the fact that Tanu is known to be the sister of Xalpen, the significance of which is not at all clear. The implications of the opposition between the earth and sky spirits can only be surmised. The symbolism of the disguise of the men for the phallic dance is not known, nor are the specific reasons for its insertion in the ceremony. Lola repeated to me often, 'There is much, much of the Hain. I can never tell you all.' More could perhaps have been learned from Garibaldi but when he died in 1981 there was no one living, to my knowledge, who had been a *kloketen* or had participated in a Hain.

The Hain hut was a microcosm of the Selk'nam universe, and the Hain ceremony had at least four principal objectives: to initiate the young men, to discipline and overawe the women, to serve as the main focus of social intercourse and to be a religious observation. Every individual was related to this complex imaginative edifice and its associated mythological and shamanistic lore through the 'skies' (divisions) and 'earths' (territories) with which everyone was identified as part of their everyday existence.

The Hain may be viewed from a number of perspectives: in terms of its functions within the society, its symbolic representations, its ideology and its animistic philosophy. It can be studied for its sociological context, the psychological conflicts it manifests or attempts to resolve, its metaphysical aspirations, its poetry, or its music. It lends itself to comparisons with religions, rituals, ceremonies, mythologies and even theatres of other cultures both past and present. I have chosen to centre my analysis on the problem of the 'secret' of the Hain; on whether or not the women knew that the spirits as they appeared during the ceremony were represented by the men. I am concerned with the symbolism of the Hain, what it represents in terms of ideology and the socio-economic structure of Selk'nam society, and with the Hain as ritual and as theatre.

The Hain utilizes two symbolic codes or semantic systems, one of which is sacred and the other profane. In terms of the sacred code, the 'actors', it will be recalled, were not only playing the roles of the spirits, they were also representing the sacred *hoowins* (mythical ancestors). For example, the seven principal Shoorts each embody one of the seven great shamans, who were the founders of the first men's Hain and in whose honour the seven principal posts of the Hain were named. These seven great *hoowins* played the parts of seven Shoorts in that first men's Hain, and inspired the tradition that Shoorts representing each of the seven founders (and posts) should be presented in the Hain ceremonies for all time to come. But not only does each Shoort have the attribute of one of the *hoowin* founders, he also has those of the *k'tétu* owl. K'tétu is the name of another outstanding *hoowin* shaman and it was he who played the part of a subordinate Shoort to perfection in the first men's Hain. I have postulated that K'tétu represents the Sun (Krren) (see chapter 6). If this is so, each of the seven principal Shoorts, and probably also the subordinate Shoorts, personify at least two *hoowin* ancestors.

Many of the *hoowins* played the same spirit roles in the mythology as they do in the real Hains, but others, such as Shocits and Háchai, have a purely metaphoric relationship with the spirits with which they are identified. The painted symbols with which the spirits were decorated linked them to their respective *hoowins*. The masks, as symbols of the *hoowins*, were treated with much respect and caution. The impersonators of Shoort, for example, were possessed by their *hoowins* and this rendered acting a dangerous game. If the rules were not respected, the *hoowin* ancestors would take vengeance on the 'actors'. This sheds light on why the men took the spirit roles so much to heart. If the Hain were only a farce to beguile the women, the *hoowins* would not have participated in the ceremony.

The sacred code is also exemplified in the myth of the matriarchy when Sun discovers the women's hoax and Moon sends a Shoort to camp to incite the men to comment and find out if they were making plans to attack the Hain (see chapter 3). The women went close to the camp and listened intently to the men's comments as the female Shoort went through the camp. One woman heard a man say, 'Who knows if that's really a Shoort?' Another man shouted, 'Perhaps one of our women has painted herself, and we believe that she's a Shoort!' This text reveals that the spirits were thought to exist independently of their representation in the Hain. The men did not accuse the women of inventing the spirits, but rather of pretending to incarnate them. The human men were putting on a show exactly like that of the *hoowin* men who in turn had learnt it from the matriarchs as a power mechanism for keeping the opposite sex in submission.

Many decades after the culture had ceased to exist, Lola made it apparent to me that she still believed in the underworld existence of Xalpen, even though she had learnt that Xalpen was represented in the ceremony by an effigy. While we were talking about Xalpen, Lola would pound the floor of the hut with her foot and point downwards exclaiming, 'That bad woman is below!'

The profane code consists of all that is not sacred, all that which does not directly involve the *hoowins*, such as the game of female vengeance (see chapter 7). The majority of scenes, however, manifest a combination of both codes as we shall see below.

The two codes have specific functions in terms of the objectives of the ceremony. While the sacred code links the ceremony to its mythological past, and the society both to its origins and to the powers which emanate from the universe through the metaphysics of the sky concept (see chapter 4), the profane code serves the more pragmatic objectives of the ceremony: to initiate the young men, to discipline the women, and to amuse and heighten the pleasure of the social gathering.

The sacred/profane dichotomy is analogous to the ritual/theatre distinction. Ritual may be defined as symbolic performances for religious or sacred usages, and theatre as similar displays for secular or profane usages. And just as the sacred and profane intertwine in the ceremony itself, so do the ritual and theatre. For example, the clown Ulen (see chapter 7) may be placed at the profane/theatre pole, since he is simply the object of amusement and has no sacred or ritual significance. In contrast to Ulen, Xalpen's position is almost purely sacred and ritual, even though she is not painted to represent a *hoowin*. She is the only spirit presented in effigy. Neither the manner in which she was decorated nor other data indicate that she symbolized a *hoowin*. Apparently her effigy was not intended as a representation but was rather regarded as being the monster which in no way resembled a human. All the other spirits shown to the public had a human shape, even Tanu whose legs protruded beneath her bulky structure. The men constructed a Xalpen not only in order to impress the women but also to embody and to control the terrible female divinity. The women were convinced that the effigy was Xalpen herself, although they knew that the other spirits shown during the ceremony were men in disguise. Even when a Xalpen effigy was not presented during a ceremony, the women still believed that she rose from the underground into the Hain hut.

The only *hoowin* with which Xalpen can be compared is Moon, and there are a number of indications that the two shared an identity. First, Xalpen's husband is Shoort, who was presented as having attributes of the *k'tétu* owl, apparently in order to signify that he represented the Sun (see chapter 6); thus Xalpen can be considered analogous to Moon, the wife of Sun. Secondly, the texts of the chants sung by the women to pacify Xalpen are almost identical to those which they sang to Moon to calm her when she was in eclipse (see chapters 3 and 7). Next, the Hain hut, whose mistress is Xalpen, is an inversion of Moon's heavenly domicile in which she received the shaman's spirits who visited her during an eclipse. Also, both Xalpen and Moon, when in a fit of rage, threaten to kill the men and even to eat them. Finally, certain attributes of both Xalpen and Moon form paired oppositions, such as earth (Xalpen)/sky (Moon), married (Xalpen)/divorced (Moon), misogyny (Xalpen)/phallogyny (Moon). It seems, therefore, that these divinities are mirror-images of one and the same symbol: a female monster who has the power to annihilate all humanity. The purpose of this complementarity of contrasting attributes is to endow the symbol with greater force by rendering it more powerful and more terrifying than would be the case were it expressed by Xalpen or Moon alone. The complementarity also reinforces the credibility of the symbol, because it encompasses a large semantic field of meanings and connotations. For example, even though the men put on the Xalpen 'show', they were full of dread of Xalpen's other self, that is, Moon. From the point of view of the men, the Xalpen scenes may be explained as their means of controlling the threatening aspects of the symbol, as well as a technique for intimidating the women. Moon escaped from the men (see chapter 3), but Xalpen was in their control, at least for the duration of the Hain ceremony.

The Xalpen—Moon figure is central to the Selk'nam religious complex. 'She' was firmly believed in by all members of society. But she was not worshipped nor were prayers addressed to her. Offerings of meat and other foods were made to Xalpen and the women sang to both Xalpen and Moon to placate their fury. Both epitomized the destructive force of female power, which was believed to threaten the patriarchal society. Moon was even capable of destroying the entire universe. If she regained ascendancy, first of all she would wreak her vengeance on Sun. Were he demolished there would be no day, no light. The world would cease to exist and the firmament would probably split wide open. The rituals dedicated to Xalpen and Moon had a dialectic objective; they transformed the mythical female power into a plausible and immediate danger of annihilation and thus united the entire society in self-defence. These rituals formed a closed circuit. They could not be contested nor taken lightly. Angela commented, after telling me about how the women played imitating Shoort, 'They never did this with Xalpen because she was of much respect' (see chapter 9).

Between Ulen, who was entirely theatrical, and Xalpen, who was almost exclusively ritual, the majority of other spirits were presented as theatre as well as ritual, as both profane and sacred. The women could take liberties with the theatrics of the Hain, with the spirits as performers, as make-believe. Matan, the ballet dancer, and Koshménk, the cuckold, were pleasing and ridiculous respectively, although since they were painted with symbols representing the skies they also had ritual significance. Kulan, Shoort, Hayílan and Halaháches were serious, threatening and dangerous in some scenes, while in others they were comical, teasing and joyful. Kulan was not only seductive and tantalizing, she was also harsh. The women were jealous and yet some-how fearful of her. She too was decorated with the ritual symbols of the skies. Shoort was serious and completely ritual when a beautifully painted representation appeared on the stage in response to the women's chants and as the symbol of the eight periods of the day which marked the passage of the sun through the sky. But he was more theatrical than ritual when he entered the camp to admonish and castigate the women. In their theatrical functions these three male spirits (Shoort, Hayílan and Halaháches) could play with the women and also be taunted or even ridiculed by them. Even a victory of the women over the men was burlesqued in the mock battle of the female vengeance game. Thus it may be surmised that the women knew the men were acting the roles of all the spirits, with the exception of Xalpen, and that they recognized the human forms, though probably not the individual ident-ity of the 'actors'. I also suggest that they knew that the spirits had been presented in this fashion in the *hoowin* epoch, that the presentation was traditional and therefore not only justified but also a necessary part of the ceremony.

The Hain is comparable to the theatre in our society as a secular perform-ance, and also on a psychological level in terms of the relationship between audience and actors, even though in the Hain the audience (the women) had a far more active role in the performance than in the theatre as we know it. But no theatre audience is purely passive. The applause, laughter and tears of the audience in modern theatre are only the most evident manifestations of the public's adherence to the 'mythology' of the scene. If the audience is moved, it experiences the drama as if it were real, on whatever level of consciousness this may occur.

Viewed as theatre, the problem of whether or not the women were party to the 'hoax' is resolved. My evidence suggests that the women knew the 'secret' even though they did not realize that Xalpen was only an effigy. They were certainly wary of revealing their knowledge of the secret to the men, though, for fear of arousing aggression, or even for fear that a shaman might 'kill' them (which could actually result in death). But the women were not just pretending to believe in the spirits; they did believe in them while the scenes were being enacted, because they were participating in a theatrical representation. Moreover, just as they knew that the spirits (except Xalpen) were only men, they also 'knew', as did the men, that the spirits existed. Thus the psychology of theatre fused with the certainty of religious faith in the supernatural; the profane fused with the sacred.

The Hain symbolized the daily experiences of the women. They lived in a patriarchal society in which male authority was real, though not usually manifested through violence or as tyranny. Moreover, the women were not without defence (see chapter 2), nor were the men police or truant officers. They were husbands, kin and friends. Yet discontinuities did exist between the sexes which on a symbolic level appeared irreconcilable. The men were the Sun, the women the Moon. The diurnal forces were posited against the nocturnal forces; warm, life-giving rays against cold, barren, tenebrous beams. But if Moon (female) forces were so annihilating, how could it be that women gave and nourished life? This dilemma is exemplified by the males' symbolic assimilation to the female in their contention that they had 'invisible' menses (see chapter 6) on the one hand, and the exaltation of their maleness in the phallic dance on the other. This unresolved problem is also highlighted in the contradictory attributes of the Xalpen—Moon symbol in that it represents both a cannibalistic monster and the mother of a beautiful child (Xalpen's baby K'terrnen and Moon's daughter Tamtam).

Woman (the Xalpen—Moon symbol) is at once destructive and creative. 'She' is dangerously ambivalent and must be controlled. During the Hain the men attempt to dominate the women, especially by means of Shoort's daily visits to the camp, and through the ritual they seek to impress the women with the enormity of their struggle with Xalpen. The *kloketens* and even the adult men are 'killed' in an effort to placate her. Men are superior to women because they make the ultimate sacrifice in order to save society and safeguard the universe. Therefore women owe them absolute allegiance.

Once the ideological premises are admitted, it becomes imperative that women remain submissive, that they never regain ascendancy, that they be powerless. So long as husbands keep their wives in subservience a catastrophe can be averted. But if a wife be insubordinate or disobedient to her husband, her behaviour might be imitated by other women and the latent Moon quality which exists in all women might begin to express itself, gain momentum and culminate in a general insurrection.[1] Urged on by Moon, the women might reestablish the matriarchy. Hence the vital role of Shoort in the ceremony. He had to inspire fear in the women. He threatened them daily during the entire ceremony, often harassing them and even beating them.

Concretely woman was considered by the men as a threat to society in terms of the power relations in the family context. She was not a threat as a shaman, for she could not 'kill' or even inflict sickness. A female shaman could cure and participate in the mystical beyond-world, the realm of shamanistic power, but this activity did not endow her with tangible authority over her husband or others. Nor was she feared as a sage, for supposedly she was ignorant of the dangerous knowledge of the ancient matriarchy.

It was not prestige that was to be kept from women, but rather the specific power in the man—woman relationship. She could have prestige in so far as it did not impinge upon her husband, so long as she did not play the role of Moon.

During the Hain the women were frequently submissive and fearful. They obviously dreaded the visits of Shoort and were in terrified awe of Xalpen, quite as the men were afraid of Moon during an eclipse. But at certain

154

moments of the ceremony the women would gang up on one of their own sex, humiliate her, verbally castigate her and force her to repent for a misdemeanour she had not committed (see chapter 7). At other times, the women were amused, joyful and provocative. Among themselves they even parodied the ceremony, making fun of it and hence the men, though they never ridiculed Xalpen.

The phantom of a matriarchy haunts the patriarchies. In this patriarchy the men ruled the society as a stratum. The only dynamics of the society which had political significance were the latent conflict between men and women. No one could speak in the name of the poor, the humble, the disinherited or the exploited because there were none. No one could oppose the true religion to a false one, for the same reason.

The shamans, sages and prophets did not compete as corporate groups. The prophets were often also shamans as were many of the sages (see table 1). Moreover the egalitarian and individualistic nature of the society limited the authority to which they could aspire. Individuals and lineages were highly competitive for prestige but not for political power; this was a chiefless society. Status afforded prestige but little or no economic prerogatives. There were no major power cleavages except the sexual one. Power was invested in the men as a homogeneous group, as a stratum. It was not contested. But even though the women never imagined revolting against the patriarchy, logically they might because they were suppressed.

The sexual inequality of Selk'nam society inspired its anti-woman ideology. The dynamics were above all economic. The relations of production (which in this context includes hunting, gathering and fishing as well as tool making) were communal yet hierarchic. They were communal in the sense that the entire population participated in and contributed to the livelihood of all. There was no deviation from the principle that the labour be performed by all the physically capable members of the society. But the relations of production were at the same time sexually stratified. Only the men were schooled in the techniques of large game hunting and the manufacture of the basic tools. Women were dependent on men for the main staple, meat, for the basic materials for clothing and shelter, that is skins and furs and the stone tools they needed, namely scrapers and cutting instruments. Women's labour, though indispensable to the survival of the group and the continuity of the culture, was largely invested in activities which served to maintain an equilibrium within the male sector of the population.

As for the means of production, not only were the men the only producers of the basic tools, but the land, though communal, was largely controlled by the men. Everyone was a fully fledged member of a lineage and could therefore claim a share of the communal rights of their lineage over a tract of land. The economic differences in the size of the land-holdings did not alter the basic principle of the communal distribution and usufruct of the land, nor did these differences create a hierarchy of the land-holding groups, that is the lineages. However, given the patrilineality and patrilocality of the lineages, the men were the virtual owners of the land where the family normally lived.

It may now be proposed that the communal yet sexually stratified nature of the relations of production was functionally complementary to and articulated with the means of production (tools and land).

The men as a stratum ruled the women. Without the egalitarian (communal) form of the relations and means of production, this would not have been possible. Vertical cleavages in these relations would have shattered the horizontal sexual stratification. Had this occurred, the men would not have ruled as a homogeneous group, as a stratum, and the society would have presented a very different configuration.

In the communal yet stratified instances of the mode of production lies a fundamental contradiction: the society was egalitarian yet patriarchal. This conflicting force constituted the society's dynamics and, as such, a radical contradiction which the ideology strove, in one way or another, to justify.

The Selk'nam society will, I believe, be recognized as a classical example of a truly traditional hunting—gathering culture, rich, vibrant and almost perfectly adapted to its environment.

The last generations of Selk'nam and Hoaush bore tragic witness to the ruthless expansion of capitalism. This book is dedicated to their heroic struggle to survive. It was written in friendship for Lola Kiepja, Angela Loij, Esteban Ichton, Francisco Minkiol, Santiago Rupatini, Alejandro Cortés, Federico Echeuline, Luis Garibaldi Honte and Segundo Arteaga.

Notes

Introduction

1 This group is better known in the literature as the Ona, which is the designation used for them by the Yámana, a neighbouring fishing people. The term Ona was first popularized in the publications of Lista (1887), Bridges (1893) and Gallardo (1910), though Beauvoir (1915) and Gusinde (1931) employed the term Selk'nam, which is their real name. See Bridges 1948: 402; Gusinde 1931: 122–4.

2 Gusinde, and most of the other authors who have written on this ceremony, mistakenly refer to it as the *kloketen* ceremony. According to my information, this latter term was employed almost exclusively for the young man being initiated in the ceremony. My informants rarely spoke of this ceremony using the term *kloketen*. They all insisted that Hain was its true name, as well as the name of the ceremonial hut. Bridges (1948: chapter 42) is one of the few writers who employs the term correctly, for both the ceremonial hut and the ceremony itself. Most authors used it only in the former sense. This confusion is probably due to the overemphasis of the *kloketen* (initiation) part of the ceremony at the expense of its other aspects. The Indians undoubtedly talked to the White men more freely about the initiation of the *kloketens* than they did about the 'secret' which they were adamant in preventing the women from discovering, or about the esoteric symbolism of the ceremony. My informants' words, together with the lexicon of the ceremony, confirm the usage of the name Hain, for example: the 'spirits' were called *hain-káspi*; the women's chants were termed *k'méyu* as well as *hain-né-mai* ('belongs to the Hain'); the name of one of the spirits is Hainxo-héuwan.

3 Gusinde 1931: 814, 824–5, 907.

4 *Ibid.*: 825.

5 For bibliographies concerning the Selk'nam see Cooper 1917; Gusinde 1931: 41–116.

6 Nearly all of the ninety-two chants we recorded that year have been issued on four records under the title *Selk'nam Chants of Tierra del Fuego* (Chapman 1972a and 1978).

7 An article dedicated to Lola was published in *Natural History* (Chapman 1971).

8   This film, entitled, *The Ona People: Life and Death in Tierra del Fuego*, was produced by Ana Montés de Gonzalez and realized in collaboration with Ana Montés de Gonzalez, Jorge Preloran, Oscar Gamardo and the author. For an article on the film see Chapman 1977b.
9   See note 12 of chapter 1.
10 For an article dedicated to Angela see Chapman 1975a.
11 For a poem dedicated to the Selk'nam see Chapman 1975b (in Spanish) and 1977b: 28–30 (in English). Garibaldi died in August 1981.

1. History and environment

1   See Laming-Emperaire (1976) for a summary of the data and a discussion of the dating. According to this author, the possibility that humans first arrived in America sometime between 80,000 and 100,000 years ago or even earlier should not be ruled out.
2   Bird 1938, 1946a, 1969.
3   Caldenius 1932. Concerning this problem, Lliboutry (1956: 423–4) writes, 'Caldenius' fourth system, that is, the moraines of the Second Narrows, limited on the east by Useless Bay, form the Second Narrows of Magellan Strait . . . The study of the varves made by Caldenius makes it possible to date these moraines at 10,000 years ago. This coincides with what Auer deduced from the study of the peat bogs as the time passed since the last glaciation.' The earliest times for the presence of man in southern Patagonia are 11,000 ± 170 years ago and 10,720 ± 300 years ago, according to two samples studied by the archaeologist Junius Bird. He comments (1969: 52): 'If these figures are valid, then the associated projectile points are, at this time, the oldest dated points known in South America.' These points were found in association with bones of the extinct horse *Parahipparion saldasi*, the giant ground sloth *Mylodon listai* and the guanaco. Laming-Emperaire discovered what is so far the earliest evidence for the presence of man on the Great Island of Tierra del Fuego near the shore of Useless Bay at a site called Marazzi. The earliest carbon-14 date there is 9,590 ± 210 years ago. For several reasons she concluded that man appeared there shortly after the retreat of the last glacier (1968b: 138).
4   Although Gusinde (1931: 131, 1057) considered that the Selk'nam and the Haush had largely identical cultures and thus subsumed the Haush under the term Selk'nam, he was aware of certain distinctions between the two groups. Koppers, who accompanied Gusinde to Tierra del Fuego in 1921, remarked (1924: 38) that the differences between the two groups were probably greater formerly than when he and Gusinde visited the island. This is accurate without doubt. After the occupation of the island by the Whites in 1880 a rapid process of assimilation occurred between the Haush and the Selk'nam, and as their numbers decreased, this process was accelerated, particularly in the central part of the island where their territories met. They lived together here at the time of Gusinde's visits (1919–23) on land which was set aside in

1926 as a reservation for the survivors of both groups. Gusinde's tendency to assimilate the two groups reflected a contemporary reality. Most, if not all, of his Haush informants (Tenenésk, Inxiol, Toin and Knoskól) spoke Selk'nam as well as their own language. But the situation before the arrival of the Whites was very different. Almost all of the authors cited in the bibliography were aware of the existence of the Haush. On the latter see Bridges 1948; Cooper 1917: 49–52; Chapman and Hester 1975; Furlong 1917a; Gusinde 1931: 127–31.

5   Beauvoir 1915: 171; Bridges 1948: 443; Cooper 1917: 49–52, 1946c: 108; Furlong 1917a, 1917b; Gusinde 1931: 129–31; Lothrop 1928: 107–10.

6   For maps indicating this area see Cooper 1942: 9; Steward and Faron 1959: 375; Willey 1971: 18–23; Wissler 1938: 2. Serrano (1947: 116–31, 143–66, 182–240) designates the following groups in Argentina as mainly hunters, though they also gathered and fished: Chanás, Guayanás, certain groups of the Huarpes, Pehuenches, Chiquillames, Guénaken, Chechenet, Charruas (who occupied mostly Uruguay), the Pampa people, Querandiés, Patagones or Chonecas and the Onas. Concerning the vast area of the Chaco (some 260,000 square kilometres) Métraux (1946: 213–14) writes, 'It is probable that, together with the Fuegian and Patagonian tribes, the Chaco Indians represent an ancient population who, until recently, have preserved several features of a very archaic culture, which in remote ages might have been common to primitive tribes of both North and South America.' While hunting was practised by the Chaco groups, gathering (particularly of the algarroba) and river fishing were more important due to environmental constraints. Apparently a number of Chaco tribes also engaged in farming. Within this great area of hunter–gatherers and fishermen, the Guarani most certainly represent the most important group of agriculturalists. Guarani enclaves in the Paraná Delta mark the southern limit of farming on the eastern side of the continent, according to the data presented by Lothrop (1946: 179).

My calculation of approximately two million square kilometres for the extension of the area occupied mainly by hunters and gatherers (and some fishing peoples) includes all of Uruguay and the following provinces in Argentina: the Chaco, all of the provinces of the eastern littoral, La Pampa and approximately half of Santa Fé, Cordoba and San Luis. According to Cooper (1924: 418) a Tehuelchean type of culture prevailed as far north as the Chaco. All of the source material on these cultures merits careful reappraisal. For a prehistorical perspective on the Fuegian cultures, see Gusinde 1974: 627–54.

7   With respect to horticultural groups which reverted to hunting as their main subsistence technique see Lathrap 1968a, 1968b; Lévi-Strauss 1968; Martin 1969: 257–8. Sahlins (1972: 38–9) evokes the problem of cultural loss in this general context, as follows: 'I must raise the possibility that the ethnography of hunters and gatherers is largely a record of incomplete cultures. Fragile cycles of ritual and exchange

may have disappeared without trace, lost in the earliest stages of colonialism, when the inter-group relations they mediated were attacked and confounded.'

8 Laming-Emperaire 1968b: 87–90, 1968c, 1972: 219–20; Laming-Emperaire *et al.* 1972.

9 Laming Emperaire 1968a: 309–10, 1972: 218–19.

10 Vignati 1926a, 1927; Bird 1969.

11 Lothrop 1928: 110–15.

12 Chapman and Hester 1975. The material collected in these surface finds, and that from the excavations carried out at False Clove, referred to in this article, were deposited by the author in the Department of Archaeology of the Museo de Historia Natural de La Plata, Argentina. The other lithic material found mostly along the Atlantic coast in the Selk'nam area was left in 1976 in the care of Mr Roberto Wilson in his small museum in Río Grande, Tierra del Fuego, Argentina. I hope to complete this study in collaboration with an archaeologist.

13 Morison 1974: 313, 380.

14 Sarmiento 1768: 243–7.

15 Oliver van Noort, in Brosse 1756: I, 295–302; also Furlong 1917b: 185–6.

16 Bartolomé Garcia and Gonzale de Nodal, in Brosse 1756: I, 421–5; also Gusinde 1931: 26–9.

17 Jacques L'Hermite, in Brosse 1756: I, 439.

18 Père Labbe, in Brosse 1756: II, 434–5. Frezier's expedition was in Good Success Bay in 1712 but he did not encounter the Indians. In Brosse (1756: II, 207–8) he cites a certain Captain Brunet as having visited there later the same year and Villemorin the following year. He states that the latter had contact with the Indians, who boarded the vessel from two bark canoes. This source should be sought in its original and carefully studied because neither the Haush nor the Selk'nam were known to use canoes and Good Success Bay was Haush territory. The Indians in canoes may have been Yámana on a visit.

19 Cook 1893: 38.

20 Darwin 1962: 205.

21 Martinic 1971: 45–6.

22 Fitz-Roy 1839: 177.

23 Bridges 1948: 430–2; Popper 1891: 138; Chapman 1966–76.

24 For accounts of, and comments on, the genocide perpetuated against the Selk'nam see Agostini 1934: 370–5, 1956: 286–97; Barclay 1926: 142–50; *Boletín Salesiano* 2–17 (1887–1902) *passim*; Bridges 1948: 153–4, 251, 265–73, 277, 315; Dabbene 1907: 40–1; Fuentes Rabe 1922: 175–81; Furlong 1910, 1917b; Gallardo 1910: 98–9; Gusinde 1931: 150–61, 1951: 99–105; Holmberg 1906: 52–4; Lista 1887: 26, 73, 99; Martinic 1973 *passim*; Popper 1891: 138–41.

25 Furlong 1910: 228; Gallardo 1910: 120.

26 Thomas Bridges (1893) estimated that there had been at least 10,000 Indians in Tierra del Fuego but that by 1893 the population had been reduced to 1,000. The estimates used in the present text are based on

Furlong 1917a: 433, 1917b: 184; Gallardo 1910: 98–9; Gusinde 1931: 148, 1951: 96–7, 125. Several authors propose lower figures for the Selk'nam population, but those given by Gusinde seem to me to be the most reasonable.

Luis Garibaldi Honte and Enriqueta de Santín, both of Haush descent, were living on the island in 1980, together with four other persons whose mothers were Selk'nam. With respect to the number of surviving Alakaluf and Yámana see Clair-Vasiliadis 1972; Emperaire and Laming 1954; Ortiz-Troncoso 1973.

27 Main references for this section: Agostini 1956; Baez 1945; Bird 1946b; Cooper 1917, 1924, 1946b, 1946c; *Encyclopaedia Britannica*; Feruglio 1946; Furlong 1917a, 1917b; Goodall 1975; Gusinde 1931: 2–8; Humphrey *et al.* 1970: 21–34; Nordenskjold 1897; Popper 1887: 86–91, 97–103; Rudolph 1934; and author's observations.

28 Gusinde (1951: 96) writes that over two-thirds of the island, some 35,000 square kilometres, was occupied by the Indians. Assuming that the total population of the four groups which inhabited the island was 6,000, there would have been about six persons per ten square kilometres. However, the analysis of my demographic data may modify these figures.

29 The temperature figures are from *Encyclopaedia Britannica*; Goodall 1975: 24; Humphrey *et al.* 1970: 21–2.

30 Humphrey *et al.* 1970: 21.

31 Martial 1888: 184.

32 *Ibid.*; Furlong 1917a: 434.

33 See Orquera *et al.* for archaeological work done recently near Ushuaia.

34 Pertuiset (1877: 216–17), one of the first explorers of the late period in the area of Useless Bay, observed the tall, strong, square shouldered Indians (the Selk'nam) exercising tyranny over other Indians whom he described as small, puny, humble and timid (undoubtedly the Alakaluf). The former obliged the latter to fish for them, while they hunted guanaco in the hinterland.

35 See note 26 above.

36 For example Cooper 1946a: 13–15; Lévi-Strauss 1949: 134; Steward and Faron 1959: 374.

37 Braun Menéndez (1945: 37, 172); Lothrop, an archaeologist, wrote (1928: 203–4): 'This point is one to recall in estimates of all or any phases of Fuegian culture, for it will be found that deficiencies arose not from any innate mental or physical handicap, but from laziness and lethargy . . . Clearly then they were laggards or backsliders in the development of mankind, so that in depicting their manner of life we are justified in assuming that we are recreating a vista of life in Europe or elsewhere many thousands of years ago.'

38 Bird 1946b: 57.

39 Gallardo 1910: 170, 183; Lothrop 1928: 31; Spears 1895: 124–5.

40 Humphrey *et al.* 1970.

41 All the references for this section are primary sources: Beauvoir 1902;

Bridges 1948: 250, 268, 282—6, 313—14, 332—6, 447—54; Chapman 1966—76, 1977a; Chapman and Hester 1975: 189—93; Furlong 1910, 1917a, 1917b; Gallardo 1910: 53—84, 167, 205, 238—50; Gusinde 1931: 269—92, 302—5; Lothrop 1928: 28—35, 81—4; Pertuiset 1877: 171—6, 192—4, 202—5, 216—22; Segers 1891: 64—9, 75. Analyses on the territoriality of hunting and gathering societies such as those in Lee and DeVore 1968, Stuart 1977 and Williams 1974 will be commented upon in another study.

42 Gallardo 1910: 240, 246.

43 Lothrop 1928: 87.

44 Gusinde 1931: 428.

45 A detailed study of the land tenure, based on the new data, will be made in the future.

46 Gallardo 1910: 240—1 (my translation).

47 For example one of my informants, Angela Loij, recalled over 650 toponyms in Selk'nam. These include names of small clusters of trees, patches of peat bog and tiny lagoons.

48 Lothrop 1928: 62.

49 *Ibid.*: 80—1.

50 Gallardo 1910: 146—7, 228, 251; Bridges 1948: 305.

51 Gallardo 1910: 344 (my translation).

52 Bridges 1948: 257.

53 Gusinde 1931: 270—1.

54 Bridges 1948: 446.

55 Gusinde 1931: 277—8. According to Gallardo (1910: 190) and Popper (1887: 84) as many as 400 were killed at one time.

56 Segers 1891: 64. Gallardo (1910: 272) writes of the preservation of tucotuco meat.

57 Gusinde 1931: 277—8.

58 Gallardo 1910: 205, 241.

59 The most common seals on the Great Island were the fur seal (*Arctocephalus australis*), the sea lion or hair seal (*Otaria byronia*) and the elephant seal (*Mirounga leonina*). According to Maxwell (1967: 60—2, 79—80) the latter two do not undertake true migrations and the sea lion does not even travel seasonally, its only journeys being to and from the feeding grounds. Therefore the herds of these two species which inhabited the Great Island probably remained there throughout the year. Possibly there were also other species there, including those mentioned in note 60 below.

60 Agostini (1956: 111) mentions the 'leopard seal', *Hydrurga leptonyx*, in this context. According to Cabrera (1940: 182) the crabeater seal (*Lobodon carcinophagus*) migrated from the Antarctic to as far north as Buenos Aires, and therefore may also have frequented the Great Island.

61 See Bridges 1948: 332—6, 449—51; Gallardo 1910: 95, 188; Gusinde 1931: 282—6.

62 Gallardo 1910: 191—2 (my translation).

63 Bridges 1948: 333.
64 Gallardo 1910: 193; Gusinde 1931: 282.
65 Humphrey *et al.* 1970: 35. The latter figure is calculated from the index.
66 Bridges (1948: 250) writes that the women used a small spear to kill a large scale-less fish, called *dahapi* in Selk'nam, which I have not been able to identify.
67 Chapman 1977a: 141.
68 Gusinde 1931: 292.
69 Gallardo 1910: 173.
70 *Ibid.*: 144–5.
71 Bridges 1948: 336. While Furlong (1917a: 438) writes that a dearth of food forced the Selk'nam to live in small clan and family groups, both Gallardo (1910: 169–71, 217) and Gusinde (1931: 292) stress the adequacy or abundance of the food available. In the early photographs of the Selk'nam taken in 1896, when they were still largely living in their own cultural context, they appear to be strong and healthy.
72 Primary sources for this section: Beauvoir 1902; Bridges 1948: 211; Coiazzi 1914: 32; Furlong 1910: 218, 1917a: 442; Gallardo 1910: 241–8; Gusinde 1931: 193–9; Lothrop 1928: 59–64; Segers 1891: 64, 94; Vignati 1926b. Others are cited below in note 76.
73 Gusinde 1931: 195.
74 Gallardo 1910: 243.
75 *Ibid.*: 244.
76 Lista 1887: 72, 85; Pertuiset 1877: 175; Popper 1887: 85; Segers 1891: 94.
77 Furlong (1910: 218 and 1917a: 442) mentions four types of 'wigwams'. Besides the two mentioned here, he describes a third type as consisting of logs leaning against one another along a centre line, thus forming a gable-like roof which was supported on the inside by two logs and a cross beam. Gusinde (1931: 196) refers to a similar type of hut which was constructed in 1923 as the family dwelling during the Hain ceremony. It seems to me that this type was an imitation of the wooden hut built by Whites and I have therefore omitted it. Furlong's fourth type consists of a mere bower of interlaced branches stuck in the ground and inclined toward the centre. This is simply a windbreak, without a hide covering or specially made poles.
78 Gallardo 1910: 241.
79 Bridges 1948: 260.
80 Chapman 1971.
81 Primary sources for this section: Bridges 1948: 263, 283, 362, 368–73, 377–8; Coiazzi 1914: 34–6; Gallardo 1910: 150, 154–62; Gusinde 1931: 208–19, 228–9; Lothrop 1928: 51–9.
82 Lothrop 1928: 51.
83 The director of the Hain ceremony, however, wore his cape with the fur inside.
84 Gallardo 1910: 265; Lothrop 1928: 52.

85 Gallardo 1910: 155 (my translation).
86 Chapman 1966–76; Coiazzi 1914: 36; Gallardo 1910: 311.
87 Bridges 1948: 369–70.
88 Lothrop 1928: 57.
89 Bridges 1948: 373.
90 *Ibid.*: 369.
91 *Ibid.*
92 Martínez-Crovetto 1968.
93 Bridges 1948: 211, 272, 366–7, 526; Gallardo 1910: 149–52; Gusinde 1931: 224–7.
94 Gusinde 1931: 226 (my translation).
95 Primary sources for this section: Beauvoir 1902; Bridges 1948: 171 note 2, 309, 367; Coiazzi 1914: 22, 36–41; Chapman 1966–76, 1977a; Gallardo 1910: 253–90; Gusinde 1931: 230–69; Martínez-Crovetto 1968; Lothrop 1928: 68–93; Outes 1906; Popper 1887: 105–6; Segers 1891: 67–72.
96 In the sources consulted, flint is the only type of rock mentioned as being used for arrow heads. The enumeration of rocks is based on my own archaeological surveys (Chapman and Hester 1975). See Popper (1887: 101–3) for rocks and minerals found on the Great Island.
97 See Cooper (1917: 210), though Gusinde (1931: 238) states that arrow heads were not made of bone.
98 Bove 1883: 133; Gallardo 1910: 273; Popper 1887: 106.
99 Gusinde 1931: 268; Lothrop 1928: 115.
100 Chapman 1966–76; Gusinde 1931: 232; Lothrop 1928: 71; Martínez-Crovetto 1968: 16.
101 Bridges 1948: 376.
102 Gusinde 1931: 232.
103 Chapman 1966–76.
104 Bridges 1948: 376; Lothrop 1928: 73.
105 Chapman 1966–76; Martínez-Crovetto 1968: 15.
106 Lothrop (1928: 73) names four woods used for shafts, the fourth being *shiterhen* in Selk'nam, a currant bush, which Martínez-Crovetto (1968: 17) identifies as *Ribes magellanica*. The latter author also states that this wood was used for arrow shafts.
107 Beauvoir 1915: 203; Chapman 1966–76; Coiazzi 1914: 37, 57; Gusinde 1931: 9, 234; Martínez-Crovetto 1968: 12.
108 Beauvoir 1915: 203; Chapman 1966–76; Lothrop 1928: 73; Martínez-Crovetto 1968: 12.
109 Gusinde 1931: 9, 234; Lothrop 1928: 73.
110 Beauvoir 1902: 163.
111 Primary sources for this section: Chapman 1966–76, 1977a; Coiazzi 1914: 57; Gallardo 1910: 272, 291, 309, 354–5; Gusinde 1931: 436–8.
112 Gusinde 1931: 437–8 (my translation).
113 Chapman 1966–76.
114 Gusinde 1931: 436–7 (my translation); Chapman 1980b.

115 Coiazzi 1914: 57 (my translation).
116 Gallardo 1910: 272 and 291 (my translation).

2. The socio-economic structure

1 Bridges 1948: 216, 283; Chapman 1966–76; Gallardo 1910: 207–22; see the section in this chapter on warriors for Gusinde's concept of the *kemal* as a leader.
2 Bridges 1948: 376, 379; Chapman 1966–76.
3 Gusinde 1931: 230; Lothrop 1928: 71.
4 Bridges 1948: 256; Chapman 1966–76, 1977a; Gallardo 1910: 188; Gusinde 1931: 275–6; Lothrop 1928: 81.
5 Chapman 1966–76, genealogies. Lothrop (1928: 86) writes that Halimink had seven wives but according to my data he only had two wives, one after the other.
6 See the section on social organization in this chapter.
7 *Ibid.*
8 Gallardo 1910: 198, 215; Gusinde 1931: 277–9.
9 Gusinde 1931: 290; also chapter 1 above.
10 Durkheim 1960: 24; Mead 1967: 188–9; Sahlins 1964: 193, 1969a; Wilson 1975: 568.
11 Chapman 1966–76 contains data from Angela Loij concerning these abilities of the Alakaluf women; Gusinde 1961: part I, 252, part II, 457–62, and 1951: 202. On the sexual division of labour in this context see Edholm *et al.* 1977.
12 Primary sources for this section: Bridges 1948: 242–3, 266–8, 289–91, 383; Chapman 1966–76, notes in the 1972a album, 1972b; Gallardo 1910: 209, 296–302, 340, 343; Gusinde 1931: 724–807.
13 Chapman 1966–76; also Gusinde 1931: 778–9.
14 See Chapman 1980a.
15 Primary sources for this section: Chapman 1966–76; Gallardo 1910: 312; Gusinde 1931: 422–3, 440–53.
16 In the last 'war' among the Selk'nam a number of women and children were killed. This was very exceptional according to my data, which are quite detailed for thirteen combats or skirmishes. The last combat occurred in 1903, when firearms were used. This subject will be treated in another study.
17 Gallardo 1910: 222.
18 Sources for this section: Bridges 1948: 225, 230, 317–24, 357, 436, 440–1; Chapman 1966–76; Gallardo 1910: 344–8; Gusinde 1931: 454, 1134–6; Lothrop 1928: 88–9.
19 Gusinde 1931: 455 (my translation).
20 Primary sources for this section: Bridges 1948: 369; Chapman 1966–76; Coiazzi 1914: 57–8; Gallardo 1910: 347–8; Gusinde 1931: 1136–8.
21 Popper 1887: 105 (my translation).
22 Primary sources for this section: Bridges 1948 *passim*; Chapman 1966–

76 and genealogies; Furlong 1917a, 1917b; Gallardo 1910: 119, 207–51; Gusinde 1931: 319–21, 342–4, 347–8, 416–29, 459–61, 619–23; Lothrop 1928: 84–6.

23   Gusinde 1931: 844, 1008–9.

24   Fox 1969: 164–72. This author stipulates that 'kindreds can and do co-exist quite easily with unilineal descent groups' (p. 168), which is the case among the Selk'nam. My use of this term is also based on Murdock (1949: 56, 60).

25   I plan to publish an article on the kinship terminology.

26   Gusinde was unaware of the existence of the kindreds as he was also of the exogamous nature of the divisions (the 'skies'). He realized that the 'local group' was exogamous and stated that first cousins and distant kin should not marry. But he thought that no one knew the exact limits of the kin (1931: 319–21, 342).

27   Here lineage is used as defined by Murdock (1949: 46): 'A consanguineal kin group produced by eithei rule of unilinear descent is technically known as a *lineage* when it includes only persons who can actually trace their common relationship through a specific series of remembered genealogical links in the prevailing line of descent.' Fox (1969: 49–50) clarified the relation between lineage and clan as follows: 'Where the actual relationship between members of such a group [descent group] can be demonstrated . . . and not simply assumed, the group is called a *lineage* . . . Higher order units often consisting of several lineages in which common descent is assumed but cannot necessarily be demonstrated are most often referred to as *clans*. Here I will use *clan* and *lineage* as the terms for higher and lower order descent groups of whatever variety.'

28   Gusinde 1931: 420, 425, 459; Furlong 1917b: 186; Lothrop 1928: 84.

29   Baer and Schmitz 1965; Lowie 1933, 1949: 327; Service 1966: 96–7; Steward 1955: 132, 1968: 333; Steward and Faron 1959: 405.

30   Fox 1969: 49; Murdock 1949: 46.

31   Gusinde 1931: 417–19, 619–23. He writes in this respect: 'According to the old myth *K'aux* [the Owl] had [given] to each of the then existing family groups or sibs a precisely limited tract of land as sib property, and indeed the right to appropriate it, to hunt and to acquire useful things there. Thereby this family group was made into a true proprietor. There was no alienation nor exchange [of the land], therefore each family to our day has considered the hereditary portion [inheritance] of its ancestor as its exclusive belonging . . . As this myth relates, the Great Island was divided into thirty-nine regions, which includes the number of all the then existing family groups . . . Each knows precisely the boundaries which were drawn up in mythological times; for this knowledge is passed on from children to children's children, because of its extraordinary significance for the sib itself' (425–6; my translation).

32   *Ibid.*: 623 note 94, translated in Wilbert 1975: 70 note 42.

33   These are: 25 Washar (*wash* or *waash* signifies fox and by connotation smelly, and is a morpheme of several common names), 26 Ketaitel (*tel*

signifies thin and forms part of many names), 27 Koshpashe (*kosh* signifies face and often is a morpheme of the names), 28 Kaukmiélek and
34 Kauwéri (*kau* might be either a prefix of a sacred name or signify
finger nail and be part of a common name), and finally 38 Chashkelp
(*chash* means mouth and also appears in other names).

34   Lévi-Strauss 1962, 1969.
35   Steward 1955: 132.
36   Service 1966: 32–4, 96–7.
37   Gusinde 1931: 426.
38   A detailed analysis of the genealogies will be published in a future study.
39   Gusinde (1931: 417) mentions the case of a widow who married some-
     one from another *haruwen* group and took her children there to live,
     noting that the latter do not lose their affiliation with their father's kin
     and sometimes return to their father's territory when adults.
40   Martin 1969: 245; Murdock 1962: 388. An exceptional case of uxori-
     locality was Lola's paternal grandfather, Terrumkan, who went to live
     in his second wife's territory where he died soon afterwards. Angela
     commented, 'He didn't have the right to do it but he did it anyway.'
41   See Lee and DeVore 1968: 9; Lee 1976: 75, 91, 97.
42   Gusinde 1931: 890–3, 1038, 1077.
43   *Ibid.*: 304, 349, 414–16.
44   Bridges 1948: 223.
45   *Ibid.*: 307.
46   *Ibid.*: 363–4.
47   Gallardo 1910: 220–4 (my translation). Lothrop (1928: 81) also
     reports wife beating with bow staves.
48   Bierstedt 1974: 222–6.
49   Sahlins 1969b: 114.
50   For comments on these controversies, as well as problems concerning
     the analyses of territoriality, see the papers by Denham, Lee, Morris
     and Peterson presented at the International Conference on Hunters and
     Gatherers, held in Paris, 27–30 June 1978. The last three papers are
     published in Leacock and Lee 1982. See also Peterson 1975 and Spence
     1974. For a reinterpretation of Steward's (1955) band typology see
     Service (1962, 1966) and the former's last comments (Steward 1968,
     1969). Birdsell (1970) and Stanner (1965) maintain Radcliffe-Brown's
     version of the Australian local group (the horde) as a land-owning group,
     in the face of the critiques by Hiatt (1962, 1966) and Meggitt (1962)
     principally. Williams (1968, 1974) argues in favour of Service's band
     model for hunter–gatherers in general. Adams (1975: 222–32), some
     of the contributors to Damas (1969), Gough (1975: 63), and Lenski
     (1966: 96–100), among others, have utilized it in their writings. The
     flexible–bilateral model has been developed principally by Lee and
     DeVore (1968: 7–9) and Lee (1974: 171–2, 1976: 75, 77, 90–1, 97)
     from basic data on the !Kung of South Africa. Yellen and Harpending
     (1972: 244) also generalize from the !Kung material. Woodburn (1968)
     published a similar analysis of the Hadza of Tanzania, and so forth.

Stuart (1977) addresses himself to the problem of 'flexibility' with respect to the Onas (Selk'nam), but unfortunately he frequently misinterprets Bridges (1948) and barely uses Gusinde.

51 Leacock (1974: 217–19, 1975, 1978) is one of the principal exponents of an egalitarian 'model' and other anthropologists such as Lee (1974) and Meillassoux (1972: 99) write of egalitarianism as a general pattern among hunter–gatherers. Gough (1975: 63, 69) states the problem as follows: 'Social life is egalitarian. There is of course no state, no organized government. Apart from religious shamans or magicians, the division of labor is based only on sex and age. Resources are owned communally; tools and personal possessions are freely exchanged. Everyone works who can. Band leadership goes to which ever man has the intelligence, courage, and foresight to command the respect of his fellows. Intelligent older women are also looked up to . . . Even in hunting societies it seems that women are always in some sense the "second sex", with greater or less subordination to men.' Moore (1977) and Webster (1975: 148–9), among others, have been critical of the egalitarian concept as it applies to women in the context of these societies.

52 Damas (1968: 116–17, 1969: 130–1), Eggan (in Lee and DeVore 1968: 116–17, and in Damas 1969: 233, 261–5) and Helm (1969: 216–17) express doubts as to the validity or usefulness of a generalized hunter–gatherer band concept.

53 Service 1962: 108–9 (my italics). Meggitt (1962: 71) makes a criticism somewhat similar to mine, but with reference to Radcliffe-Brown's 'horde' with respect to the Walbiri of Australia. He writes: 'The only Walbiri group that possessed some of the attributes ascribed by Radcliffe-Brown to the horde was the community, but this was clearly a much more extensive, populous and complexly-structured group than that which he had in mind. It was not a simple patrilineal and patrilocal band.'

54 Also if the mother's 'division' (sky) had greater prestige than the father's, a man might insist upon being assigned a place in the Hain ceremonial hut which corresponded to his matrilateral 'division'. See chapter 4 below.

3. The ideology

1 Principal sources for this chapter: Bridges 1948; Gusinde 1931; Salesian Missionary; Wilbert 1975; Chapman 1966–76, informants Lola Kiepja, Federico Echeuline, Angela Loij and Luis Garibaldi Honte.

2 I have not included here 'The spread of the kloketen', translated by Wilbert (1975: 165–70) from Gusinde 1931: 873–83 because it is not pertinent to the subject of this chapter, although one remark should be made: the various renderings of this myth (also in Bridges 1948: 444–5; Angela and Federico in Chapman 1966–76) illustrate very clearly their function in terms of social prestige. Gusinde comments upon the way in which the raconteur oriented this myth to favour his

homeland sky. If he was from the south, he would narrate this myth placing the origin of the Hain ceremony in the south. But were he from the north, the ceremony would be described as originating there. The second myth summarized in this chapter, 'The first men's Hain', is another case in point. It stipulates that the first men's Hain took place on a mountain named Máustas located in the south. Actually this was Haush area and the territory of Tenenésk, who was Gusinde's informant for this myth. I will discuss these problems in a future study.

3 Bridges 1948: 412.
4 Gusinde 1931: 860 as translated by Wilbert 1975: 148.
5 I employ Bridges' spelling for the names of Moon (Kreeh) and Sun (Krren).
6 Gusinde 1931: 1025.
7 Gusinde 1931: 861 as translated by Wilbert 1975: 149.
8 *Ibid.*
9 Gusinde 1931: 862 as translated by Wilbert 1975: 150.
10 Gusinde 1931: 864–5 as translated by Wilbert 1975: 152–3.
11 Gusinde 1931: 865–7 as translated by Wilbert 1975: 153–5.
12 Gusinde 1931: 867 as translated by Wilbert 1975: 155.
13 *Ibid.*
14 *Ibid.*
15 *Ibid.*
16 Angela Loij in Chapman 1966–76.
17 Federico Echeuline in Chapman 1966–76.
18 Luis Garibaldi Honte in Chapman 1966–76.
19 For comparable myths in the northwestern Amazon area (Colombia and Brazil) see Bamberger (1974: 272–80). The author relates these myths to the Hain and Kina (Yámana) matriarchy myths. She concludes (p. 280): 'The myth of matriarchy is but the tool used to keep woman bound to her place. To free her, we need to destroy the myth.' For a similar context in New Guinea see especially Godelier 1976, Langness 1977 and Meggitt 1964.
20 Federico Echeuline in Chapman 1966–76.
21 Bridges 1948: 413.
22 Gusinde 1931: 873 note 204 as translated by Wilbert 1975: 163. Gusinde (1931: 871) describes how Tenenésk was aroused when the name of the Spaniard who had rented land near the mountain Máustas was mentioned.
23 Gusinde 1931:872 as translated by Wilbert 1975: 162.
24 Gusinde 1931: 599–606, 1025; Lola Kiepja and Angela Loij in Chapman 1966–76.
25 Gusinde 1931: 599–606.
26 *Ibid.*
27 *Ibid.*, and p. 869.
28 *Ibid.*
29 All the data on eclipses are from either Lola Kiepja and Angela Loij or Gusinde.

30   This data is from Lola and Angela. Gusinde (1931: 604) cites Coiazzi
     (1914, which is a Spanish translation of his 1911 article in Italian cited
     by Gusinde) to the effect that, among the Haush, the shamans knew
     just how furious Moon would be during an eclipse. If she were to be
     calm, the eclipse passed without much notice.
31   Gusinde 1931: 604.
32   The term *swáren* means 'to clear the sky using shamanistic power'; to
     clear it of an eclipse, rain clouds or snow. See Chapman (1972a) for
     Lola's *swáren* chant (no. 30).
33   See Chapman 1972a for Lola's chant no. 5 which Lola sang without
     words but was later recorded from Angela, who did sing it with words.
     Both quotations are from Angela's text of this chant, which has not
     yet been issued on a record. Also Chapman 1972b.
34   *Ibid.*
35   Gusinde 1931: 827.
36   *Ibid.*: 1038.
37   Bridges 1948: 424–5.
38   *Ibid.*: 410.
39   Gusinde 1931: 893–9.
40   *Ibid.*: 883–7, 900–1, 940–1.
41   For Lévi-Strauss' concept of primitive societies as 'cold' see 1962:
     41–4 and Charbonnier 1961: 37–48.

4. The setting and symbolism of the Hain ceremony

1   For sources on the Hain ceremony in general see note 1 of chapter 6.
    Principal sources for this chapter: Gusinde 1931: 831–44, 870–3,
    909–15, 1006–10, 1014, 1018, 1052; Bridges 1948: 405–29; and my
    four principal informants in Chapman 1966–76.
2   Gusinde 1931: 832 and diagram on p. 833.
3   Bridges 1948: 414.
4   Gallardo (1910: 205) asserts that in Tierra del Fuego the fat of a whale
    lasted for a year without decomposing.
5   See note 1 of chapter 6 below.
6   See note 2 to the Introduction above.
7   See chapter 1. In this chapter reference to the Selk'nam will include the
    Haush unless otherwise indicated.
8   Among Gusinde's informants of Haush origin there were four
    (Tenenésk, Inxiol, Toin and Knoskól) who belonged to the territory of
    Kal which was associated with the south sky. A number of other people
    named by Gusinde were also Haush or Selk'nam–Haush.
9   Bridges (1948: 414) writes that it was so oriented 'merely because the
    prevailing winds came from the west'. It should be noted however that
    the prevailing wind shifted. For instance, Gusinde (1931: 1061) notes
    that the entrances to the dwelling huts in camp were toward the north
    as protection against the south wind. This was undoubtedly true as

there is no indication that the entrances to the dwellings were in any way symbolically oriented.

10　Gusinde has no information on the concept of 'central' and 'peripheral'. Unlike my informants, he does not define the four posts as Flamingo, Owl, Shag and Wind. In different parts of his work these words, with different spellings, are so defined but not in relation to the posts of the Hain hut.

11　Chapman 1972a: chant no. 24. See note 50 of chapter 7.

12　*Ibid.*: chant nos. 1, 3, 8, 13 and 15.

13　*Ibid.*: chant nos. 3, 29, 30, 36. Rain was brother and sister, see p. 67.

14　Lola Kiepja in Chapman 1966–76.

15　Compare the diagram of the Hain in this text with that of Gusinde (1931: 839). He placed Páhuil (Pawus) just north of the entrance, undoubtedly because it was there in 1923. Federico told me that, after colonization, the post was placed there though in the past it had been located at the centre of the entrance, sometimes a few feet beyond the ground circle, but always directly opposite the west post. This would be done in order to facilitate the entry of the men into the hut. According to my data, Gusinde was mistaken in the placement of two posts. Shag (Keyáishk) was placed northeast instead of due north as it appears on Gusinde's diagram, while Flamingo (Télil) was located due north and not northwest as on Gusinde's drawings. Angela confirmed this in the context of mythological data. My information is identical to that of Gusinde with respect to the location of the remaining posts. However, on the identities of two other posts there is a divergence. Wechúsh, according to my data, was not considered an east post but rather southeast (peripheral to the south) following its location. Jóichick (Yoichik) was not a south post as Gusinde indicates, but rather the southwest post (peripheral to the west).

16　Gusinde 1931: 1009.

17　As far as I know, this dual division has no particular significance but was only a function of the mystical existence of the chasm. Gusinde often speaks of the southern and northern Selk'nam, distinguishing them from the eastern Selk'nam who were the Haush. In effect there was such a distinction. Those north of the Río Grande (Hurr) were called *párika*, 'people of the pampa', while those to the south were called *hérska*, 'people of the forest' (see chapter 1 above). As far as I know, this classification was not operative in the Hain, nor did it play a part in the mythology. There were territories (*haruwen*) assigned to the north sky in the south (*hérsk*) region. The west territories were also located to the north and south of the Río Grande, though all the south sky territories were in effect south of the Río Grande in the so-called *hérsk* area. The Haush were called 'easterners' (*Wínteka*) by the Selk'nam, as a generic name, because they occupied that part of the island. So outside the context of the Hain, Gusinde's observations are perfectly reasonable. Bridges (1948: 415) thought that the 'chasm' divided the Hain hut into north and south groups with men assigned in contradiction to their kin relations or place of birth, so that a man from the north would sit on the south side, and vice versa. This author is obviously confused. He states also that if a man's mother and father were from opposite sides, one from the north and the other from the south, he could enter the Hain from either direction. In a sense this was true. As I mentioned in the text, if a man's mother's sky and the post which corresponded to it were more prestigious than his father's, he might manage to be seated in the former, and if the two posts of his parents were located on opposite sides of the Hain, theoretically he could enter from either side, though actually he would enter on the side corresponding to the post to which he had been assigned. Bridges did not understand the system. He was misled by the place where he was ordered to sit. As he was born on the south coast of the island (on the Harberton farm on the coast of the Beagle Channel), he assumed that he should have been assigned to one of the south poles. But instead he was told to sit under a north pole (Keyáishk) and consequently he entered the Hain on that side. For this reason, I suppose that he assumed that the southerners entered and were placed on the north side and vice versa. Obviously he did not know what Angela told me, that he was assigned to a north post because he was a foreigner and that his place of birth was not taken into consideration. In addition he was born in Yámana territory which did not enter at all into the scheme of the Hain. Gusinde as a foreigner was also assigned a seat near a north pole.

Here I might add that my data confirms Gusinde's (1931: 840) to the effect that the ceremonial hut was not used as a bachelor's or counsel house when the ceremony was not in function. Bridges, Furlong and others asserted that it was so employed.

18 Bridges 1935: 36.

5. Girls' puberty rite and the organization of the Hain ceremony

1 The details of the girls' puberty observations are in Gusinde 1927: 169, 1928: 38, 1931: 410—13; Angela Loij added some more data (in Chapman 1966—76).

2 Main sources for this section: Gusinde 1931: 809—10, 1015—38; Angela, Federico and Garibaldi in Chapman 1966—76.

3 Gusinde 1931: 829, 1031.

4 Gusinde 1931: 1020. Bridges (1948: 405) gives thirteen to seventeen as the age range of the *kloketens*. Beauvoir (1915: 202) states that they were about fourteen to fifteen years old; Gallardo (1910: 330) that they were at the age of puberty. Gusinde specifies (1931: 829) that around 1923 the average age was between fourteen and eighteen. I think his estimates are the most reliable. When the society was disintegrating (from the beginning of the decade of 1890 in the central part of the island), the age level was lowered. All the authors cited

above made their observations after this period, and none but Gusinde was aware that the upper age limit had been higher in the past.

5 Gusinde 1931: 812–13.

6 Bridges 1948: 419.

7 Agostini 1929: 267; Beauvoir 1915: 206; Fuentes Rabe 1922: 171; Gallardo 1910: 330–1.

8 Sources for this section: Gusinde 1931: 1039–47; Chapman 1966–76 (Lola Kiepja and Angela Loij).

9 Gusinde (1931: 1042) states that only the mother of the eldest *kloketen* was called by this term, but Lola and Angela referred to all the '*kloketen* mothers' as *kai kloketen.*

10 Sources for this section: Gusinde 1931: 844; Federico and Garibaldi in Chapman 1966–76.

11 Sources for this section: Gusinde 1931: 829–31, 841, 857, 1010–15, 1023; Angela and Federico in Chapman 1966–76.

12 I do not know the exact meaning of *órien*, but a *kloketen* who proved to be a good student and diligent worker was called *tul-órien. Tul* signifies heart, sentiment or temperament, as in the term *tul-ulichen* (beautiful heart) meaning a person with a generous or pleasant temperament.

13 Gusinde (1931: 829–30) understood that formerly the father of the oldest *kloketen* was automatically the principal director and that the father of the next oldest *kloketen* was the second director. But this could not be true if the director were a *chan-ain* because even in pre-White times there were apparently relatively few men of this status. As Gusinde states, the Hain of 1923 was directed by Tenenésk who was not the father of either of the two *kloketens* then presented. Tenenésk was undoubtedly chosen because he was the most prestigious man of his epoch. According to Gusinde the fathers of the *kloketens* of 1923 were the subordinate directors. One, Halimink, did participate as such but the other, whose name was Nana, did not seem to do much counselling let alone directing.

14 Gusinde 1931: 830–1.

15 The sole source for this section is Gusinde 1931: 907–8, 1012–13, 1076.

16 *Ibid.*: 907–8.

17 The sole source here is Gusinde 1931: 1011–12, 1075.

6. The first day

1 The principal primary sources for the Hain ceremony are Gusinde 1925, 1926a, 1931: 808–1083, 1951, 1964; the anonymous Salesian Missionary and all the informants in Chapman 1966–76. Bridges (1948: chapters 42, 43) has some very valuable data though it is not entirely reliable. The fact that he considered the Hain 'a ludicrous show' (p. 412) may have affected his interest and judgement. Several authors who discussed the Hain did not apparently gain most of their

information directly from the Selk'nam but rather from the Bridges family who were often obliging hosts to foreign visitors. The texts concerning the Hain in the works of the following authors are very similar to the data published by Lucas Bridges and they repeat many of the same errors: Barclay 1926; Coiazzi 1914: 25–7; Dabbene 1907: 74; Gallardo 1910: 326–35; Holmberg 1906: 57–8; Lothrop 1928: 92–5. Two of my informants, Luis Garibaldi Honte and Federico Echeuline, had been *kloketens*. The former had spent a month in the Hain in about 1921 and the latter several months in 1920. Lola Kiepja remembered participating in Hains, though mostly in the twentieth century. Her first husband 'Aneki' had been Lucas Bridges' sponsor in the Hain. Angela Loij was present in the 1923 Hain and had of course met Gusinde. In his 1931 book there are three photographs of her taken at this period: nos. 95 (first left), 96 (centre) and 113. Gusinde also published one of Federico (no. 42 first left). But Federico, Garibaldi and Lola did not participate in the 1923 Hain. Angela had witnessed other Hains including the one which was presented in 1920. She also learned about the Hain from her husband 'Nielsen' (no. 98 first left in Gusinde 1931) who also took part in the 1923 Hain. He was given this name by the Bridges family. Angela also learned a great deal about the Hain from the old Selk'nam women in the Salesian mission, where she lived for some ten years. Specific sources for this section: Federico Echeuline in Chapman 1966–76; Gusinde 1931: 845–8 and the Salesian Missionary.

2   This is taken from Federico. Gusinde (1931: 933) only mentions that the performers were helped to put on the masks. The Ténin-nin and the Shoort actor had to be kin of the *wiik stirin* category; described in Federico's words as 'those with whom one can play'. This category includes brothers, near male cousins and grandfathers and corresponds to kin of the 'joking relation' type.

3   Chapman 1978: chant no. 5.

4   *Ibid.*: chant no. 3.

5   *Ibid.*: chant no. 4.

6   Gusinde 1931: 848.

7   Main sources for this section: Gusinde 1931: 838, 871–3, 929–42; Bridges 1948: 411, 413, 418–21; Salesian Missionary; Federico and Angela in Chapman 1966–76.

8   Federico in Chapman 1966–76; Gusinde 1931: 872. In 1923, all of the Shoorts photographed by Gusinde were painted with white splodges, but not all the masks were painted with white bands around the eyes. See the album of photographs in the cited volume.

9   Notwithstanding the fact that the myth of the men's Hain as published by Gusinde (1931: 872, translated in Wilbert 1975: 163) in which the owl K'tétu is described as a subordinate Shoort, the data given by Federico, as well as other data, indicate that K'tétu was not a subordinate Shoort but rather the prototype of Shoort as such and hence incarnated in each of the seven principal Shoorts. In turn, each of these

represented another *hoowin*, which symbolized their respective skies and hence posts in the Hain hut. Gusinde's data is confirmed by what I was able to gather regarding the characterization of *hoowin* K'tétu as a *hauwitpin* (a man with a 'perfect' physique) who played the role of Shoort exceptionally well in the first men's Hain.

10 Bridges 1935: 36, 1948: 413; Angela and Federico in Chapman 1966–76; Gusinde 1931: 930–1.

11 Gusinde spells Krren (Bridges' spelling for the Sun) as Kran, with the a pronounced like the 'e' in hen. Of the five words mentioned in the text which lack definitions, the second (Koxó) may well be derived from the word for 'sea', *kox* or *koox*, and the last (Sanenkepáuwen) is very likely to be partly derived from the word for 'wind', *shénu*. In the time of *hoowin*, Wind was the brother of Sun and like him is associated with the west sky. Shénu represents the west post in the Hain. But in this context he is associated with the sunset.

12 Bridges (1948: 413) refers to Shoort as emerging from the grey rock. He may have confused his place of origin with his substance. Lothrop (1928: 95) quotes several authors to the effect that Shoort was the spirit of the white stone. This is the same sort of error and may have been derived from Bridges as a common 'informant' for many of the scientists and travellers who wrote about the Selk'nam.

13 Esteban Ichton died in 1969 shortly after I began working with him.

14 Principal sources for this section: Federico and Garibaldi in Chapman 1966–76; Bridges 1948: 413, 420–2; Gallardo 1910: 331; Gusinde 1931: 846, 850–7; Salesian Missionary.

15 Gusinde 1931: 848 (my translation).

16 Chapman 1978: chant no. 4.

17 Gusinde 1931: 849 (my translation).

18 *Ibid.*: 851.

19 Fuentes Rabe (1922: 173) describes a different sort of torture; the *kloketen* is held firmly from behind while Shoort burns him with an enormous fire-brand, so that the *kloketen* can smell his own burning flesh.

20 Gusinde 1931: 852.

21 Bridges (1948: 421) states the contrary, but in this context it does not seem likely. This part of the account is taken from Gusinde 1931: 852.

22 Federico Echeuline in Chapman 1966–76.

23 *Ibid.*

24 *Ibid.*

25 *Ibid.*

26 *Ibid.*

27 *Ibid.*

28 Lothrop (1928: 93) asserts that the *kloketen* 'had to prove indifference to pain by allowing wood splinters thrust in his arm to burn themselves out against his flesh'. According to Angela Loij, this was the normal technique of scarification, ashes being pressed into the wound so that the mark remained. She said that almost everyone had these marks on

their hands and forearms in the past but that the technique was not practised on *kloketens* during the Hain. Bridges (1948: 421) was also mistaken when he wrote that there was no torture of any kind during the initiation.

29 This is a quote from the manuscript by the Salesian Missionary. Gusinde (1931: 1018–19) describes the same rite, although the words of the *kloketen* are not as significant. According to Gusinde's account, the *kloketen* held his body very stiff, rolled Shoort's (leather) mask up and fastened its ends together. First he laid it under his genitals then he stretched it out over the upper part of his body, slowly lifting it up toward his neck and down. This he did several times. Finally he jumped up and down, his legs stiff, repeating the words spoken to him by the men who played the role of Shoort; that he is very happy to learn about the Hain, of which he had previously been in ignorance. He repeated these words five times in the same fashion. This rite was performed every day during the first week of the ceremony and less frequently during the next three weeks. Gusinde commented that he was not able to learn the significance of this rite.

30 Gusinde 1931: 853, 898.

31 The young men would have been warned that premature sexual relations would stunt their growth.

32 Garibaldi in Chapman 1966–76. Tenenésk asked Garibaldi this question when the latter was a *kloketen*.

33 Gusinde 1931: 853–4. Here the ambiguity of the word 'killed' should be recalled; it could mean either actual killing or to 'kill' by use of shamanistic powers.

34 Bridges 1948: 422.

35 Garibaldi in Chapman 1966–76.

36 Gallardo 1910: 331.

37 Bridges 1948: 422.

38 Garibaldi in Chapman 1966–76.

39 *Ibid.*

40 Federico in Chapman 1966–76.

41 *Ibid.*

42 Gallardo 1910: 331.

43 *Ibid.*

44 *Ibid.*

45 Gusinde 1931: 1031.

46 *Ibid.*: 1030.

47 *Ibid.*: 1020.

48 *Ibid.*: 1026.

49 Federico in Chapman 1966–76; Gusinde 1931: 1032.

50 *Ibid.*; Salesian Missionary.

51 Salesian Missionary.

52 *Ibid.*; Gusinde 1931: 854, 1037.

53 Gusinde 1931: 1037.

54 Federico in Chapman 1966–76; Gusinde 1931: 215, 853, 1016.

55 Federico in Chapman 1966–76; Gusinde 1931: 1018.
56 Garibaldi in Chapman 1966–76; Gusinde 1931: 1036–7.
57 Gusinde 1931: 1017.
58 Garibaldi in Chapman 1966–76; Gusinde 1931: 1034–5.
59 Gusinde 1931: 854.
60 Federico in Chapman 1966–76; Gusinde 1931: 1018; Salesian Missionary.
61 Federico and Garibaldi in Chapman 1966–76; Gusinde 1931: 855–7,
    1034–5; Salesian Missionary.
62 Chapman 1978: chant no. 20; Gusinde 1931: 923, 958–9, 1069.

7. Daily and frequent scenes of the Hain

1 Chapman 1978: chant no. 1.
2 Gusinde 1931: 1039.
3 Gusinde 1931: 875–80; the myth in question 'The spread of the
   klóketen', is translated by Wilbert (1975: 165–70); quotation is from
   ibid.: 167.
4 Chapman 1978: chant no. 2.
5 Main sources for this section: Federico in Chapman 1966–76; Bridges
   1948: 414–18; Gusinde 1931: 938–41, 1040–6; Salesian Missionary.
6 This is the category of kin, called *wiik óijen* according to Federico,
   which was comprised of a man's mother-in-law, his mother's brother's
   wife, his sister-in-law and perhaps other female affines.
7 Bridges 1948: 418.
8 Gusinde 1931: 938 note 130.
9 Federico in Chapman 1966–76.
10 Chapman 1978: chant no. 6; Gusinde 1931: 1046.
11 Bridges 1948: 414.
12 These chants were also called *hain-né-mai* (belong to the Hain). See
    Chapman 1978: chant nos. 26, 27, 29–42. According to Federico the
    kloketens were strictly forbidden to hear them. If they were near camp
    when the women began to sing them, the *kloketens* had to move out of
    hearing distance or at least turn their backs on the women singing.
13 Sources for this section: Angela and Federico in Chapman 1966–76;
    Gusinde 1931: 942–53.
14 Federico in Chapman 1966–76.
15 Gusinde 1931: 951 (my translation).
16 Gusinde 1931: 947.
17 Gusinde 1931: 948. These phrases have undoubtedly lost some of the
    flavour of the original Selk'nam as they were translated to Spanish,
    then German and finally into English.
18 According to Gusinde (1931: 950) the women usually sang while
    Hayílan was in camp, though he does not specify which chant they
    sang. I assume it was the *ho kreek* chant (see note 10 above).
19 Gusinde 1931: 953.
20 Sources for this section: Angela and Federico in Chapman 1966–76;
    Gusinde 1931: 925–8.

21 Chapman 1978: chant no. 7.
22 Angela said that *hashé* is a 'power' (*poder* in Spanish) which is introduced into the body of Hu-ku-hu. But she could give no further explanation.
23 Sources for this section: Bridges 1948: 412, 416; the four principal informants of Chapman 1966–76; Gusinde 1931: 900, 916–29, 1045–6; Salesian Missionary.
24 In 1923 according to my count (Gusinde 1931: 1059–76) Xalpen appeared eight times during the fifty days the ceremony lasted.
25 Chapman 1978: chant no. 8.
26 Gusinde (1931: 922) quotes the expression 'that bad women devoured some [men]'. He comments in note 118 (p. 922) that this concept is unclear, that it does not mean man-eating but rather extermination (*Vernichten*). But Lola, Angela and Federico told me that Xalpen would eat her victims if she was not given enough guanaco meat. This however does not in any way imply that the Selk'nam were cannibals, nor were any of the other Fuegian groups. See Beauvoir 1915: 212; Bridges 1948: 34–6.
27 Chapman 1978: chant no. 9.
28 Furious, *aime-ré*, is my spelling from Lola and Angela. Gusinde (1931: 919) renders it as *aimerán*.
29 The terrifying noise of the voice of Xalpen produced by the rolled-up guanaco skins may be functionally comparable to the 'bull-roarers' employed by the Australian men during their initiation rites. See for example Eliade 1959: 36–41 and *passim*.
30 Gusinde 1931: 1046 my translation.
31 *Ibid.*
32 *Ibid.*
33 Probably Bridges (1948: 418) described Xalpen as white because during the Hains he witnessed she was painted with this colour. But why he said she was from 'the white cumulus clouds' is not clear. Both Gusinde's informants and mine stated time and again in many different contexts that she inhabited the interior of the earth. She was in no way associated with the clouds, as far as I know. The description of the effigy is based on Bridges 1948: 416; Gusinde 1931: 928, 1071–2 and all five informants of Chapman 1966–76.
34 Gusinde 1931: 916.
35 Main sources for this section: Bridges 1948: 425–7; Gusinde 1931: 989–93. Also Lola, Angela and Federico in Chapman 1966–76.
36 Chapman 1978: chant no. 10.
37 Bridges 1948: 425.
38 *Ibid.*: 426.
39 *Ibid.*
40 Gusinde 1931: 992. See Gallardo 1910: 347 and Gusinde 1931: 1136 for the description of an ordinary game which somewhat resembles this 'dance'.

41 Sources for this section: Lola, Angela and Federico in Chapman 1966– 76; Bridges 1948: 426; Gusinde 1931: 993–7.

42 Gusinde (1931: 997–8) states that the Hóshtan spirit and a Haush spirit and scene both of which were called Hapashkan are variants of the same, although he is not sure which is the original. According to my data this spirit is of Haush origin.

43 Chapman 1978: chant no. 11.

44 Bridges 1948: 426.

45 Lola's husband was a friend of Bridges, known as Aneki, and was Bridges' supervisor when he was presented in the Hain. Any man, except the *kloketens*, could participate in this dance.

46 Gusinde 1931: 994.

47 The sources here are Angela and Federico in Chapman 1966–76; Gusinde 1931: 967–74; Salesian Missionary.

48 Chapman 1978: chant no. 12.

49 Federico told me that each *kloketen* impersonates a Kulan.

50 Chapman 1978: chant no. 13. *Maukel* or *pémaulk* in this context simply means the far heavens, to the east. It has no reference (here at least) to a supreme deity, as Gusinde (1931: 486–509) interprets this term. This problem will be taken up in another study.

51 Sources for this section: Angela, Federico and Lola in Chapman 1966– 76; Gusinde 1931: 967–74.

52 Chapman 1978: chant no. 14.

53 Main sources for this section: Angela, Federico and Lola in Chapman 1966–76; Gusinde 1931: 964–7; Salesian Missionary.

54 The Salesian Missionary describes this spirit as having two manifes- tations, a husband and wife, each distinctively painted. He adds that they were flesh and blood like all the sky spirits and that the earth spirits were made of rock. The latter statement does not entirely con- form either to Gusinde's data or to mine.

55 Gusinde 1931: 863, 869.

56 Chapman 1978: chant no. 15.

57 Gusinde 1931: 964.

58 Principal sources for this section: Bridges 1935: 37, 1948: 417; the four main informants of Chapman 1966–76; Gusinde 1931: 976–81.

59 Although Gusinde suggests that this spirit is masculine both Bridges' and my data agree that it was feminine.

60 Both Angela and Federico told me that Tanu is 'the same as' Hainxo- héuwan. I think this is the key to the problem. I submit that Gusinde confused several elements, which is not difficult to do with reference to such a complex ceremony and the problems of working with four languages: Selk'nam, Haush, Spanish and German. He writes that Hainxo-héuwan is a feminine spirit who appears only in the night and that she is the good natured wife of Hainxo, the latter being a frail, sickly earth spirit who only presents himself during the day. I do not know the meaning of *héuwan*. Nor did I ever hear the name Hainxo by

itself, though obviously it is derived from Hain. In any event, it now seems apparent to me that neither the wife nor the husband are distinctive spirits but rather that they are different manifestations of the Tanu spirit. Gusinde states that the wife, Hainxo-héuwan, was not presented in 1923. However he does describe (1931: 979) her appearance as being similar to that of her husband, Hainxo, who in turn is very similar to Tanu. Furthermore he was told (p. 980) that the wife, Hainxo-héuwan, carries two pointed little sticks with which she jabs the men's noses inside the Hain hut, in preparation for the dance which would follow. As we have seen, an identical pointed stick, serving the same purpose, was described by my informants as an attribute of Tanu. As for the husband, Hainxo, Gusinde says that his data is not satisfactory even though he did see one. As noted above he describes this spirit's appearance as being very similar to Tanu. This is one of the reasons why I propose that Hainxo was simply one of the Tanus.

With reference to the term Hainxo-héuwan, I learned from Lola that this term, and a variation, is repeated during the chant sung for the dance in honour of Tanu (chant no. 17 in Chapman 1978). This is not surprising as a second name for Shoort is used in the chant in honour of him (chant no. 6) and the same thing occurs with respect to Hashé in chant no. 7. However, these names are probably not full equivalents of the commonly used names. They may well have had different connotations, but what these could have been, I do not know. To return to the differences of the appraisals of Bridges and Gusinde with respect to the personality of Tanu, I submit that neither are correct, that Tanu was neither cruel as Bridges reported nor agreeable as Gusinde wrote. I propose that Tanu had no personality, that she was conceived as an abstract symbol of the Hain and that this explains her great importance in the ceremony. She is a witness, a spectator and hence a kind of judge. In this context she was the envoy, and the sister, of Xalpen. This role of Tanu will become clearer in the description of Kewánix, the profession of almost all of the participants, at the end of this chapter. Tanu is obviously not the same type of spirit as the others. She is on a different conceptual level.

61 According to Gusinde (1931: 977) Tanu Korukánh is of the west. But he is mistaken, for the second term means south. Also Tanu Knaekánh is not of the east as he thought, but of the west as the term defines him. His other two designations of Tanu are correct, according to my Hain and linguistic data. Therefore two of Gusinde's four Tanus are of the south, one of the west and one of the north.

62 This is from Federico. However, Angela told me that Shocits is the name of a *hoowin* woman and of her son of the south sky. The latter was a *kloketen*. They were lazy and dirty and (hence) became transformed into a bird which had these defects. There is probably a certain difference in the interpretation of the Hain spirits given by the men and the women. Matan, cited in the text, is another example. Lola and Angela said it was a female spirit while Gusinde's men informants

described it as a male spirit. This problem will be dealt with in another study. Bridges writes (1948: 417) that Tanu is of the red clay. He may have confused the fact that she is painted with red clay (*ákel*) with her place of origin.

63 This is from Federico. See Gusinde 1931: 980–1 for a slightly different account.

64 Chapman 1978: chant no. 16.

65 *Ibid.*: chant no. 17.

66 That is, a distant cousin (see chapter 2) or, according to the levirate custom, her sister's husband, as his second wife.

67 Sources for this section: Federico in Chapman 1966–76; Gusinde 1931: 1000–3.

68 Chapman 1978: chant no. 18.

69 *Ibid.*: chant no. 19.

70 The only reference here is Gusinde 1931: 999–1000.

71 *Ibid.*: 985.

72 Source for this section: Gusinde 1931: 1003–6.

73 Gusinde 1931: 974–6.

74 Bridges (1948: 414) mentions another Hain spirit called Kmantah which he describes as the spirit of the beech tree. Other authors, who probably received their information directly from the Bridges family, describe this spirit in a few lines in similar terms, namely Fuentes Rabe 1922: 173; Furlong 1917a: 414; Gallardo 1910: 333–4 and Lothrop 1928: 95. Neither Gusinde nor I have any data on such a spirit. Moreover, I am puzzled because *k'manta* signifies a small dolphin and appears as such in the mythology as a *hoowin* of the west sky and according to my data and Gusinde's (1931: 622, 871) it is in no way associated with the beech tree nor with the Hain spirits.

75 References for this section: Angela, Federico and Lola in Chapman 1966–76; Bridges 1948: 427; Gusinde 1931: 979, 982–8, 1068, 1072.

76 This term is from Gusinde. My informants called this dance or procession *héuwan tien*, 'to present or presenting *héuwan* and Tanu *tien*' as another Tanu scene (see note 63). Bridges also employs the former term which he spells as Ewan.

77 See note 60 above.

78 Gusinde 1931: 984, photograph no. 94 right.

79 *Ibid.*: 983, photograph no. 94 left, 97 right.

80 Chapman 1966–76.

81 Gusinde 1931: 984, photograph no. 94 centre. Photograph no. 93 centre according to my data is a man of the west 'sky', although his step-father was of the north 'sky'. He was a kin of Lola and belonged to the same territory as her mother.

82 Gusinde 1931: 985, photograph no. 95 left which is of Angela Loij, who in effect belonged to the north 'sky'.

83 Gusinde 1931: 984, photograph no. 96 centre (also of Angela) and right.

84 Chapman 1966–76. For *ksámenk* see also Gusinde 1931: 620.

85 Gusinde 1931: 984, photograph no. 93 left and right.
86 Gusinde 1931: 984 photograph no. 95 right.
87 Chapman 1966–76; Gusinde 1931: 622.

8. The climax and anti-climax of the Hain

1 Sources for this section: Angela, Federico and Lola in Chapman 1966–76; Gusinde 1931: 922, 953, 959, 1068, 1071; Salesian Missionary.
2 Chapman 1978: chant no. 21.
3 *Ibid.*: chant no. 22.
4 Gusinde 1931: 953.
5 *Ibid.*: 1063, 1071.
6 Sources for this section: Bridges 1948: 422–4; Angela, Federico and Lola in Chapman 1966–76; Gusinde 1931: 923, 958–9; Salesian Missionary.
7 Chapman 1978: chant no. 23.
8 Gusinde (1931: 923, 959) relates that small groups of men had gone to camp taking game which they had just killed, and that the women were happy to see them and to be reassured that little Olum had restored life to them. Just before their visit to camp, other men had gone into the Hain and started to clap their hands softly.
9 Federico Echeuline in Chapman 1966–76.
10 Bridges 1948: 422–4.
11 Sources for this section: Bridges 1948: 414; Angela, Esteban Ichton, Federico in Chapman 1966–76; Gusinde 1931: 953–60, 1069, 1072; Salesian Missionary.
12 Gusinde 1931: 955.
13 Chapman 1978: chant no. 24.
14 Gusinde 1931: 943.
15 Federico in Chapman 1966–76.
16 Gusinde 1931: 958.
17 *Ibid.*: 959–60.
18 *Ibid.*: 1069, 1072. Bridges observed (1948: 414) that only this spirit was kindly disposed towards the women. He mistakenly describes him as exclusively male and as the son of Shoort. Also he fails to mention his mother, Xalpen.
19 Sources for this section: Bridges 1948: 413, 417–18; Angela, Federico and Lola in Chapman 1966–76; Gusinde 1931: 921, 960–4, 1068–70.
20 Gusinde 1931: 960.
21 Chapman 1978: chant no. 25.
22 Bridges (1948: 413) writes that Háchai is the usual name for this spirit. According to him, Halaháches or Háchai came out of the lichen-covered rocks and was rubbed with grey down to represent the lichen. This description has not been confirmed by any other first-hand source and is probably based on a misinterpretation. This spirit was very probably adorned with grey down at times, like K'terrnen. When the Indians saw the White man's cattle, the impersonators of this spirit may well have

mimicked the bulls, though the horns were an important traditional attribute of this spirit. Bridges was impressed by how realistically one of the Indians who played this role imitated a well-horned charging bull.

23 Gusinde 1931: 964.
24 Bridges 1948: 417.

9. For women only

1 Sources for this section: Angela and Federico in Chapman 1966–76.
2 In Spanish, *haciendo travesias*, to quote Angela.
3 Federico, who was told about this by his mother, said that women could only wrestle together if they were sisters-in-law or female cousins, that is, the *wiik stirin* category of kin. See note 2 of chapter 6.
4 Federico.
5 This is a little round white or yellow parasite that grows in the branches of trees. After Martínez-Crovetto (1968: 10) it is *Rumex hippiatricus*.
6 According to Federico she would take the gift to the hut of a sister-in-law or female cousin. See note 3 above.
7 Sources for this section: Angela and Federico in Chapman 1966–76; Gusinde 1931: 1040, 1044.
8 Gusinde 1931: 1040.
9 *Ibid.*: 1044.
10 Angela related this.
11 *Ibid.*
12 This is the austral pygmy owl (*Glaucidium nanum*) according to Humphrey *et al.* 1970. The authors quote (p. 239) an authority to the effect that an imitation of the whistles of this owl invariably attracted a half dozen or more of this species, especially the males who would fly directly towards the source of the imitated whistling.
13 Angela was the source here.

10. Concluding remarks

1 For the latent Moon quality in women see Chapman 1972b.

Bibliography

Adams, R.N. 1975. *Energy and Structure. A Theory of Power.* Austin, University of Texas Press.

Agostini, Alberto M. de. 1929. *Mis Viajes a la Tierra del Fuego.* Milan.

1934. *I Miei Viaggi Nella Terra del Fuoco.* 3rd edition. Turin.

1956. *Trenta Años en Tierra del Fuego.* 3rd edition. Buenos Aires, Ediciones Peuser.

Baer, G. and C.A. Schmitz. 1965. 'On the Social Organization of the Ona (Selk'nam)', *Journal de la Société des Américanistes* 54: 23–9.

Baez, Gregorio. 1945. 'El Territorio Nacional de Tierra del Fuego', *Anales del Musee de la Patagonia* 1: 243–52.

Bamberger, Joan. 1974. 'The Myth of Matriarchy: Why Men Rule in Primitive Society', in M.Z. Rosaldo and L. Lamphere (eds.) *Woman, Culture and Society.* Stanford, Stanford University Press.

Barclay, William S. 1926. *The Land of Magellan.* London, Methuen.

Barth, Fredrik. 1948. 'Cultural Development in Southern South America: Yahgan and Alakaluf vs. Ona and Tehuelche', *Acta Americana* 6: 192–9.

Beauvoir, José Maria. 1902. 'Memorias del Rev. D. Beauvoir', *Boletín Salesiano año XVII* 5: 128–30, 6: 163–4.

1915. *Los Shelknam: Indigenas de la Tierra del Fuego.* Buenos Aires, Libreria del Colegio Pio IX.

Bicchieri, M.B. (ed.) 1972. *Hunters and Gatherers Today.* New York, Holt, Rinehart and Winston.

Bierstedt, Robert. 1974. *Power and Progress: Essays on Sociological Theory.* New York, McGraw-Hill.

Bird, Junius B. 1938. 'Antiquity and Migrations of the Early Inhabitants of Patagonia', *Geographical Review* 28: 250–75.

1946a. 'The Archeology of Patagonia', in Steward 1946–59: I, 17–24.

1946b. 'The Alacaluf', in Steward 1946–59: I, 55–79.

1969. 'A Comparison of South Chilean and Ecuadorian "Fishtail" Projectile Points', *Kroeber Anthropological Society Papers* 40: 52–71.

Birdsell, Joseph B. 1970. 'Local Group Composition among the Australian Aborigines', *Current Anthropology* 11: 115–42.

Boletín Salesiano. Libería Salesiana Sarría Barcelona, 1886–.

Borgatello, Maggiorino. 1915. *Patagonia Meridionale e Terra del Fuoco. Memorie di un Missionario nel Cinquantenario delle Missioni Salesiana.* Turin, Societa Editrice Internazionale.

Bibliography

Bove, Giacomo. 1883. 'Expedición Austral Argentina. Informes Preliminares', *Institute Geográfico Argentino.*
Braun Menéndez, Armando. 1945. *Pequeña Historia Fueguina.* Buenos Aires, Emecé Editores.
Bridges, E. Lucas. 1935. 'Supersticiones de los Onas', *Argentina Austral* 73: 33–9.
   1948. *Uttermost Part of the Earth.* London, Hodder and Stoughton.
Bridges, Thomas. 1893. 'La Tierra del Fuego y sus Habitantes', *Boletín del Instituto Geográfico Argentino* 14: 221–41.
Brosse, Charles de. 1756. *Histoire des Navigations aux Terres Australes.* 2 vols. Paris.
Brown, Judith K. 1970. 'A Note on the Division of Labor by Sex', *American Anthropologist* 72: 1073–8.
Burton, M.L., L.A. Bruder and D.R. White. 1977. 'A Model of the Sexual Division of Labor', *American Ethnologist* 4: 227–52.
Cabrera, A. 1940. *Historia Natural. Mamíferos Sud-Americanos.* Buenos Aires.
Caldenius, C.C. 1932. 'Las Glaciaciones Cuaternarias en la Patagonia y Tierra del Fuego y sus Relaciones con la Glaciaciones del Hemisferio Boreal: Estudio Geocronológico', *Anales de la Sociedad Científica Argentina* 113: 49–70.
Canals Frau, Salvador. 1946. 'Expansion of the Araucanians in Argentina', in Steward 1946–59: I, 761–6.
Cancian, Frank. 1976. 'Social Stratification', *Annual Review of Anthropology* 5: 227–48.
Ceballos, Rita. 1972. 'Les Habitants de la Patagonie Continentale Argentine', *Objets et Mondes* 12: 117–28.
Chapman, Anne. 1966–76. Ethnographic Journal: Selk'nam, Tierra del Fuego (diary of field work; 1966: three months; 1967: three months; 1968–70: two years; 1972–4: two years; 1976: three months). Additional material includes seventy-nine genealogies concerning approximately 3,386 individuals, and fifty-five tapes. About half of the latter are recordings of Lola Kiepja's chants which have now been issued on four records (see below 1972a and 1978). The remaining tapes comprise largely linguistic data (lexicons). Other material consists of photographs and archaeological findings, the great majority of which is deposited in the Museo de la Plata, Argentina and in a small museum directed by Mr Roberto Wilson in Río Grande, Tierra del Fuego.
   1971. 'Lola', *Natural History* 80–3: 32–41.
   1972a. *Selk'nam Chants of Tierra del Fuego, Argentina*, vol. I (album of two records of shamanistic and mourning chants sung by Lola Kiepja), Folkways Inc. no. FE 4176.
   1972b. 'Lune en Terre de Feu. Mythes et Rites chez les Selk'nam', *Objets et Mondes* 12: 145–58.
   1973. 'Donde los Mares Chocan. La Tierra de los Antiguos Haush, Tierra del Fuego', *Karukinka. Cuaderno Fueguino* 3: 5–14.
   1975a. 'Angela Loij, la Ultima Selk'nam', *Journal de la Société des Américanistes* 62: 232–4.

185

1975b. 'Llanto por los Indios de Tierra del Fuego', *Journal de la Société des Américanistes* 62: 235–6.

1977a. 'Economía de los Selk'nam, Tierra del Fuego', *Journal de la Société des Américanistes* 64: 135–46.

1977b. 'The Ona People: Life and Death in Tierra del Fuego', *Film Library Quarterly* 10: 21–30.

1978. *Selk'nam Chants of Tierra del Fuego, Argentina*, vol. II (album of two records of the Hain (*kloketen*) ceremony sung by Lola Kiepja), Folkways Inc. no. FE 4179.

1980a. 'What's in a Name? Problems of Meaning and Denotation apropos of a Corpus of Selk'nam Personal Names', *Journal de la Société des Américanistes* 67: 329–57.

1980b. 'Barter as a Universal Mode of Exchange', *L'Homme* 21: 33–83.

Chapman, Anne and Thomas R. Hester. 1975. 'New Data on the Archaeology of the Haush: Tierra del Fuego', *Journal de la Société des Américanistes* 62: 185–208.

Charbonnier, Georges. 1961. *Entretiens avec Claude Lévi-Strauss*. Paris, Union Générale d'Editions.

Clair-Vasiliadis, Christos. 1972. 'Les Alakaluf de Puerto Eden (1971)', *Objets et Mondes* 12: 197–200.

Cohen, Abner. 1969. 'Political Anthropology: the Analysis of the Symbolism of Power Relations', *Man* 4: 215–35.

Coiazzi, Antonio. 1914. 'Los Indios de Archipélago Fueguino', *Revista Chilena de Historia y Geografía* 13.

Cook, James. 1893. *Captain Cook's Journal during his First Voyage Round the World. Made in H.M. 'Endeavour' 1768–71*. Edited by Captain W.J.L. Wharton. London, Elliot Stock.

Coon, Carleton S. 1971. *The Hunting Peoples*. Boston, Little Brown.

Cooper, John M. 1917. 'Analytical and Critical Bibliography of the Tribes of Tierra del Fuego and Adjacent Territory', *Bureau of American Ethnology Bulletin* 63.

1924. 'Culture Diffusion and Culture Areas in Southern South America', *International Congress of Americanists, Proceedings* 21: 406–21.

1942. 'Areal and Temporal Aspects of South American Culture', *Primitive Man* 15: 1–38.

1946a. 'The Southern Hunters: An Introduction', in Steward 1946–59: I, 13–15.

1946b. 'The Yahgan', in Steward 1946–59: I, 81–106.

1946c. 'The Ona', in Steward 1946–59: I, 107–25.

1946d. 'The Patagonian and Pampean Hunters', in Steward 1946–59: I, 127–68.

Dabbene, Robert. 1907. 'Viaje a la Tierra del Fuego y a la Isla de los Estados', *Boletín del Instituto Geográfico Argentino* 21: 3–78.

Dahrendorf, Ralf. 1968. *Essays in the Theory of Society*. Stanford, Stanford University Press.

Damas, David. 1968. 'The Diversity of Eskimo Societies', in Lee and DeVore (eds.) 1968: 111–17.

(ed.) 1969. 'Contribution to Anthropology; Band Societies', *National Museum of Canada Bulletin* (Ottawa) 228.

Darwin, Charles. 1962. *The Voyage of the Beagle.* Edited by L. Engle. New York, The Natural History Library.

Denham, Woodrow W. 1978. 'Some Theoretical and Methodological Problems in the Study of Pleistocene Social Organization', unpublished paper presented at the International Conference on Hunters and Gatherers, Paris, 27–30 June.

Denich, Bette S. 1974. 'Sex and Power in the Balkans', in M.Z. Rosaldo and L. Lamphere (eds.) *Woman, Culture and Society.* Stanford, Stanford University Press.

Divale, William and Marvin Harris. 1976. 'Population, Warfare and the Male Supremacists Complex', *American Anthropologist* 78: 521–38.

Dowling, John H. 1968. 'Individual Ownership and the Sharing of Game in Hunting Societies', *American Anthropologist* 70: 502–6.

Durkheim, Emile. 1960. *De la Division du Travail Social.* 7th edition. Paris, Press Universitaire de France.

Edholm, Felicity, Olivia Harris and Kate Young. 1977. 'Conceptualizing Women', *Critique of Anthropology* 3 (9 and 10): 101–30.

Eliade, Mircea. 1959. *Initiation, Rites, Sociétés Secrètes.* Paris, Gallimard.

Ember, Melvin and Carol R. Ember. 1971. 'Conditions Favoring Matrilocal versus Patrilocal Residence', *American Anthropologist* 73: 571–94.

Emperaire, José and Annette Laming. 1954. 'La Disparition des derniers Fuégiens', *Diogène*, November: 48–81.

Encyclopaedia Britannica. 1953 edition. 'Tierra del Fuego', 22: 208–9.

Evans-Pritchard, E.E. 1965. *The Position of Women in Primitive Society.* New York, Free Press.

Feruglio, E. 1946. *Geografía de la República Argentina.* Buenos Aires, Sociedad Argentina de Estudios Geográficos.

Fitz-Roy, Captain Robert. 1839. *Narration of the Surveying Voyages of his Majesty's Ships 'Adventure' and 'Beagle' between the years 1826 and 1836,* vol. II. London.

Fox, Robin. 1969. *Kinship and Marriage.* Harmondsworth, Penguin Books.

Fried, Morton H. 1967. *The Evolution of Political Society.* New York, Random House.

Friedl, Ernestine. 1967. 'The Position of Women: Appearance and Reality', *Anthropological Quarterly* 40: 97–108.

1975. *Women and Men. An Anthropologist's View.* New York, Holt, Rinehart and Winston.

Fuentes Rabe, Arturo. 1922. *Tierra del Fuego.* 2 vols. Valdivia, Chile.

Furlong, Charles W. 1910. 'Vanishing People of the Land of Fire', *Harpers Monthly Magazine* 120: 117–29.

1917a. 'The Haush and Ona: Primitive Tribes of Tierra del Fuego', *International Congress of Americanists* 19: 432–44.

1917b. 'Tribal Distribution and Settlements of the Fuegians', *Geographical Review* 3: 169–87.

Gallardo, Carlos R. 1910. *Los Onas.* Buenos Aires, Cabaut y Cía.

Godelier, Maurice. 1975. 'Modes of Production, Kinship and Demographic Structures', in Maurice Bloch (ed.) *Marxist Analyses and Social Anthropology.* London, Malaby Press.

1976. 'Le Problème des Formes et des Fondements de la Domination Masculine: Les Baruya de Nouvelle Guinée', *Les Cahiers du Centre d'Etudes et de Recherches Marxistes* 128: 1–42.

Gonzalez, Alberto Rex. 1977. *Arte Precolombino de la Argentina.* Filmediciones Valero, Buenos Aires.

Goodall, R. Natalie Prosser de. 1975. *Tierra del Fuego, Argentina.* Buenos Aires, Ediciones Shanamaiim.

Gough, Kathleen. 1975. 'The Origin of the Family', in Reiter 1975: 51–76.

Gusinde, Martin. 1925. 'Geheime Männerfeiern bei den Feuerländern', *International Congress of Americanists* 21: 40–60.

1926a. 'Männerzeremonien auf Feuerland und deren Kulturhistorische Wertung', *Zeitschrift für Ethnologie* 58: 261–312.

1926b. 'Das Lautsystem der Feuerländischen Sprachen', *Anthropos* 21: 1000–24.

1927. 'Wertung und Entwicklung des Kindes bei den Feuerländern', *Mitteilungen der Anthropologischen Gesellschaft in Wien* 57: 163–70.

1928. 'Die Stellung der Frau bei den Feuerländern', *Tagungsberichte der Deutschen Anthropologischen Gesellschaft* (Leipzig) 49: 36–41.

1931. *Die Feuerland-Indianer*, vol. I, *Die Selk'nam.* Mödling bei Wien, Anthropos Verlag.

1951. *Hombres Primitivos de la Tierra del Fuego.* Sevilla, Escuela de Estudios Hispano-Americanos de Sevilla.

1961. *The Yamana.* 5 vols. Translated by Frieda Schütze. New Haven, Conn., Human Relations Area Files.

1964. 'Die Religionsform der Selk'nam auf Feuerland', *Völkerkundliche Abhandlungen* 1: 153–62.

1974. *Die Feuerland-Indianer*, vol. III, *Die Halakwulup.* Mödling bei Wien, Anthropos Verlag.

Guyot, Mireille. 1968. 'Les Mythes chez les Selk'nam et les Yamana de la Terre de Feu', *Travaux et Mémoires de l'Institut d'Ethnologie* 75.

Harris, Marvin. 1977. *Cannibals and Kings: The Origins of Cultures.* New York, Random House.

Helm, June. 1965. 'Bilaterality in the Socioterritorial Organization of the Arctic Drainage Dene', *Ethnology* 4: 361–85.

1969. 'Remarks on the Methodology of Band Composition Analysis', in Damas 1969: 212–17.

Héritier, Françoise. 1978. 'Fécondité et Stérilité: la Traduction de ces Notions dans le Camp Idéologique au Stage Préscientifique', in E. Sullerot and O. Thibault (eds.) *Le Fait Féminin.* Paris, Fayart.

Hiatt, L.R. 1962. 'Local Organization among the Australian Aborigines', *Oceania* 32: 267–86.

1966. 'The Lost Horde', *Oceania* 37: 81–92.

1971. 'Secret Pseudo-Procreation Rites among the Australian Aborigines',

Bibliography

in L.R. Hiatt and C. Jayawardena (eds.) *Anthropology in Oceania.* New York, Chandler.

Holmberg, Edwardo A. 1906. 'Viaje al Interior de Tierra del Fuego', *Anales del Ministerio de Agricultura, sección de Inmigración, Propaganda y Geografía: República Argentina* 1 (1).

Hugh-Jones, Stephen. 1979. *The Palm and the Pleiades. Initiation and Cosmology in Northwest Amazonia.* Cambridge, Cambridge University Press.

Humphrey, Philip S., D. Bridge, P.W. Reynolds and R.T. Peterson. 1970. *Birds of Isla Grande (Tierra del Fuego).* Washington, D.C., Smithsonian Institution.

Kolata, Bari. 1974. '!Kung Hunter-Gatherers: Feminism, Diet and Birth Control', *Science* 185: 932–4.

Koppers, Wilhelm. 1924. *Unter Feuerland-Indianern.* Stuttgart.

Laming-Emperaire, Annette. 1968a. 'Quelques Etapes de l'Occupation Humaine dans l'Extrême Sud de l'Amérique australe', *International Congress of Americanists* 37 (3): 301–14.

1968b. 'Missions Archéologiques Françaises au Chili Austral et au Brésil Méridional', *Journal de la Société des Américanistes* 57: 77–100.

1968c. 'Le Site de Marassi en Terre de Feu', *Rehue* (Concepción, Chile) 1: 133–44.

1972. 'Les Sites Préhistoriques de Patagonie et de Terre de Feu', *Objets et Mondes* 12 (2): 201–24.

1976. 'Le Plus Ancien Peuplement de l'Amérique', *Bulletin de la Société Préhistorique Française* 73: 280–7.

Laming-Emperaire, Annette, Danièle Lavallée and Roger Humbert. 1972. 'Le Site de Marazzi en Terre de Feu', *Objets et Mondes* 12: 226–44.

Langness, L.L. 1977. 'Ritual, Power and Male Dominance in the New Guinea Highlands', in R.D. Fogelson and R.N. Adams (eds.) *The Anthropology of Power.* New York, Academic Press.

Lathrap, Donald W. 1968a. 'The "Hunting" Economies of the Tropical Forest Zone of South America: An Attempt at Historical Perspective', in Lee and DeVore 1968.

1968b. 'Discussion. Part II', in Lee and DeVore 1968.

Laughlin, William S. 1968. 'Hunting: An Integrating Biobehavior System and Its Evolutionary Importance', in Lee and De Vore 1968.

Leacock, Eleanor B. 1974. 'The Structure of Band Society', *Reviews in Anthropology* 1: 212–22.

1975. 'Introduction', in Frederick Engels, *The Origin of the Family, Private Property and the State.* Edited by E.B. Leacock. New York, International.

1978. 'Women's Status in Egalitarian Society: Implications for Social Evolution', *Current Anthropology* 19: 247–75.

Leacock, Eleanor B. and Richard B. Lee (eds.) 1982. *Politics and History in Band Societies.* Cambridge, Cambridge University Press.

Lee, Richard B. 1974. 'Male–Female Residence Arrangements and Political

Bibliography

Power in Human Hunter–Gatherers', *Archives of Sexual Behavior* 3: 167–73.

1976. '!Kung Spatial Organization', in Lee and DeVore 1976: 73–97.

1978. 'Issues in the Study of Hunter–Gatherers 1968–1978', paper presented to the International Conference on Hunters and Gatherers, Paris, 27–30 June. In Leacock and Lee 1982.

Lee, Richard B. and Irven DeVore (eds.) 1968. *Man the Hunter.* Chicago, Aldine.

1976. *Kalahari Hunter–Gatherers.* Cambridge, Mass., Harvard University Press.

Legros, Dominique. 1977. 'Chance, Necessity and Mode of Production: A Marxist Critique of Cultural Evolutionism', *American Anthropologist* 79: 26–41.

Lehmann-Nitsche, Roberto. 1913. 'El Grupo Tachon de los Paises Magallánicos', *Revista del Museo de la Plata* 22: 217–76.

1927. 'Estudios Antropológicos sobre los Onas', *Anales del Museo de la Plata* 2 (2): 57–99.

Lenski, G. 1966. *Power and Privilege: A Theory of Social Stratification.* New York, McGraw-Hill.

Lévi-Strauss, Claude. 1949. *Les Structures Elémentaires de la Parenté.* Paris, Presses Universitaires de France.

1962. *La Pensée Sauvage.* Paris, Plon.

1968. 'The Concept of Primitiveness', in Lee and DeVore 1968: 348–52.

1969. *Totemism.* Translated by Rodney Needham. Harmondsworth, Penguin Books.

Lista, Ramón. 1887. *Viaje al Pais de los Onas. Tierra del Fuego.* Buenos Aires.

Lliboutry, Luis. 1956. *Nieves y Glaciares de Chile. Fundamentos de Glaciología.* Santiago, Chile, Ediciones de la Universidad de Chile.

Loeb, E.M. 1931. 'The Religious Organizations of North Central California and Tierra del Fuego', *American Anthropologist* 33: 517–55.

Lothrop, Samuel K. 1928. 'The Indians of Tierra del Fuego', *Contributions from the Museum of the American Indian* (Heye Foundation), 10.

1946. 'Indians of the Paraná Delta and La Plata Littoral', in Steward 1946–59: I, 177–90.

Lowie, Robert H. 1921. *Primitive Society.* London, Routledge.

1933. 'Selk'nam Social Kinship Terms', *American Anthropologist* 35: 546–8.

1949. 'Social and Political Organization of the Tropical Forest and Marginal Tribes', in Steward 1946–59: V, 313–67.

Martial, Louis Ferdinand. 1888. 'Histoire du Voyage', in *Mission Scientifique du cap Horn 1882–83,* vol. I. Paris.

Martin, M. Kay. 1969. 'South American Foragers: A Case Study in Cultural Devolution', *American Anthropologist* 71: 243–60.

Martínez-Crovetto, Raul. 1968. 'Nombres de Plantas y su Utilidad, según los Indios Onas de Tierra del Fuego', Universidad Nacional del Nordeste, Facultad de Agronomía y Veterinaria, Corrientes, Argentina, *Estudios Ethnobotánicos* 4 (3).

Bibliography

Martinič, B. Mateo. 1971. 'José Nogueira, Primer Pionero y Hombre de Fortuna de la Antigua Colonia de Magallanes, a la Luz de Papeles Ineditos', *Anales del Instituto de la Patagonia* (Punta Arena, Chile) 2 (1–2): 41–75.

1973. 'Panorama de la Colonización en Tierra del Fuego entre 1881 y 1900', *Anales del Instituto de la Patagonia* (Punta Arena, Chile), 4: 5–69.

Mason, Otis T. 1958. *Women's Share in Primitive Culture.* London, Macmillan.

Maxwell, Gavin. 1967. *Seals of the World.* London, Constable.

Mead, Margaret. 1967. *Male and Female.* New York, William Morrow.

Meggitt, M.J. 1962. *Desert People: a Study of the Walbiri Aborigines of Central Australia.* Sydney, Angus and Roberton.

1964. 'Male–Female Relationships in the Highlands of Australian New Guinea', *American Anthropologist* 66: 204–24.

Meillassoux, Claude. 1972. 'From Reproduction to Production. A Marxist Approach to Economic Anthropology', *Economy and Society* 1: 93–105.

1975. *Femmes, Greniers et Capitaux.* Paris, François Maspero.

Métraux, Alfred. 1946. 'Ethnography of the Chaco', in Steward 1946–59: I, 197–370.

1949. 'Boy's Initiation Rites', in Steward 1946–59: V, 375–82.

Montagu, Ashley. 1974. *The Natural Superiority of Women.* London, Collier Macmillan.

Moore, John H. 1977. 'The Exploitation of Women in Evolutionary Perspective', *Critique of Anthropology* 3 (9 and 10): 83–100.

Morison, Samuel Eliot. 1974. *The European Discovery of America. The Southern Voyages 1492–1616.* New York, Oxford University Press.

Morris, Brian. 1978. 'The Family, Group Structuring and Trade amongst Hunter–Gatherers', paper presented to the International Conference on Hunters and Gatherers, Paris, 27–30 June, in Leacock and Lee 1982.

Murdock, George P. 1949. *Social Structure.* New York, Macmillan.

1962. 'Ethnographic Atlas', *Ethnology* 1: 113–34, 384–404.

1965. 'Ethnographic Atlas', *Ethnology* 4: 343–8.

Murdock, George P. and C. Provost. 1973. 'Factors in the Division of Labor by Sex: A Cross Cultural Analysis', *Ethnology* 12: 203–25.

Murphy, Robert. 1959. 'Social Structure and Sex Antagonism', *Southwestern Journal of Anthropology* 15: 89–98.

Musters, George C. 1871. 'On the Races of Patagonia', *Journal of the Anthropological Institute of Great Britain and Ireland* 1: 193–206.

1969. *At Home with the Patagonians.* First printing 1897. New York, Greenwood Press.

Najlis, Elena. 1973. 'Lengua Selknam', *Filología y Linguistica* (Buenos Aires) 3.

1975. 'Diccionario Selknam', *Filología y Linguistica* (Buenos Aires) 4.

Nordenskjold, Otto. 1897. 'Algunos Datos sobre la Naturaleza de la Región Magallánica', *Anales de la Sociedad Científica Argentina* 44: 190–7.

191

Olrog, C.C. 1959. *Las Aves Argentinas. Una Guía del Campo.* Instituto Miguel Lillo, Universidad Nacional de Tucumán.

Orquera, Luis Abel, Arturo Emilio Sala, Ernesto Luis Piana and Alicia Haydee Tapía. 1977. *Lancha Packewaia. Arqueología de los Canales Fueguinos.* Buenos Aires, Editorial Huemul.

Ortiz-Troncoso, Omar T. 1973. 'Los Yámana, Vienticinco Años después de la Mision Lipschutz', *Anales del Instituto de la Patagonia* (Punta Arenas, Chile) 4: 77–107.

Outes, Felix F. 1905. 'La Edad de Piedra en Patagonia', *Anales del Museo Nacional de Buenos Aires* 12: 203–574.

1906. 'Instrumentos Modernos de los Onas', *Anales del Museo Nacional de Buenos Aires* 13: 287–96.

Owen, Roger C. 1965. 'The Patrilocal Band: A Linguistically and Culturally Hybrid Social Unit', *American Anthropologist* 67: 675–90.

Pertuiset, Eugène. 1877. *Le Trésor des Incas à la Terre de Feu.* Paris.

Peterson, Nicolas. 1975. 'Hunter–Gatherer Territoriality: the Perspective from Australia', *American Anthropologist* 77: 53–68.

1978. 'Territorial Adaptations among Desert Hunter–Gatherers: the !Kung and Australians Compared', presented to the International Conference on Hunters and Gatherers, Paris, 27–30 June. In Leacock and Lee 1982.

Popper, Julio. 1887. 'Exploración de la Tierra del Fuego', *Boletín del Instituto Geográfico Argentino* 8: 74–115.

1891. 'Apuntes Geográficos, Etnológicos, Estadísticos e Industriales sobre la Tierra del Fuego', *Boletín del Instituto Geográfico Argentino* 12: 130–70.

Reiter, Rayna R. (ed.) 1975. *Toward an Anthropology of Women.* New York, Monthly Review Press.

Rogers, Susan Carol. 1975. 'Female Forms of Power and the Myth of Male Dominance: a Model of Female/Male Interaction in Peasant Society', *American Ethnologist* 2: 227–56.

Rosaldo, Michelle Z. 1974. 'Woman, Culture and Society: a Theoretical Overview', in M.Z. Rosaldo and L. Lamphere (eds.) *Woman, Culture and Society.* Stanford, Stanford University Press.

Rossi, Ino. 1973. 'Verification in Anthropology: the Case of Structural Analysis', *Journal of Symbolic Anthropology* 2: 27–46.

Rudolph, William E. 1934. 'Southern Patagonia as Portrayed in Recent Literature', *Geographical Review* 24: 251–71.

Sacks, Karen. 1976. 'State Bias and Woman's Status', *American Anthropologist* 78: 565–9.

Sahlins, Marshall D. 1964. 'The Social Life of Monkeys, Apes and Primitive Men', in M.H. Fried (ed.) *Readings in Anthropology*, vol. II. New York, Crowell.

1969a. 'The Origin of Society', in Y.A. Cohen (ed.) *Man in Adaptation: the Biosocial Background.* Chicago, Aldine.

1969b. 'Social Stratification in Kinship Societies', in A. Beteille (ed.) *Social Inequality: Selected Reading.* Baltimore, Penguin.

Bibliography

1972. *Stone Age Economics.* Chicago, Aldine.

Salesian Missionary. 1914. Manuscript notebook on the Hain Ceremony. Written in Spanish at the Candelaria Mission, Río Grande, Tierra del Fuego. Most of the text of this document is published in *Karukinka. Cuaderno Fueguino* 9, 1974.

Sanday, Peggy R. 1973. 'Toward a Theory of the Status of Women', *American Anthropologist* 75: 1682–700.

Sarmiento de Gambóa, Pedro. 1768. *Viage al Estrecho de Magallanes por el Capitán Pedro Sarmiento de Gambóa en los años de 1579 v 1580.* Madrid, Imprenta Real de la Gazeta.

Segers, Polidor. 1891. 'Habitos y Costumbres de los Indios Aonas', *Boletín del Instituto Geográfico Argentino* 12: 56–82.

Serrano, Antonio. 1946. 'The Charrua', in Steward 1946–59: I, 191–6.

1947. *Los Aborigines Argentinos.* Buenos Aires, Nova.

Service, Elman R. 1962. *Primitive Social Organization.* New York, Random House.

1966. *The Hunters.* Englewood Cliffs, New Jersey, Prentice Hall.

Slobodin, Richard. 1969. 'Criteria of Identification of Bands', in Damas 1969: 191–6.

Slocum, Sally. 1975. 'Woman the Gatherer: Male Bias in Anthropology', in Reiter 1975: 36–50.

Spears, John R. 1895. *The Gold Diggings of Cape Horn: A Study of Life in Tierra del Fuego and Patagonia.* New York and London, G. Putman's Sons.

Spence, Michael W. 1974. 'The Study of Residential Practices among Pre-historic Hunters and Gatherers', *World Archaeology* 5 (3): 346–57.

Siffredi, Alejandra. 1969–70. 'Hierofanías y Concepciones Mítico-religiosas de los Tehuelches Meridionales', *RUNA* (Buenos Aires) 12: 247–72.

Stanner, W.E.H. 1965. 'Aboriginal Territorial Organization: Estate, Range, Domain and Regime', *Oceania* 36: 1–26.

Steward, Julian H. 1946–59 (ed.) *Handbook of South American Indians.* 7 vols. Reprinted Michigan, Scholarly Press.

1949. 'South American Cultures: An Interpretative Summary', in Steward 1946–59: V, 669–772.

1955. *Theory of Culture Change: the Methodology of Multilinear Evolution.* Urbana, University of Illinois Press.

1968. 'Causal Factors and Processes in the Evolution of Pre-farming Societies', in Lee and DeVore 1968: 321–4 *and passim.*

1969. 'Observations on Bands', in Damas 1969: 187–90.

Steward, Julian H. and Leslie C. Faron. 1959. *Native Peoples of South America.* New York, McGraw Hill.

Stuart, David E. 1977. 'Seasonal Phases in Ona Subsistence, Territorial Distribution and Organization: Implications for the Archaeological Record', in L.R. Binford (ed.) *For Theory Building.* New York, Academic Press: 251–83.

Terray, Emmanuel. 1969. *Le Marxisme Devant les Sociétés 'Primitives'.* Paris, François Maspero.

Tonelli, Antonio. 1926. *Grammatica e Glossario delle Lingua degli Ona–Selknam Terra del Fuoco.* Turin, Missioni Salesiane.

Tuden, Arthur and Leonard Plotnicov. 1970. 'Introduction', in A. Tuden and L. Plotnicov (eds.) *Social Stratification in Africa.* New York, The Free Press.

Vignati, Milcíades A. 1926a. 'Consideraciones Generales Relativas al Instrumental Humane Hallado en "Conchales" Fueguinos', *Physis. Revista de la Sociedad Argentina de Ciencias Naturales* 8 (30): 396–401.

1926b. 'El Tipo de Habitación Actual de los Indios Onas de Tierra del Fuego', *Physis. Revista de la Sociedad Argentina de Ciencias Naturales* 8 (30): 363–7.

1927. 'Arqueología y antropología de los "Conchales" Fueguinos', *Revista del Museo de la Plata* 4 (3): 79–143.

Webster, Paula. 1975. 'Matriarchy: A Vision of Power', in Reiter 1975: 141–56.

Wilbert, Johannes. 1975. 'Folk Literature of the Selknam Indians: Martin Gusinde's Collection of Selknam Narratives', *UCLA Latin American Studies Series* (Los Angeles), 32.

Willey, Gordon R. 1971. *An Introduction to American Archaeology*, vol. II, *South America.* Englewood Cliffs, New Jersey, Prentice Hall.

Williams, B.J. 1968. 'The Birhor of India and Some Comments on Band Organization', in Lee and DeVore 1968: 126–31.

1974. 'A Model of Band Society', *American Antiquity* 39 (4): part 2, Memoir 29.

Wilson, E.O. 1975. *Sociobiology: the New Synthesis.* Cambridge, Mass., Harvard University Press.

Wissler, Clark. 1938. *The American Indian.* New York, Oxford University Press.

Woodburn, James. 1968. 'Stability and Flexibility in Hadza Residential Groupings', in Lee and DeVore 1968: 103–10.

Yellen, John and Henry Harpending. 1972. 'Hunter–gatherer Populations and Archaeological Inference', *World Archaeology* 4 (2): 244–53.

Index